D0849278

Beyond a Christian
Commonwealth

BEYOND
A CHRISTIAN
COMMONWEALTH

The Protestant Quarrel with

the American Republic,

1830–1860

Mark Y. Hanley

The University of North Carolina Press

Chapel Hill and London

© 1994 The University of North Carolina Press
All rights reserved
Manufactured in the United States of America

The paper in this book meets the guidelines for permanence and durability of the Committee on Production Guidelines for Book Longevity of the Council on Library Resources.

Library of Congress Cataloging-in-Publication Data
Hanley, Mark Y.
    Beyond a Christian commonwealth : the Protestant quarrel with the American Republic, 1830–1860 / by Mark Y. Hanley.
        p. cm.
    Includes bibliographical references and index.
    ISBN 0-8078-2121-7 (alk. paper)
    1. Protestant churches—United States—History—19th century. 2. Christianity and culture—History of doctrines—19th century. 3. United States—Church history—19th century.
    I. Title.
    BR525.H324   1994
    280′.4′097309034—dc20   93-8467
                                                             CIP

98 97 96 95 94   5 4 3 2 1

For Janet, Matthew, and Kelly

Contents

Acknowledgments

It is finally my privilege to acknowledge my debts to the many people and institutions that contributed to this book. The David Ross Foundation at Purdue University awarded me a two-year fellowship that eased the financial burdens of writing and research. Northeast Missouri State University generously granted two summer research stipends. My wife, Janet, contributed immeasurably to the lives of her first graders and provided a steady income while I was buried under chapter drafts.

The helpful and competent people and the resources available at several fine libraries made my work possible. I wish to thank the staffs of the American Baptist Historical Society, Rochester, New York; the General Commission on Archives and History for the United Methodist Church, Madison, New Jersey; the Historical Foundation of the Presbyterian and Reformed Churches in the United States, Montreat, North Carolina; Lutheran Archives, Ohio Synod, Wittenburg University, Springfield, Ohio; Depauw University Archives, Greencastle, Indiana; Wabash College Archives, Crawfordsville, Indiana; Franklin College Archives, Franklin, Indiana; and the Purdue University Library. Access to the magnificent nineteenth-century collections at the University of Illinois Library in Urbana proved indispensable.

I have benefited from the suggestions of several fine scholars along the way. Harry S. Stout and Theodore Dwight Bozeman generously offered encouragement coupled with unflinching criticism of the manuscript that guided my revisions in the later stages. I also benefited from the thoughtful suggestions of Susan Curtis, Jan Shipps, Thomas J. Davis, and James Farr. Lewis Bateman, Ron Maner, Jan McInroy, and the excellent staff of the University of North Carolina Press receive my deepest thanks for their guidance throughout the publication process. My student assistants Roger Wohletz, Jason Bainter, Jeff White, and David Welky made copyediting and reference checking easier. The gifted teaching and scholarship of Harold D. Woodman, Linda Levy Peck, Lester H. Cohen, and

Robert E. May have contributed to my scholarly efforts beyond the confines of this endeavor. My teacher and friend John L. Larson, who directed the project at the dissertation stage, lent his assistance and support in so many ways that I can only issue to him a global thank-you. I remain personally and professionally in his debt. I myself, however, must claim sole responsibility for the errors that remain.

Thanks also are due Indiana University Press and the Center for the Study of Religion and American Culture for allowing me to use material from my article that appeared in *Religion and American Culture: A Journal of Interpretation* (Summer 1991).

Finally, I have the privilege of thanking a wonderful family, who pocketed their doubts and maintained their faith that the work would finally be completed. Winifred S. Hanley and Jared W. Young made a difference long ago. To Lucy and Jack, Jimmy and Ellen, and, most especially, to my parents, Harold and Marcia Hanley, I offer love and gratitude for teaching me how to live. Janet, thanks for sharing your life with me. Matthew and Kelly, I continue to learn from the richness and wonder of your lives.

Beyond a Christian Commonwealth

Introduction

Antebellum mainline Protestant leaders are commonly portrayed as scions of a cultural "faith in progress" that reached high tide in the three decades before the Civil War. These modernizers shed ancient doubts about human nature, blended national and millennial hopes, and conjured up a new evangelical vision, consonant with American success and the earthly paradise to come. Emboldened by the demise of Calvinism and a "sanctified" republican ideology, the argument runs, Protestantism sheathed its "critical edge" and warmed to a cultural frenzy of "progressivism, bravado, and boasting." Church leaders administered a full dose of moralism and reformist zeal to sustain this collective destiny, but only a few renegade naysayers—notably Herman Melville and Nathaniel Hawthorne—sailed into the cultural headwind. Indeed, Protestant confounding of sacred and secular purposes has become a thematic constant of works rich in insight and diversity. The sheer preponderance of this scholarship makes the possibility of significant Protestant dissent seem all but incredible.[1]

The central argument of this study is twofold: First, the muscular liberal culture that emerged in America between roughly 1830 and 1860 seriously eroded mainstream Protestant confidence in the spiritual yield of republican liberty and faith. The economic freedom, political democracy, and social and intellectual diversity pillaring this new liberal order prompted clerical rebukes of an expansive materialism that promised a new freedom beyond faith. Second, these cultural alarms pealed loudest in the clergy's "spiritual discourse," the vast body of sermons and sermonic literature that elevated transcendent religious concerns above civic and narrow denominational agendas. In sum, even as some mainline Protestants recalled republican and millennial hopes, the creative spark of democratic mind and material ambition ignited widespread cautions against facile rapprochement with the nation's shifting cultural agenda. An analysis of those themes of resistance that developed widely within mainline orthodoxy can yield essential insight into one of the great but neglected religious struggles of the age.

To be sure, Protestant civic discourse had historically tempted ministers to sacralize republican advance and to bless the nation's material agenda. Fourth of July, Thanksgiving, and other commemorative discourses still offered opportunity to synchronize Christian morality and American progress. Several fine studies suggest the alacrity with which American clergymen succumbed to nationalistic blustering during wartime.[2] But the riches of this vein have also relegated the equally compelling story of Protestant cultural resistance to the fringes of recent scholarship. This analysis aims at recovering the vigor and passion of antebellum mainline cultural dissent without denying its real limits. Beyond civic addresses that affirmed the temporal interests of mainline ministers, their more combative spiritual discourse weighed the religious consequences of liberal triumph and revealed the encroachment of the new order upon the community of faith. Within this context, spiritual vaunts, more than cultural confidence or nationalistic bias, contoured Protestant exceptionalism. Collective bows to "respectable" moral or political imperatives, clerical defenders argued, could not mark spiritual progress or secure the glories of a supranational, supernatural world beyond the commonwealth.

Unitarian divine Henry Bellows bared the historic irony that pressed his orthodox sparring partners to the ramparts: "Protestantism little knew what she was doing when she combined with the other free influences of the times, to set the human mind at large. . . . A power that would not be controlled was set loose in the earth; and the great and anxious question since, becoming every day more serious and pressing, is this: Whether man, left perfectly at liberty . . . will choose Christianity for his religion, or will have any religion at all?" Bellows struck close to the mark in 1852, but the mainline ministers who were his quarry were already scrambling to contain the power of liberty unbounded by faith. They boldly announced the risks. Addressing "the great questions of liberty and social order," warned Congregationalist divine Austin Phelps, could indulge the culture's mandate for reform at the expense of those "critical transitions of destiny," the "transactions on which individual destiny for eternity is suspended." In short, antebellum ministers like Phelps found their immediate spiritual vision focused not on the threshold of the millennium but at the edge of an uncertain destiny. How they explained and plotted a strategy with which to combat this unanticipated cultural challenge is explored in the chapters that follow. First, however,

I shall describe my analytical strategy and the historiographic context of this study.[3]

Since the breakdown of consensus history in the late 1960s, scholars have explored how competing visions of the Revolutionary promise spurred intense ideological conflict in the early Republic. Millennialism—the belief that man was to spread the gospel throughout the earth and effect Christ's spiritual reign—is often recognized as a signal component of this volatile intellectual mix.[4] Many historians argue that as millennialism blended with American nationalism and republicanism, it developed into a secularized and intensely parochial vision of divine purpose. Revolutionary success confirmed the new nation as Jehovah's favorite. Calvinist circumscriptions bowed to an optimistic moralism and a rational faith in human potential. Confident Protestants proclaimed the nation "God's New Israel" and assigned redemptive status to republican ideology and American institutions in a secularized eschatology.[5]

Millennial studies multiplied in tandem with scholarly interest in early American ideological beliefs. These new approaches to sacred and secular motivation rejected older notions of a Lockean or Enlightenment consensus in America. Aided by sociological, anthropological, and linguistic models, scholars have set the American intellectual landscape ablaze with competing visions of the republican task.[6] This new work rescued American religious history from the "exile" imposed by a generation of "Progressives." Historians like Vernon Parrington had pronounced Calvinism a "retrograde" philosophy and effectively denied its explanatory potential. Perry Miller countered in 1961, blasting scholars for assuming that rational philosophy alone fueled the resistance in 1776. Reason may have guided elites, Miller admitted, but only the common folk's discernment of an angry God in the Revolutionary crisis nerved them to support independence and fight a war. Miller's patriots marched in the shadow of the jeremiad, the Puritan clergy's occasional political thrashing of the larger community that urged retreat from the collective sinfulness that eroded social solidarity and invited divine retribution. Only warring against sin and weathering the Revolutionary travail could restore divine favor.[7]

Building on Miller's work in the late 1960s, a new generation of scholars reintegrated religion into the mainstream of the historical narrative by portraying it as a rhetorical vehicle for political ideologies.[8] In the vigorous debate that followed, investigators explored the interpenetration of civil religion, sanctified nationalism, classical republicanism, and millennialism as conceptual frameworks for redefining the relationship between religion and American culture.[9] Church leaders often occupied a pivotal position in these studies. Preaching patriotism and morality in defense of the Standing Order became the clergy's antidote for religious decline. The underlying assumption is that in the absence of an established church, "religious nationalism" replaced "national religion" in the American Protestant mind. According to such an analytical dichotomy, champions of national religion foster reverence for divine authority and providential guidance without assuming automatic congruence between the will of the nation and the will of God. Religious nationalists, to cite one scholar, give "uncritical religious endorsement" to the state agenda, replacing the worship of a transcendent deity with an essentially political faith that offers "unconditional reverence for the nation."[10]

To identify the American clergy as religious nationalists connects them with what Clifford Geertz calls the two most destructive forces in world history.[11] Sacvan Bercovitch contends that American ministers between 1630 and 1850 constructed a jeremiadic and millennial road map that linked redemption to the ascendancy of bourgeois culture. "Only *America*," he asserts, "united nationality and universality, civic and spiritual selfhood, secular and redemptive history, the country's past and paradise to be, in a single synthetic ideal." Martin Marty concludes that the confounding of sacred and secular purposes signaled nineteenth-century Protestantism's "fatal compromise" with the rising American empire and silenced its "critical note." Obsessed with the "trivial" and unwilling to rebuke the culture, ministers compelled outsiders like Melville and Hawthorne to sound the "note of reservation" and "challenge the pretensions of the people." Evangelicals, James Turner agrees, "seldom worried" about civil religion's threat to faith's transcendent purposes "if only because they conflated the nation's future with the coming Kingdom of God."[12]

The mission of unearthing the roots of American civil religion and national arrogance took on justifiable moral urgency for scholars writing in the aftermath of the Vietnam War. Focusing on Protestant civic discourse spawned by previous national crises, historians found ministers to be hard-sell vendors of a peculiar prophetic role for an "American Israel." Church historians have had their own reasons for indicting forebears who "secularized" the faith. Together with other scholars of religion, they have justly denounced racial bigotry, mindless patriotism, and the prostitution of religion to inhumane causes. Modern sensibilities prefigure a contempt for millennial visionaries and secular scions of endless progress blissfully aloof from environmental limitations and social travail.[13] This congruence of sentiment has provided a particularly important interpretive nexus for shaping assessments of late antebellum religion. When the agnostic Miller lamented the critical impotence and sentimentalism of post-Revolutionary divines and yearned for the intellectual toughness of the Puritan fathers, his assault dovetailed with neo-orthodox attacks on nineteenth-century Protestantism as spiritually flaccid and culturally "captive."[14] Consequently, two scholarly traditions, driven by separate purposes and both productive of rich insights, offered subsequent researchers few reasons to move beyond the frameworks of declension and accommodation.

In sum, recent scholarship demonstrates the hopes of Protestant leaders for a "Christian America," as well as their willingness to pronounce Christianity an elixir for social and political ills. But exploring the complexity of Protestant motivation requires equal attention to how parochial religious interests could structure priorities and limit cultural optimism.[15] Theodore Bozeman's brilliant study of seventeenth-century Puritanism, for example, severely circumscribes Miller's "errand" thesis and other works that stress the faith's modernizing, progressive impulse. He reveals a transatlantic New England "fixed firstly upon the past," not on the progress of an American "city upon a hill." The insightful works of Nathan O. Hatch and Jon Butler together invite scholars to examine more closely the dynamic tension between democratic freedom and religious authority that shaped the Protestant experience in the early Republic.[16]

Bernard Bailyn and Gordon Wood have urged scholars to grant ideas the same potential for explaining behavior as they have granted material forces. Affording Protestant religious perceptions the same integrity and explanatory potential now granted to social facts and political ideologies reveals a "critical edge" to the antebellum Protestant message still sharpened by transcendent hopes and a traditional dialectic of sin and salvation. By the 1830s, clerical warriors against intemperance, slavery, and moral turpitude charted the advance of a more dangerous and elusive adversary resistant to material renovations—the turbulent popular freedom of what Robert Wiebe calls an "opening society."[17]

To mark the three decades before the Civil War as the point of liberal culture's emergence provides essential context to the clerical discourse examined here. It also requires some additional explanation. For the purposes of this study, "emergent liberalism" may be defined as the broad and chaotic surge of democratic principles throughout the culture. Individual freedom, self-interested material striving, and the expansive liberty of both marketplace and mind were, quite simply, becoming a way of life. This nineteenth-century liberalism employed democracy and market capitalism as a "template for society."[18] Wiebe's insights underscore the new order as nothing less than a "revolution in choices"— political, social, economic, and intellectual. His assessment also captures the essential "liberalism" that fired the Protestant dissent that we will examine: "After 1825, an extraordinary popular passion for personal freedom fought to extend the range of these exhilarating new rights in a self-fueling process that propelled the participants as fast and as far as their impulses drove them. In each area their objective was self-determination, and in sum they generated a revolution in choices that transformed the character of American society."[19] It is hardly surprising that muscular freedom alloyed with unprecedented cultural flux and uncertainty spurred critical ministers to examine liberty's yield anew.

Liberal culture did not, of course, report neatly in 1830. Indeed, well before the century's fourth decade, religious malcontents set the democratic pace in their denominational zeal to divide and conquer. But this celebration of religious freedom clashed with Protestant circumscription by the 1830s. Ministers jockeying within the sectarian free-for-all now engaged in a war on two fronts as liberal culture set popular freedom beyond faith astride a "steeply rising curve of material productivity as the dynamic of a new kind of society."[20] Jacksonian politicians promised the triumph of individual opportunity over privilege. Popular democracy forced at least verbal deference to "the people" as full political players. Stump orators heralded the "common man" as arbiter of his own progress and the nation's destiny. In the wake of the Mexican War, economic opportunities expanded to the Pacific rim. Nothing could obstruct the "diffusion of the Anglo-Saxon race over the North American continent."

A concurrent revolution in communication gave unprecedented visibility to change and encouraged a clerical watch on Europe's cultural ferment. Young European positivists like Auguste Comte, David Strauss, and Ludwig Feuerbach railed against orthodoxy and linked progress to a new faith in humanity. American lyceums, steam transportation, and a cheap press assured domestic outlets for all kinds of radical theory. The lecture podium and the democratic political platform in particular undermined the sanctity of the pulpit and "the Word." Swelling immigration, especially following Europe's revolutions of 1848, also hardened

American links with Continental rationalism. Transatlantic visionaries tapped unprecedented popular enthusiasm for "progress," while their multiplying agendas for improvement mocked clerical hopes for spiritual consensus. Protestant critics decried a unifying materialist ethos as the unruly midwife of this ideological diversity.

While some ministers soothed republican ears with millennial promises or innocuous messages of morality and benevolence, a growing contingent of Protestant defenders railed against the nation's material pretensions and plotted a traditional path in the wake of change. The Republic needed Christian virtue, they argued, but God's spiritual designs did not depend on temporal renovations. Connecticut Congregationalist divine Horace Bushnell extolled the virtues of a "Christian commonwealth" but placed his Hartford flock's destiny and purpose beyond republican or material maneuvering: "Christianity . . . is not any doctrine of development, or self-culture; no scheme of ethical practice, or social reorganization; but it is a salvation; a power moving on fallen humanity from above its level, to regenerate and so to save."[21] His rapid-fire assault rebuked the diverse material strategies of emergent liberal culture and gave dominion to a traditional message of sin and salvation. Neither his bluntness nor his quarry was exceptional. Blending innovative dissent with pleas for individual, supernatural regeneration gave traditional preaching immediate relevance, restored the tension between spirituality and the material order, and formed the central dialectic of the Protestant quarrel with the Republic.

This dialectic of cultural criticism and calls for traditional faith gave strategic coherence to the spiritual discourse examined in this study. One of its components is regular pulpit sermons. In recent studies of the Protestant relationship to the larger culture, this most voluminous body of Protestant communication typically escapes the close scholarly analysis afforded ministers' speculative treatises, civic discourse, and moral reform commentary. Certainly these latter modes demonstrate that bids for cultural influence and accommodation were always an adjunct to Protestant dissent. But understanding antebellum Protestantism's more critical religious turn requires the construction of productive analytical bridges between ministers' workaday preaching and their complex responses to cultural change. In his groundbreaking study of colonial New England sermons, Harry Stout argues that scholarly emphasis on occasional civic discourse too often "[extracts] a pattern of meaning that distorts the larger spiritual context in which political ideas were expressed and given meaning." Stout demonstrates that colonial civic discourse dovetailed

with regular Sunday homilies emphasizing a spiritual triad of "sin, salvation, and service."[22] The persistence of otherworldly themes between
1830 and 1860, however, offers far more than testimony to pulpit continuity. Protestant spiritual discourse must be studied within the context
of the immediate cultural realities that sustained it.

Significantly, antebellum ministers used cultural criticism to revital-
ize a transcendent spiritual agenda in their "religious jeremiads," the
second major component of the spiritual discourse that we will examine. By the 1830s, cultural and intellectual diversity was rendering the
political jeremiads (grounded in an older tradition of continuity between
religion and social community) increasingly anachronistic. Ministers still
addressed the collective national community in election, fast day, and
other commemorative sermons, but these were remnants of an older tradition. As democracy and disestablishment sped the clergy's transition
from "office" to "profession," the political sermons gave way to their more
insular counterparts.[23] The religious jeremiads, aimed primarily at the
family of faith, announced a widening gulf between the Protestant "spiritual community" and the larger culture. They reached inward to the
"exclusive" world of Protestant believers rather than outward to "Americans" or the "nation." Consequently, the faithful could be addressed as a
distinct and "superior" community within the culture. Like regular sermons, the jeremiads extolled the eternal purposes of Christianity, but
they did so within a broader framework, one that allowed specific analysis and drubbing of cultural challenges to the faith. They were often the
rhetorical centerpieces of ministerial conferences and denominational
gatherings—indeed, any assemblage where the "regenerate" were the
primary audience. In addition, religious jeremiads could take the form
of sermonic pieces in religious journals, newspapers, and pamphlet literature, where instructions to the faithful also served notice of Protestant
resolve to interested outsiders.

This assumption of a special, spiritual bond between speaker and
hearer—a relationship that seemed increasingly important but removed
from the dynamics of liberal culture—sharply separated the religious
jeremiad's purpose from that of its political counterpart. The jeremiad
gave ministers a critical outlet for elevating Protestant spiritual hopes
above earthbound agendas for progress that dismissed the claims of religion. Without civic themes to prefigure content, the clergy refocused
these critical sermons on key religious concerns of particular interest to
believers. They defined threats to the faith and confessed cultural doubts
with the confidence that their listeners possessed the requisite "spiritual"

understanding. The larger culture's material ambitions became a foil for reaffirming the spiritual claims of religion. Extolling Protestant faith as sole arbiter of man's eternal fate, in other words, became a defensive act of cultural dissent. Religious jeremiads and regular sermons—the core of antebellum spiritual discourse—together defended a spiritual kingdom beyond the Republic or the millennium. Ironically, jeremiads and regular sermons celebrating historic faith and an uncomplicated salvific theme also underscored growing contradictions between orthodoxy and liberal democratic culture. Clerical defenders openly admitted Protestant cultural vulnerabilities with an intensity that gave collateral legitimacy to the question of faith's relevance in a materialistic age. Anxious church leaders also reached for the "enemy within," using cultural analysis as a basis for self-criticism and winnowing among the faithful themselves.

Finally, I must give fuller character to the "clergymen" who inhabit my pages. My goal is to recover the character of "Protestant" cultural dissent as it developed broadly—*not* universally—within the boundaries of spiritual discourse as I have defined it for this study. I concentrate on ministers both prominent and "ordinary" from mainline evangelical and confessional groups—specifically Baptists, Methodists, Congregationalists, Episcopalians, Lutherans, Presbyterians, and German Reformed groups. This orientation includes the largest and most influential orthodox groups. These are also the denominations most commonly targeted in studies emphasizing the accommodative side of Protestantism. I wish to show that emergent liberal culture kindled historically significant resistance among all these groups through the complex, dynamic interplay of traditional messages and religious jeremiads. Within this framework, clerical dialogue with the culture sustained critical distinctions between sacred and secular purpose that merit closer analysis. My "clergymen" (variously cultural "critics" and "dissenters") and "spiritual discourse," then, speak to complaints and strategies widely shared within a significant body of religious discourse and not to clerical or denominational homogeneity. Nor, it should be emphasized, does this study seek to replace equally important analyses of Protestant civic commitments. Rather, it explores how civic lures generated a concomitant critical tension that fed equally into a complex antebellum Protestant response to cultural change.

A necessary connection between analytical purpose and level of generalization is further explained by the extended reach of the religious jeremiads themselves. They typically drew battle lines in the broadest possible terms, eschewing sectarian particulars and engaging in a more inclusive struggle between freedom and faith. At this level of prescriptive analysis, denominational markers gave place to a more general "Protestant quarrel." From such common ground, however, ministers *did* laud the defensive resources peculiar to their own folds. I address this diversity particularly in the last three chapters. The first chapter suggests the historic critical and spiritual traditions available to antebellum ministers and is necessarily a broad sweep.

This study exploits a variety of sources. Geographically, it draws heavily on sources from the South and the Midwest, as well as New England. (Chapter 5, for example, examines in detail the regular preaching of "ordinary" Lutheran, Baptist, Methodist, and Presbyterian ministers from Ohio, western New York, Indiana, and Virginia.) Materials include religious jeremiads that often gained a wide audience in the journal press; circular letters issued by denominational associations to local congregations; annual reports, sermons, and publications issued by evangelistic societies; and the unpublished preaching diaries and sermon sketches produced by ordinary ministers North and South. For nationally known figures like Francis Wayland, Charles Grandison Finney, and Bushnell, regular sermons and religious jeremiads take precedence over speculative or civic pieces. Within these vehicles of spiritual discourse, the continuities between confessional Protestants—Episcopalians, Lutherans, and German Reformed—and "pietistic" groups such as Methodists and Baptists regularly transcend sectarian jealousies and lend coherence to a "Protestant" quarrel. British sources, especially from ministers whose work gained a transatlantic following, suggest the international scope of Protestant concerns.

The analysis begins by tracing a pattern of clerical dissent that began as early as Augustine's fourth-century defense of spiritual faith over classical virtue. Puritan suspicions of resurgent Renaissance classicism and post-Revolutionary Anglo-American attacks on classical republican ideology establish the Protestant counterparts of Augustine's vision. I then explain how historic concerns about classical political theory translated into clerical indictments of liberal culture. By mid-century, Protestant critics explained how pursuits of liberty and equality could become ideologically amorphous epicenters from which endless competing systems of progress could radiate. Their jeremiads warned of a new infidelity, an "angel of light" that exalted human potential and material riches in place of faith. The final chapter examines the thematic emphasis of approximately one thousand sermon deliveries recorded in the sketches and preaching diaries of five ordinary ministers. I examine thematic bonds among regular sermons, popular evangelical literature, and religious jeremiads that formed the rhetorical boundaries of an exclusive "community of the Word" that sharply contradicted the fundamentals of liberal culture.

Remarkably, the critical power of the religious jeremiads and the widespread Protestant defense of *spiritual culture* remained vigorous during the 1850s, even as the rising sectional crisis challenged ministers to enlist in a national war of words that tragically culminated in the Civil War. This study illuminates a struggle between religion and the Republic whose distinctive character should not be lost against the larger conflagration that eventually consumed the nation's political soul.

In sum, antebellum church leaders may have hoped for what Robert Handy calls a "complete Christian commonwealth."[24] But the central bias and core purpose intrinsic to that vision may have derived less from an essential linkage of cultural and religious destinies than from resurgent doubts and religious certitudes geared to preserving the transcendent possibilities of Protestant faith in an increasingly liberal society. We must explain why ministers' spiritual discourse so often subordinated temporal prescriptions and millennial speculations to a message that sustained and even intensified distinctions between Christianity and the culture of the young Republic. These dissenters turned a critical eye to their own sins and brooded in the shadow of diverse challengers who, they believed, eagerly awaited their demise.

1

Spiritual Visions, Political Fears, and the Origins of Antebellum Protestant Dissent

Francis Asbury Hester was barely twenty-one years old in 1843 when he accepted a charge as a licensed Methodist exhorter in his native southern Indiana. Born in Vernon, Indiana, Hester had experienced conversion under the preaching of his father in 1836 at a Jefferson County camp meeting. Although early in his career he had had little formal schooling, he exuded the energy and enthusiasm that made him one of the most noted expository preachers in the state. With "joy unspeakable" he claimed "entire sanctification" to Christ in 1844, believing that such a complete transformation was the special blessing of the Holy Spirit reserved for born-again believers who put total "faith in the merits of Christ." "In my arms and my legs the blood seemed almost stagnated," he wrote, "while my willing soul invited the Sanctifier and the Comforter." Hester's spiritual euphoria must have been especially welcome after a month of confronting sinners with whom, he complained in his diary, "politics was the all-absorbing matter." He detested the competition offered by lecturers from New Harmony, Robert Owen's nearby experimental socialist community. But even more threatening was the growing religious indifference and discreet infidelity of ordinary folks "more interested in hoisting poles and flags than hearing the gospel." [1]

On July 4, 1845, Hester joined in a Methodist and Presbyterian gathering on his New Harmony circuit in a "sabbath school celebration." The picnic was "'got up,'" he explained, in order to encourage children in their Sunday School attendance. With acid wit, Hester contrasted his group's religious efforts with "'the Citizens'" who planned to celebrate the day with political speeches and "their 'Barbecue'" (which Hester refused to attend). He caught enough of "'Judge Green's'" Fourth of July oration to decide that "infidelity [was] increasing and that few statesmen retained any genuine "fear of God." Religion, he lamented a few days later, had for too many people become a "matter of but little consideration."[2] Hester, no doubt, would have rebuked anyone who questioned his patriotic, republican sentiments. He had no interest in inciting hostility toward republicanism or democracy. The growing power and self-sufficiency of the nation's political culture did worry him, however. That the day's political revelry implicitly declared his Sunday school gathering inappropriate and curiously out of place signaled for Hester an ominous erosion of religion's place in the new Republic.

The youthful Hester, born in 1822, was no aging malcontent grumbling at the sins of a new generation. He was responding to the realities of a democratic political order that had matured with him. His early years witnessed the last gasps of federalism, the growth of the second American party system, and the popularization of politics under the rubric of Jacksonian democracy. Fewer than 27 percent of the electorate cast ballots in 1824 when the House of Representatives selected John Quincy Adams from among four Democratic-Republicans unable to muster a majority. In 1844, Hester's second year in the ministry, almost 80 percent of the eligible voters participated in the contest between Democrat victor James K. Polk and Whig challenger Henry Clay. It was a new age of mass meetings, party platforms, nominating conventions, and appeals to the "genius of the common man" on both sides of the political fence.

The soul dividends that accrued to fast-growing populist groups like the Baptists and Hester's own Methodists demonstrated Protestantism's investment in the new order. Indeed, popular politics borrowed generously from the mass revival strategies that stirred trans-Appalachian settlers in the early nineteenth century. Barely a hundred miles from Hester's native Vernon, at Cane Ridge Church near Paris, Kentucky, Barton Stone initiated a revival in 1801 that became the "archetype of frontier camp meetings" and inspired the urban revivalism of evangelist Charles Grandison Finney during the late 1820s and 1830s in western New York's "Burned-Over" District.[3] In the spiritual conflagration at Cane Ridge, Baptist, Methodist, and Presbyterian preachers sidestepped Calvinist predestinarian theology and urged the 25,000 seekers to repent and be saved. The message had little to do with preserving order or securing the Republic. The emphasis was on individual accountability to God in eternity; the preachers urged seekers to protect their souls from the devil. Spreading eastward and into urban areas by the late 1820s, the revival earned recognition among historians as the Second Great Awakening.[4]

Hester's complaint amid emergent liberal culture provides a useful introduction to an examination of the historic political sources of an antebellum Protestant quarrel with the Republic. While late antebellum clerical dissent pressed well beyond politics in the narrow sense to attack "democracy" as a diverse cultural phenomenon, an uncontrolled proliferation of choices and individual power, it nevertheless had antecedents in historic Protestant suspicions of the political order. Protestant relationships with the political state since the Reformation had ranged widely, from Cromwellian-style rebellion to the celebratory embrace of the American Revolution by New England's "black regiment." One chronic theme that emerges from the ambivalence is Protestant distrust engendered by the rebirth of classic political morality during the Renaissance. Historic suspicions of human virtue free of sin and located fully within the civil state bore distinct resemblance to antebellum Protestant complaints against their own culture's self-sufficient, materialistic boasts; consequently, the antebellum Protestant struggle to sustain spiritual controls on "true virtue" may be instructively linked to past anxieties. A significant historic pattern (not consensus) of dissent, which antebellum critics could hone to their own purposes, can be traced, in preparation for a fuller analysis of antebellum spiritual discourse.

"The Emptiness of Natural Virtue"

From his Virginia pulpit in the 1850s, Methodist minister David Doggett explained the compatibility of Christian and civic responsibility. Potential harmony, however, depended ironically on perpetual tension, on the recognition that "their nature and spheres are totally dissimilar." Such tension, Doggett's religious jeremiad explained, sustained critical boundaries between what "would otherwise appear the conterminous and blending lines of two very different territories." An "infinite reality" placed an exclusive "Kingdom of Truth" above the intrinsic decadence of all earthly states. Its subjects transcended temporal categories and were not even "human beings, as such." They were creatures "'of the Truth,'" beyond the "pomp and secularity" and the "principle of self-aggrandizement," that corrupted all earthly states, he declared. Doggett's charge was hardly an offering of uncritical largesse to the nation. He issued a stern warning to those who confounded temporal triumphs with transcendent truths. The "revelation of God,"—the "guide of [human] destiny"—was humankind's "true and only good," distinguished from political responsibilities by borders "never to be obliterated," he resounded.[5] Noted Congregationalist divine Horace Bushnell offered similar circumscriptions in 1840. Christ's "political" fate in Pilate's momentary deference to popular will, he thundered, provided a fair indication of the capacity of the political world to be a retainer of spiritual values.[6]

Doggett's and Bushnell's cudgels stoked a larger blaze of antebellum Protestant criticism, aimed at political schemes to renovate the human condition. Their labors renovated historic anxieties reaching all the way back to Augustine's rhetorical bout with Roman assailants. In the *City of God*, Augustine tooled a Christian response to charges that the Visigoth sack of Rome in 410 A.D. had stemmed from the enervating influence of Christianity on the state. The African bishop of Hippo distinguished sharply between classical and Christian conceptions of liberty, virtue, and community. Specifically, Greek and Roman thought defined man as a political creature and tied human purpose to the civil state. Augustine argued that Christianity required believers to transcend self and state through the "true liberty which [freed them] from the dominion of sin and death." He hurled pleas for civic virtue back at his opponents, insisting that only the "true virtue" inscribed by Christian piety could be the "salvation of the commonwealth." What could be "more fortunate for human affairs," he argued, "than that, by the mercy of God, they who are endowed with true piety of life should also have the power." Christian faith was the dynamic force in the "city of man" as well as the key to eternity.[7]

In his massive study *The Foundations of Modern Political Thought*, Quentin Skinner makes the vital point that it was Augustine's "immensely influential argument" against classical political virtue that effectively muted its discussion in the West until the Renaissance. Surmounting Augustine's legacy became instrumental to the triumph of modern secular political theory and the reemergence of civic virtue as a secular alternative to Augustine's spiritual boundaries. The Renaissance recovery of Aristotle proved to be the catalyst for success and the seedbed of political upheaval. As Skinner suggests, the Aristotelian departure from Augustine's political understanding marked the fundamental divide out of which modern political struggles emerged. Philosophers like Leonardo Bruni and Niccolò Machiavelli accepted politics as an earthbound science tied to the pragmatic contingencies of maintaining the state. "Civic" rather than "spiritual" virtue became the moral imperative of good government. Protestant bids for legitimacy amid this political change ranged from passive resistance to open revolt. Yet Augustine's legacy remained vital, even among Protestants. Martin Luther lauded the saint as a personal inspiration superseded only by the Bible.[8]

Even a surprising contingent of antebellum Protestants would tender specific tribute. As unlikely a source as the premier Baptist journal *Christian Review* praised Augustine's spontaneous piety as approached in recent times only by Jonathan Edwards. The writer pronounced his *Confessions* as the quintessential expression of human confrontation with sin and divine grace.[9] Most significant here, however, is not Protestant homage to the ancient personage or his theological rigor but the survival of what Skinner calls the "Augustinian conceptions of Christian political life."[10] This Augustinian tradition remained vital among Protestants as a mode of political and cultural exegesis. They were especially devoted to political society as a divinely ordained temporal expedient for slowing the ravages of sin; to Christian virtue as distinctly superior to classical models; and, finally, to a belief that classical virtue's seemingly admirable tenets (community, honesty, frugality) masked its "fatal" isolation from transcendent Christian truth. Doggett recognized the historical relevance of these themes when he pronounced the subordination of civic purpose to spiritual pilgrimage as the distinction that humankind had been most "prone to confound." Civil governments, he affirmed, served only "earthly and secular impulses" and inclined to the material and philosophical truths that they "vaunted and magnified."[11] In this specific sense, then, one antecedent to the Protestant quarrel with the Republic is found in the post-Reformation clerical adaptation of an "Augustinian" critical tradition.

This Augustinian vein persisted among key Protestant spokesmen, especially those whose work remained broadly accessible and influential among mainline theologians into the nineteenth century. Significantly, as a revitalized classicism eroded Augustinian doubts and injected new optimism into human political striving, Protestant doubters remained wary of what seventeenth-century Puritan divine Thomas Scot called "Machiavels and Politicians who look upon us with smiling faces, and yet do hate us in their hearts."[12] Reformation giants Martin Luther and John Calvin rejected church domination of state, but they also wanted godly magistrates and expected civil government to defend the true faith. Only extreme corruption justified resistance to civil authority that was divinely ordained to interdict the earthly toll of sin. Other Protestants fashioned routes to active resistance. But the Reformation also preserved Augustine's belief that a national political life not reined in by divine rationale bred hostility toward otherworldly faith. In sum, a "liberated" political ideology ignored religion and apotheosized its own "godless" spheres of human aspiration. Likewise, a political system deferential to the "true" faith was at least not hatching mischievous plans to attack it.

Two examples illustrate seventeenth-century Protestant concerns. English Puritans Richard Baxter and John Milton—authorities invoked regularly by antebellum clerics—feared not just Catholic domination but any political theory not based on Christian piety. In his 1659 treatise "A Holy Commonwealth," for example, Baxter reaffirmed the Augustinian tradition by condemning James Harrington's *Oceana* as a utopian political blueprint hopelessly mired in Renaissance classicism. Harrington had based his model on Venetian republicanism and faith in natural virtue and human potential. In Harrington's utopia, Baxter warned, liberty of conscience meant liberty "not to worship God at all." Without piety as the source of virtue, he emphasized, "Mr. Harrington's government cannot be good." It was a "brutish, sensual kingdom" that did not subject "corporal felicity to spiritual, and temporal to eternal."[13] Similarly, Milton assaulted classical humanism in *Paradise Regained*. When Satan offers Jesus the classical wisdom of the ancients, Milton's Christ responds:

> Much of the soul they talk, but all awry
> And in themselves seek virtue, and to themselves,
> All glory arrogate, to God give none,
> Rather accuse him under usual names,
> Fortune and fate, as one regardless quite
> Of mortal things. Who therefore seeks in these
> True wisdom, finds her not, or by delusion
> Far worse, her false resemblance only meets,
> An empty cloud.[14]

Even the millennial speculations of seventeenth-century Puritan zealots—for many scholars a clear indication of conflated political and spiritual visions—often explicitly rejected a paradise coterminous with the purification of earthly political orders. In a landmark study of Puritan restorationism, Theodore Bozeman finds no essential connection between eschatological speculation and political optimism in New

England.[15] His recounting of John Eliot's travails is illustrative. The Roxbury, Massachusetts, teacher and preeminent missionary to Native Americans took time from evangelical labors in 1651 to pen his vision of the coming millennium. *The Christian Commonwealth* was finally published in 1659, one year after the death of Oliver Cromwell and in the midst of the process of replacing the Lord Protector's English Puritan order with a restored Stuart monarchy under Charles II. Anxiously hoping to avert official disfavor, New England leaders suppressed the work and hastily ordered Eliot to recant "political" indiscretions that predicted a millennial order shorn of existing royal mechanisms. Theological integrity gave way to self-preservation.

In fact, Eliot's Scriptural exegesis was largely consonant with normative New England thinking, including that of his distinguished mentor John Cotton. His error was to complement contemporary speculations with a detailed assessment of the millennium's social and political character. As Bozeman points out, however, Eliot's new order bore little resemblance to a "political Eden." Indeed, he assumes the replacement—not the sanctification—of present political structures and depends on Scripture as "the onely 'Magna Charta' of Christian commonwealth." As a dimension of human history, the millennium would remain dependent on ordering mechanisms, but political justice and moral discipline would ensue from the perfect execution of ancient Scriptural truth, not the progressive purification of existing systems. Eliot's millennial scenario mandated a supernatural, biblical contradiction to mundane "political progress." Transcendent power alone could replace an earthly cycle of corruption and decay with an unchanging judicious harmony between ancient truth and human action. Eliot's vision accepted earthly political systems as temporally ameliorative but neither integral to redemptive purpose nor redeemable within the historical process.[16]

By the eighteenth century, Protestant political fears had been further nurtured by the classical republicanism of the English "Real Whigs" and the rationalism and skepticism of Enlightenment thought. Indeed, one scholar has recently contended that the religious heterodoxy of English classical republicans, more than any other single factor, checked their political influence among the majority of Britons who were still largely committed to a confessional state.[17] No less a figure than Jonathan Edwards, transdenominational icon among nineteenth-century Protestants, laid siege to classical and rational assumptions in his work *The Nature of True Virtue*. Edwards warned specifically against sacralizing collective devotion to finite material purposes, what he called "private systems." "True virtue," he explained, was conceivable only from the vantage point of "true *grace* and real *holiness*." Civic striving and humanitarian benevolence, pursued as means of virtue instead of subordinate effusions of "supreme regard to God," necessarily produced hostility to faith. They became, in Edwards's view, false idols that "excite enmity, and fix us in a stated opposition to the supreme Being." To seek virtue in benevolence toward a party, nation, "the whole world of mankind," or "even all created sensible natures throughout the universe," Edwards shrilled, expressed self-love at odds with complete submission to the divine will.[18]

The imperial crisis plunged Americans into a maelstrom of political experimentation and innovation that invited examination of secular political theorists and, according to many scholars, overwhelmed Protestant apprehensions. Still, recent historians have reconsidered the portrayal of Revolutionary ministers as pulpit vanguards of a "holy war" waged victoriously by "God's New Israel." Interest in theological integrity and evangelical purpose probably remained strong enough in most clerical camps to resist uncritical indulgence in political euphoria. Even Nathan Hatch's *Sacred Cause of Liberty*, an important anchor of the "holy war" thesis, notes a postwar moralistic turn that tempered the New England clergy's civic religion. A republican millennium remained central to their collective vision, he argues, but they now preached Christian morality as a vital component of civic virtue.[19] Yet it was also possible for spiritual concerns to push ministers beyond second thoughts about the precise millennium-inducing mix of religion and republicanism.

In the flush of American victory in 1783, for example, Yale University president Ezra Stiles indulged the patriotic sentiments of Governor Jonathan Trumbull and the Connecticut Assembly: "By the blessing of God, these States may prosper and flourish into a great American Republic, and ascend into high and distinguished honor among the nations of the earth," he reveled. Victory had restored the "sweet charms" of liberty to "this American Israel," a new nation "called in Providence to fight out not the liberties of America only, but the liberties of the world itself."[20] Stiles's sermon, as Hatch correctly argues, is rife with potential to explain Protestant understanding of the Revolution. Quite simply, victory and American liberty became fixed in the Protestant mind as the single greatest political blessing that God had bestowed on humanity in the Christian era. It is far from certain that Protestants suddenly decided that "history turned on the success of liberty" or that clerical willingness to distinguish classical and religious ideals evaporated in the heat of liberty's triumph. It is instructive to look beyond the political tint to the religious hues of Stiles's sermon. In fact, he brandished his genuine patriotic fervor only to strike more forcefully at citizens who would politicize or nationalize the Christian faith. "Conformity of heart and life to the divine law," he warned, constituted "true virtue." "If we defend and plead for Christianity from its secular and civil utility only," religion is stripped of "its greatest glories." Stiles demolished the notion that material progress, improvement, or even the temporal rewards of faith in the Kingdom of Providence were the benchmark of human advancement toward Christ's transcendent kingdom. "We may trifle on many things," he argued,

> but on the things that respect eternity, the things of religion, it is too solemn, too dangerous to trifle. . . . How infinitely happier they who, believing the record which God giveth of his Son, have received him, and are become the sons of God! . . . Shall this light come into the world and we neglect it? And shall it be said that these views do not animate a sublimer virtue than the motives taken from civil society? Shall the consideration of being citizens of a little secular kingdom or community be equally animating with those taken from our being citizens of the august monarchical republic of the universe?[21]

At a stroke, Stiles divided sacred and secular history and reinvigorated ancient suspicions of politics that had informed Christian thought for more than a millennium. Jean-Jacques Rousseau's plea for a politically subservient "civil religion" instead of otherworldly Christian piety angered Stiles, as similar charges by Roman political potentates had inflamed Augustine. Both divines believed that political systems and theories not based on Christian piety tied human purpose and happiness to this world, deified human wisdom, and ultimately branded religion an enemy of national progress. Connecticut Yankees could, of course, dine eclectically on Stiles's offerings and reinforce a self-styled "republican faith." That Stiles anticipated temptation explains the minefield of cautions that he laid in their paths. When Protestant leaders like Stiles insisted that the new Republic needed Christian piety, they expressed not a new faith in "republican religion" but a determination to protect traditional faith from the republic.

The pragmatic spirit that prevailed at Philadelphia in 1787 produced a Constitution that drew freely from the liberal, classical, and Calvinist traditions. The framers seemed to acknowledge Calvinist and Augustinian suspicions of human nature. James Madison argued in *The Federalist*, no. 51, that human corruption must be assumed and that government exists to overcome the "defect of better motives" in man. But the Constitution's theoretical foundations also sanctioned a classical faith in purely political and natural routes to republican stability. More important, the framers located ultimate sovereignty and political power in the people. Protestant tradition continued to prescribe national allegiance to a divine power that checked kings and popular majorities alike. Although Protestant leaders hoped for republican harmony, they also retained the religious resources for discord. European turmoil in the 1790s helped to sustain Protestant doubts. Nineteenth-century ministers commonly denounced the French Revolution's bold heresies as testament to European decadence and the stillborn promises of "godless" political theory. Conversely, their civic discourse also predicted steady dividends from girding American republicanism with Christian faith. As transatlantic tensions embittered partisan rhetoric and pushed the nation close to war, George Washington borrowed the theme and called for a deeper religious unity from factious patriots. It was fanciful, he argued, to suppose that national morality could "prevail in exclusion of religious principle." The morality of the "mere Politician" was impotent unless it sprang from religious piety. Protestant political jeremiads in the early nineteenth century continued to parade the "proud, presumptuous, and godless spirit" that had destroyed French republicanism and hopes for liberty and equality.[22] Such attacks also became useful platforms for thumping the glories of American republicanism.

Bullish civic stratagems at times allowed an uneasy alliance between classical political theory and religious interests. Washington's religious rationale for questioning the secular tendencies of democratic politics also reinforced classical republican opposition to factious, self-interested political maneuvering. But his scolding hinted at a more potent reality that would sustain and reshape ancient political doubts among a new generation of Protestant critics. That is, religion would remain relevant in a factious, liberal culture not in deference to divine ordination but at the people's pleasure. Political hopes kept cautious ministers in step with republican transformation and the growth of liberty. Cultural realities revived Augustinian tocsins. By the early 1800s, the confounding of Christian and civic purpose, historically blamed on "godless" elites, seemed equally adaptable to the extending political and material reach of the people.

The application of historic concerns to transatlantic political and cultural change at the opening of the nineteenth century can be glimpsed in the intellectual pilgrimages of New England patriot Noah Webster, Scottish theologian Thomas Chalmers, and English politician and Protestant writer William Wilberforce. All three reached intellectual maturity by the 1790s, opposed the political turmoil of the French Revolution, championed educational, social, or political reforms into the 1830s, and earned prominence among a rising generation of mainline Protestant leaders. Their broadsides illustrate the changing focus of Protestant dissent and ultimately foreshadow the more sweeping clerical critique of liberal culture. To be sure, this trio can be conveniently aligned with defenders of the standing social and political order and champions of a "Christian commonwealth." Closer inspection of their work, however, suggests the critical insights to be gained by looking beyond a conservative agenda. In fact, the reasons advanced by the three for distinguishing piety from politics had more to do with religious purpose than with socially useful material reforms.

An avowed skeptic in his youth, Webster candidly asserted in 1785 that "religion will have little or no influence in preserving the union of the states." Instead, the future Federalist demanded industry, frugality, virtue, knowledge, and the cultivation of national character as the social and moral components of republican perpetuity.[23] In 1785, his *Sketchbook of American Policy* recounted weaknesses in the Articles of Confederation and urged the centralization of power as the political route to stability. In 1802, following his retirement from public life and several years of editing the Federalist newspaper *American Minerva* in New York, Webster despaired of national harmony and attacked both parties for failing to nourish a spirit of "mutual concessions" and for allowing party strife to interdict the deliberative capacities of the people.[24] Six years later, Webster lamented that his faith in knowledge, human potential, and political virtue had been a "fatal error." Writing to his friend Thomas Dawes in 1808, he described his conversion experience and lamented the devotion to reason and knowledge which "deluded into ruin" the "more intelligent and moral part of society."[25]

For thirty-five years following his conversion, Webster championed "primitive Christianity," warned against dependence on classical morality, and preached Christian virtue as the cornerstone of the Republic. In his *History of Political Parties*, he put into contemporary context the historic keynote of Protestant political anxiety that echoed Baxter's attack on Harrington's *Oceana*: "The citizens of the United States . . . have attempted to establish a government solely by the help of *human reason*. Our constitution recognizes no Supreme Being, and expresses no dependence on Divine aid for support and success. . . . It is certain that a government thus formed, and thus administered, can not be a good government; it is not possible."[26]

Webster did not divinize republican principles. Nor did he view Christianity as merely a politically expedient collection of moral principles to secure Brahmin culture in New England. Indeed, his calls for a Republic grounded in Christian virtue still invoked an essential spirituality unburdened by cultural expedients. "When I speak of the Christian religion as the basis of government," Webster wrote in 1836, "I do not mean an ecclesiastical establishment or . . . compulsion of conscience. I mean primitive Christianity, in its simplicity, as taught by Christ and his apostles."[27] Significantly, his religious principles left him sanguine about eternal destiny, but not national. In a letter to his cousin Daniel published in 1837—praised by the Congregationalist *New Englander* as an insightful attack on classical morality—he chastised an American penchant for "self-admiration" and lamented that history offered no reason to believe that sufficient Christian virtue and humility to sustain the Republic "will ever exist."[28] Just months before his death in 1843, he acknowledged that pleas for "intelligence and virtue" had become a political shibboleth so tied to Montesquieu's legacy and classical thought in general that it could only produce "fallacious hopes."[29]

In Scotland, Webster's contemporary Thomas Chalmers shared his reservations about classical morality. Entering the Scottish Presbyterian ministry in 1799 at age nineteen, Chalmers nevertheless continued his youthful interest in chemistry, mathematics, and political economy. His early preaching, he confessed in 1819, was thoroughly intellectual, driven more by socially expedient interests in external morality and political rectitude than by piety. After absorbing the writings of eighteenth-century American divine Jonathan Edwards and publishing an article on Christianity in the *Edinburgh Encyclopedia* in 1813, Chalmers took a pietistic turn. He later gained international fame as reformer, preacher, and founder (in 1843) of the evangelical Scottish Free Church.[30] In 1815 he accepted the pastorate at the Tron Church in Glasgow. It was at Tron that he drilled his congregation on the eternal priorities of faith and the futility of social and political reform apart from spiritual renewal. Like his counterparts in America, Chalmers targeted liberty and liberalism as direct challenges to Christian faith.

In a Tron sermon titled "The Emptiness of Natural Virtue" (published in both England and the United States), Chalmers rebuked the arrogance of utilitarian theorists and educated, wealthy elites for attributing sacred motives to acts of generosity and benevolence that derived from self-interest. Mere human effort might seem "a lovely object in the eyes of the world," he contended, but "[man's] best exertions are unsound in their very principle; and as the love of God reigns not within him, all that has usurped the name of virtue, and deceived us by its semblance, must be a mockery and a delusion." He warned that man could transcend the "fact of human corruption" and exercise true virtue only by becoming a "new creature" in Christ.[31]

Chalmers used a homily on Christianity and civil government to brand the "earth-born righteousness" and "taste of many among the higher orders of society" as more akin to the "native integrity" of "Pagan antiquity" than the spirit of the gospel. He insisted that Solomon's declaration that "righteousness exalteth a nation" referred to a "deeper and more sacred character than the mere righteousness of society" than that "learned in the school of classical or civil virtue." Like Webster, Chalmers demolished notions of superior virtue among social elites, stressing that through law, civilization, and enlightened self-interest, humanity had been "altered a little in its guise" but "not, apart from the gospel, at all altered in its substance." Chalmers attacked popular "radicalism" with equal vigor and attributed it to the penetration of upper-class infidelity into the masses. With open "irreligion" expanding beyond the confines of the "sons of wealth or of lettered infidelity," he thundered, "the impiety of our upper classes now glares upon us from the people, with a still darker reflection of impiety back again." [32]

Chalmers's interest in a "godly commonwealth" and his fear of political disorder, however, were coupled with a more intense interest in "vital godliness" among the people. He believed that securing souls for the Kingdom of Grace transcended all temporal concerns. The bulk of his sermons harped on the depravity of man, the reality of heaven and hell, and the individual transforming power of divine grace. The power of the kingdom of God growing in the hearts of believers, he asserted, affirmed the natural "nothingness of man" and destroyed confidence in the "mere instrument" of God's purpose.[33]

William Wilberforce shared the concerns of Chalmers and Webster. More important, the extraordinary popularity of his writings among Protestant leaders and laymen through the 1850s demonstrates the unexceptional nature of his views. In 1798 the British politician and leader of the English antislavery reformers known as the Clapham Sect took his layman's case for Christianity to the public in *A Practical View of the Prevailing Religious System of Professed Christians, in the Higher and Middle Classes in this Country, Contrasted with Real Christianity*. It would be difficult to overstate the transatlantic influence of this work during the first half of the nineteenth century. The book went through five English editions in six months and was soon translated into French, Spanish, Dutch, German, and Italian. By 1829 it had been reprinted fifteen times in Britain and twenty-five times in the United States. The work's separation of sacred and secular purposes and its concise delineation of faith's temporal and eternal priorities suggest continuing Protestant interest in such distinctions. During the 1830s, it reached a wide popular audience through distribution by the interdenominational American Tract Society.

A single chapter in a work otherwise devoted to spirituality explained Christianity's relation to the state. Wilberforce warned that neither religion nor Christianity as a "mere system of ethics" could cure the "disease of selfishness," the "grand malady" of all political states. The Greeks and Romans rightly pursued civic spirit as the anchor of political stability, he admitted, but their quest rested on the inherently flawed principles of glory, honor, oppression, national aggrandizement, and other "puny productions of human workmanship." The single source of temporal and eternal hopes was "real, not nominal" Christianity, he contended.[34] Like Chalmers and Webster, Wilberforce excoriated the "moral vipers" of Revolutionary France, and warned that Britain could expect no better unless people were transformed individually by the "sanctified" power of the "crucified Redeemer." Yet he hastened to dispose of any notion that he was carelessly prostituting religion to a political cause. He confessed his hesitancy to explain the connection of Christianity and the national welfare, "lest it should appear as though the concerns of eternity were melted down into a mere matter of temporal advantage or political expediency." Only because such "subordinate inducements [were] not infrequently held forth . . . by the sacred writers" did he include "inferior motives" to faith with "considerations of a higher order."[35]

Freedom's "Dangerous Extreme"

Cultural change by the 1830s offered little solace to the aging critics Webster, Chalmers, and Wilberforce. As Lord John Russell and British Whigs hammered a crumbling aristocratic order, popular political participation surged in the United States after Andrew Jackson's election in 1828. The rise of the American Whigs in the 1830s assured the survival of party politics and fired passions anew. Daniel Walker Howe notes in his landmark study of Whig political culture that "politics became the nation's first national sport, and the public played and watched the game with great enthusiasm."[36] Jackson's "war" against the Bank of the United States, his brandishing of executive power during the nullification crisis in South Carolina, and the endless local squabbling over internal improvements amply testify to a factious popular gambit for political and material advantage.

Mainstream Protestants hardly remained aloof. The desire to sustain critical distinctions between Christian and political virtue strained against antipathy to political abstinence. Prominent African Methodist Episcopal divine William Douglass explained general antebellum Protestant sentiment in a sermon to his Philadelphia congregation: "Because our days are few, should we therefore leave all converse with our fellow-men, seclude ourselves in some retired cell, and there spend our time in mortifying the body for the good of the soul? This would be a superstitious absurdity, but no part of Christian duty." Since believers were the "light of the world," he reasoned, they were called to glorify God "in all their relations, whether domestic, civil, or religious."[37]

While Protestants populated the ranks of all major parties that emerged between 1830 and 1860, evangelical influence among the Whigs provided the most visible example of their commitment. Catharine Beecher, Horace Bushnell, Francis Wayland, Charles Grandison Finney, and others made Whiggery a pragmatic legacy of Washington's farewell admonition to keep republicanism firmly anchored to religious morality. The faithful made temperance, abolitionism, and opposition to Indian removal widely respectable moral causes in Whig circles, especially in the North.[38] Whig rhetoric bore the marks of Protestant political jeremiads. William Henry Harrison's 1840 inaugural affirmation was typical: "Sound morals, religious liberty, and a just sense of religious responsibility are essentially connected with all true and lasting happiness." The nation, Harrison boomed, must fully commit itself to the God who "preserved to us institutions far exceeding in excellence those of any other people." When Zachary Taylor followed Harrison's lead to become the second Whig president to die in office, the *Baptist Memorial and Monthly Record* assured readers that Providence still had "grand designs" for a Republic whose "freedom and piety" could help usher in the "glories of the millennium."[39]

It is by no means clear, however, that temporal agendas transformed moral interests and millennial speculations into consensual road maps for tracking spiritual progress. Such a friendly merger still faced resistance from historic distinctions between faith and culture that remained vital within mainstream orthodoxy. With the full bloom of a liberal political order in the 1830s, a new phalanx of clerical guardians moved from trouncing the secularism of classical virtue toward a much broader scrutiny of emergent liberal *culture*. Continuities with past struggles help explain the revitalization of Protestant dissent. Despite liberalism's anchors in individual freedom and material pursuits, both liberal and classical traditions elevated human creative potential in "fatal" isolation from Christian piety. Both placed human striving firmly in the earthly realm and ignored Christianity as the "only possible source of virtue and happiness."[40] Did not endless new schemes, an Episcopal writer queried, ultimately share a common faith in "political and philosophical regeneration"? Did not the empty search for an "Emperor yesterday, a Constitution to-day, a Republic to-morrow"—amount to mere historical vanity and reduce Christ to a "mock Redeemer"?[41] That political "liberty" could spawn a democratic *"cultural* tyranny" over traditional faith became the new and unexpected twist in a very old struggle. In other words, the Protestant quarrel with the Republic was significant precisely because it extended far beyond political categories. Constitutional democracy ignited the challenge, but religious jeremiads spoke broadly to the secular potential of liberal democratic culture that earlier divines had not anticipated.

Two examples from the 1840s suggest the spiritual interests that girded widening Protestant concerns about liberty. In summarizing the obstacles to faith in 1843, evangelical Lutheran leader Samuel S. Schmucker emphasized not political tyranny but the growing intellectual and material diversity of the culture itself. He augured the challenge of "free inquiry" that fostered "superficial views on the great and essential truths of revelation" and honored every form of "fanciful speculation" with the dignity of "theory" and the nods of "numerous advocates and followers."[42] Similarly, in an 1846 "Address to the Protestant Clergy of the United States," Catharine Beecher upbraided her male compatriots for ignoring the changing shape of liberty. Protestants content to revel in their "independence of mind" and the nation's civil and religious liberty, she cautioned, now stared at freedom's "dangerous extreme." "Independent thought" now pushed beyond "faith in Jesus Christ" toward a new agenda that challenged "every established principle and practice." The breaking of "old systems of belief" led to "doubt and distrust of everything" and, finally, to "entire skepticism."[43]

Surging interest in rebuilding the spiritual muscle of the past became a strategic adjunct to such clerical soundings of a new cultural freedom. In addition to the clerical prescriptions, the soaring publication of denominational histories and historic biography after 1830 provides a useful marker of this "backward quest." Between 1800 and 1830, American publishers released only 40 works on church history. Over the next three decades, however, 150 such tomes responded to the growing demand.[44] The transdenominational character of this restorationist impulse assured significant diversity. New England Presbyterians and Congregationalists talked endlessly of rejuvenating the faith of the fathers. Disciples of Christ founder Alexander Campbell demanded restoration of original Christian community purged of individualized doctrine and based solely on Scripture. Baptists touted their individualistic freedom from denominational shackles and pleaded for a return to the simpler unity of "Bible faith." Lutherans and Episcopalians prescribed a renewal of Reformation religion with its creedal integrity and churchly, communal piety. Protestant leaders almost to a person nurtured this vision of Protestant unity and spiritual community beyond democratic, sectarian realities.

This diverse, transatlantic quest went beyond parochial boasts of New England piety. The religious press scrambled to widen popular access to a broad array of past heroes—Augustine, John Calvin, Martin Luther, Richard Baxter, John Milton, and John Bunyan. A Presbyterian reviewer, for example, lauded the English translation of Reformed leader Phillip Schaff's *Life and Labours of Augustine* in 1854. "Patristical studies," he argued, should be accessible to "Christians in the ranks." The historic piety of "the Fathers" must continue to inspire the faith of common folks.[45] Ministers shed no tears for the ancient political structures that had dogged past saints. Yet the cultural uncertainties of the new American order ignited a complex Protestant search for spiritual security rooted deep in the Christian past.

The seeming ubiquity and complexity of this primitivist or restorationist search during the late antebellum era is amply demonstrated in Richard T. Hughes's recent volume, *The American Quest for the Primitive Church*. Well-defined categories—Confessionalists elevating Reformation structures while pietistic Baptists spurned history and grasped for the faith's primitive essence—often broke down in practice. Antebellum evangelical Episcopalians, for example, could celebrate their roles as Reformation "churchmen" and as easily claim the originality of New Testament piety. As David Holmes points out, such eclectic maneuvering to affirm continuities between a historic Protestant struggle and primitive spirituality drew from a common reservoir of Protestant suspicions that cultural encroachment had insidiously corrupted the faith's original purity.[46]

It must be emphasized, however, that Protestant dissent developed in the wake of an evangelical thrust that undeniably tapped the democratic impulse of the Republic. An earlier generation under the tutelage of William Warren Sweet emphasized religious crusaders eager to trample frontier "barbarism" and put the nation in step with advancing civilization and institutional security.[47] More recent investigators have placed religion's conservative social purpose within a broader framework of radical economic change. Paul Johnson explains how the early nineteenth century's rising entrepreneurs applied revivalism as a balm to the raw resentment of displaced workers. An evangelical faith that stressed "individual responsibility to God" could also justify a free labor system that "liberated" employers from communal and moral responsibility. Mary Ryan finds a more complex matrix of religious enthusiasm and adaptation in her study of Oneida County, New York. The relationship between women and converted children replaced patriarchal dominance as the central dynamic of evangelical faith. This bond made evangelical women central to the shaping of middle-class values and "was perhaps the most significant social change that germinated on the charred landscape of the Burned-Over District."[48] Evangelical leader Catharine Beecher endowed this new power relationship with a significance that extended beyond social purpose to the preservation of religion itself.

Most recently, Nathan Hatch's *Democratization of American Christianity* has placed post-Revolutionary Protestantism at the creative center of a progressive, democratic impulse that became the foundation of liberal, capitalist society. Leveling groups like the Methodists and Baptists made war on aristocratic structures and became architects of choice, free expression, and individualism in the new order. An older communal and hierarchical vision of Christian community was consumed in a blaze of sectarianism, denominational infighting, and the self-styled religious improvisations of the frontier. As believers stripped high culture of its religious hegemony, their notions of spiritual democracy slipped easily into an enthusiasm for the liberal, individualistic spirit of Jacksonian America. This chaotic assault on authority, Hatch argues, had unanticipated results: "Religious leaders could not foresee that their assault upon mediating structures could produce a society in which grasping entrepreneurs could erect new forms of tyranny in religious, political, and economic institutions."[49]

Hatch's analysis puts evangelical Protestants at the center of democratic transformation. In sharp contrast to Johnson's view, he outlines a class war challenging the view that "humble folks" knuckled under to traditional power. Like the structures and chieftains they battled, however, religious populists proved equally unable to contain the democratic leviathan within their own religious vision of "equality and justice." Jon Butler makes the important observation that, egalitarianism notwithstanding, Protestant plebeians soon consummated their victories with new structures of authority and power. "The Christian contribution to a developing American democracy," he emphasizes, "rested as fully on its pursuit of coercive authority and power as on its concern for individualism or its elusive antiauthoritarian rhetoric." But if this struggle for authority was more than simple conservatism or a bid for "social control" it also had dimensions beyond the "[shaping] of American society and culture."[50] By the 1830s, clerical dissent labeled partisan squabbling and denominational power plays as symptomatic of a transcendent struggle between the creative freedom of democratic culture and the authority of the religious idea itself. Here was an uncontrollable titan that could render their intramural bouts an irrelevant sideshow. Besieged clergymen struck back from an arsenal of traditional faith, an intellectual base that seemed sufficiently aloof from new alternatives strangely allied with human freedom and power.

One thing seems certain. As social processes evolving in tandem, democratic culture and mainstream Protestantism forged a complex, volatile relationship that resists easy analysis. The Reformation heritage and the American Revolutionary experience inspired Protestant leaders with hopes of religious liberty that would permanently rein in political pretensions, and they entered the nineteenth century flush with the confidence that a "novus ordo seclorum" and the separation of church and state had rendered historic suspicions anachronistic. But the indiscriminate edge of democratic cultural liberty revealed new and more threatening challenges amid the crumbling of ancient tyrannies. The direct appeals of liberal culture to popular material interests magnified its economic and social power, ministers complained, and thereby broadened its base of attack. Consequently, calls for spiritual renovations, and a tradition of jousting with secular political ideals, combined with whelming doubts about unlimited cultural freedom to sharpen mainstream orthodoxy's critical edge between 1830 and 1860. One South Carolina Episcopal bishop gave perspective to a widening materialist ethos by noting an

English comrade's confession that Catholicism and Dissent now bowed to "secularity and unbelief," as the *"grand danger"* facing the Church of England.[51] The new order's "shallow and contradictory freedom," was no cordial, another writer warned. By "baiting" its prey with "displays of speculative liberty," this new freedom could ply the congenial waters of American progress without exposing the "dark sea" of unbelief on which it rested.[52]

Few mainstream clerics renounced political democracy, the Republic, or the unprecedented religious freedom that preserved an open field for evangelism. Likewise, social benevolence and reform movements affirmed cultural commitments, while millennial speculations often masked deeper religious anxieties. In the regular sermons, sermonic literature, and religious jeremiads that composed the spiritual discourse, however, critical ministers sustained an outlet for dissent that claimed patriotism on Protestant terms and turned exceptionalist zeal to the celebration of a spiritual destiny beyond the commonwealth.

2

A Critical Republican Vision

On January 27, 1838, twenty-eight-year-old Abraham Lincoln delivered
one of his earliest public addresses, to the Springfield, Illinois, Young
Men's Lyceum. After years of struggle, the lyceum by the mid-1830s had
become Springfield's leading cultural forum. As for the city's newfound
prominence, citizens could thank Lincoln and other Whig leaders who
had led the recent struggle to move the state capital from Vandalia. The
young lawyer, state legislator, and Black Hawk War veteran was already
steeling a constitutional faith that would guide his political ascent. His
"peculiar ambition," he confessed to Sangamo County voters in 1832,
was to be "esteemed of my fellow men, by rendering myself worthy of
that esteem." Lincoln's topic for the evening, "The Perpetuation of Our
Political Institutions," prophesied his hoped-for political destiny and in-
sightfully tapped national anxieties. Lincoln masterfully turned the jeremiadic form to a purely republican purpose.[1]

In solid Whig style, Lincoln decried racially motivated violence, the
crude excesses of vigilante justice, and a "mobocratic spirit . . . abroad
in the land." Unwavering popular support for the Constitution and law
he prescribed as the political bedrock of national survival. Alluding to
antiabolitionist turmoil within the state, Lincoln decried robbing, church
burning, and violation of property as implicit repudiations of the framers'
vision. Injustice must fall not to random violence but in obedience to the
nation's founding principles.

Lincoln's protean religious faith and resistance to orthodox allegiances
did not prevent a full appropriation of spiritual metaphors. He tendered
"reverence for the Constitution," laws "religiously observed," Americans
worshiping at the "temple of liberty" as bulwarks to replace the fad-

ing memories of the Revolution. Let these, Lincoln thundered, become "the *political religion* of the nation," preached from pulpit and legislative hall alike. While Protestant political jeremiads called for religion as the foundation of political morality, Lincoln took little notice of such props. "Reason, cold, calculating, unimpassioned reason, must furnish all the materials for future support and defense," he concluded.[2]

President Lincoln's addresses would take greater stock of divine power, but his youthful explication of "political religion" illustrates precisely the kind of material strategy that would kindle Protestant return fire. At one level, critical ministers could complain about political jeremiads that sidestepped their own civic formulas, which emphasized republican dependence on orthodoxy. More significantly, the marginalization of Protestant civic discourse drove anxious ministers far beyond a defense of faith's republican relevance. The burgeoning lyceum movement that sponsored Lincoln's address was only the most visible symbol of exploding intellectual and material choices liberated from old spiritual loyalties.

Clerical critics resisted the antebellum ascendance of republican ideals more nurturing to liberal cultural transformation than to historic Christian principles. This "critical republican vision" avoided an easy convergence of religious and national purpose and focused variously on cultural adaptations of republican liberty and individualism that defied orthodox spiritual boundaries. Scholarly interest in portraying mainstream ministers as religious nationalists culturally numbed to such distinctions has directed investigations away from this critical stance. William McLoughlin's assessment illustrates the recent emphasis: "The shift from Calvinistic or Enlightenment determinism included the belief that man had free will, that he and God were partners, and that God had chosen the Americans as special people with a special mission to save the world and bring on the millennium."[3] The crisp clarity of this summation is clouded considerably, however, by an examination of the spiritual discourse of watchful ministers, which charted the spiritual risks of unbound liberty. Their religious jeremiads granted place to republican freedom and individualism of a distinctly Christian kind. Protestant "exceptionalism" did emerge from this strategy, but far more than touting American republican virtues, ministers demanded deference to the spiritual singularities of a destiny beyond the Commonwealth. This maneuvering also broadened to encompass sharp distinctions between the pretensions of transatlantic "Christendom" and the supranational, supernatural bonding of true believers.

Certainly Protestant civic discourse at times struck a celebratory note. Independence Day revelries in particular coaxed clerical vulnerabilities into full view. One zealous preacher feted the occasion by linking the "incarnation of the Son of God and the birth of Representative Republicanism" as the two greatest days in the history of humanity.[4] Lyman Beecher's verbal agility at mixing religious and political progress has made him a stalwart of recent millennial studies. Ironically, such internal muddling often sparked fierce clerical counterassaults.

As early as 1827, for example, New England's orthodox *Quarterly Christian Spectator* detected a disturbing reverence for the nation's political heritage in both secular and religious eulogies honoring Thomas Jefferson's and John Adams's fortuitous parting on July 4, 1826. In an acclaimed oration at Faneuil Hall in Boston, Daniel Webster lauded their timely demise as a "dispensation of the Divine Providence" and thanked the heavens for "receiving them both at once." Webster further dared anyone to deny that "their lives themselves were the gifts of Providence" and proof that God had made America and its benefactors "objects of his care."[5] The *Spectator* obliged. Was it not possible, the writer lamented, to acknowledge the "almost chivalrous patriotism" and accomplishments of both men without [identifying] piety with love of country?" Echoing Wilberforce, the writer denounced the "sweet delusion" often perpetuated by those in "high places of society" who confused devotion to the Republic with "love of Christ [and] reliance upon his righteousness and atonement." To claims that divine providence had distinguished both men with their coincidental departure, he responded that God was as providentially interested in the life of "the most obscure individual" as in the careers of political heroes or even the Revolution itself.[6]

Such sentiments adapted historic bouts with classical conceptions of virtue to immediate concerns about cultural transgressions and the turning of religious language to secular advantage. The strategy is not surprising. Protestant critics counted the meager returns from fusing the growth of Christ's spiritual kingdom with the selfish vacillations of national policy. Like Augustine, they envisioned the kingdom of God as expanding without regard to nationalistic contingencies and in tandem with the conversion of souls. Jehovah still punished and rewarded nations on this earth, they argued, because as finite entities they had no future existence. Consequently, national sin or virtue had temporal but not eternal significance. A Christian commonwealth might receive temporal blessings from the Almighty, but most of all it protected the primary religious mission from "pernicious" political power. As a state jettisoned its religious base, one minister explained, patriotism spiraled toward degradation. It became a "refined selfishness, which extends beyond self, only for the sake of self." Love of country became a willingness to see other nations "embarrassed, oppressed, and destroyed" for the sake of "policy and political expediency." Such a secularized state would then turn on religion itself by replacing it with "pride and vanity."[7]

Any acknowledgment of the salutary benefits of religion to the state remained subordinate and defensive. The idea of a collective spirituality defined in nationalistic terms contradicted fundamental conceptions of a supranational spiritual kingdom made up of the regenerate alone. A New York contributor to the Presbyterian and Congregationalist *Literary and Theological Review* stressed that Christianity's "essential results" did not depend on its "public influence." Power lay in its capacity to change "the hearts of individuals" and replace temporal motivations with spiritual aspirations. Like the Apostles, he argued, modern Christians must eschew the "office of politicians and moralists" and simply "preach and exemplify the gospel."[8] Distinguishing sharply between celestial and earthly realms, he concluded that Christ's spiritual kingdom existed beyond "a secular or national institution." With "objects not primarily worldly but spiritual," its citizens were people of "righteousness, and peace, and joy in the Holy Ghost." Paradisiacal visions were not the lodestar of this transcendent reality: "Those in whose hearts it is established . . . will be prompted to [labor] to accomplish in others what they have experienced of the grace of God."[9] Outrage at the corruption and self-interest that steered scions of national aggrandizement prompted such soundings within the Protestant kingdom. To their dismay, ministers spied unprecedented potential for complicity and compromise abounding within the Protestant fold and, alarmingly, within themselves. Not a sense of unassailable purity but a fear of personal and collective vulnerability jolted their complacency.

At Odds with "Christendom"

Protestant defenders often expanded this critical republican vision to encompass the broader, transatlantic pretensions of Western "Christendom." The intellectual journey of Francis Wayland, Baptist leader and for thirty years president of Brown University, is a case in point. Born in 1796 to English dissenter immigrants in New York City, Wayland early imbibed the rigorous personal discipline and deep Baptist piety of his father. "Diligence in business" enabled Francis Wayland, Sr., to prosper as a New York leather currier, but he traded material success for the ministry in 1807. Personal investments in the marine insurance business largely evaporated in the wake of Napoleon's predations on American shipping, but frugality and enthusiasm for higher education enabled the younger Wayland to graduate from Union College, in Schenectady, New York, and begin medical training in 1813. Like his father, however, Wayland drifted from secular pursuits into the Baptist ministry and accepted a Boston pastorate in 1821. Skillful preaching and writing earned him immediate prominence in the Baptist community and culminated in a call to the presidency of Brown University in 1827.[10]

Wayland's career at Brown marked his ascendance as one of the nineteenth century's most prominent educators and moral teachers. His standard portrait in most studies highlights his role as "academic moralist," committed mainly to the production of "Christian gentlemen" and the peaceful coexistence of religious principles and the social and material status quo. His 1835 textbook *The Elements of Moral Science* sold more than 100,000 copies, gained international acclaim, and became the standard at evangelical Protestant academies (his later texts on political economy and intellectual philosophy were well received but less influential).[11] Yet professional success and an aggressive interest in popular education failed to erase personal doubts about his decision to abandon the pulpit. Christian education, he became convinced, could never fulfill the essence of a higher, spiritual calling. This internal struggle sustained a dynamic tension that ultimately found public vent in religious jeremiads blasting Christian complicity with cultural arrogance.

His doubts imbued Wayland's religion with a ragged, radical edge that flayed his own compromises and bared the material interests that girded national pursuits and "aristocratic" religion. Upon resigning the Brown presidency in 1855, Wayland lamented the "entirely secular" nature of the work and avowed the complete supremacy of "preaching" over "teaching." "There is nothing I so much regret as that I did not make myself a preacher,"[12] he confessed to a friend in 1854. Within months of relinquishing the Brown presidency, Wayland assumed a full-time pastorate in Providence. The religious jeremiads that map Wayland's transformation provide key insights into a neglected component of his ministry and allow a closer scrutiny of the anxieties affecting the larger Protestant community.

In an early sermon selected for publication by the American Tract Society, Wayland destroyed sacred assumptions that informed religious nationalism. "The arm of the patriot is generally, and of necessity, bathed in blood," he cautioned. Apart from the spiritual regeneration of the heart, he argued, the "principles of this world" inevitably produced national power struggles dependent on "threatened or inflicted misery."[13] In another religious jeremiad, he further refined this discriminatory theme, upbraiding citizens who confused "Christendom" with Christianity:

> Christendom is not the Church of Christ. By this term we generally designate those nations which acknowledge the Bible to be a revelation from God, and have forsaken idolatry and paganism. . . . But these nations are not the church, for they contain multitudes who have no hope, and are without God in the world. . . . Religion is, and ever has been, the intercourse which the spirit of man holds with the unseen and uncreated Spirit; and with it no created being has any conceivable right to interfere.[14]

Wayland accepted an essentially Augustinian view of political entities. That is, as finite but "divinely ordained" institutions they interdicted temporal evils and checked the social chaos that human selfishness naturally produced. Even constitutional liberty acted mainly as a bulwark against religious tyranny, not as a positive element of the gospel. For Wayland, that Christianity mollified social evils by checking self-interest merely proved the need to secure the gospel from self-interested redefinition by political exploiters. Statesmen, of course, could join Rousseau in a celebration of "civil religion's" benefits. In other words, they patronized the "social power" of religion not out of deference to its spiritual priorities but out of secular interest in its "cohesive attraction" and its utility in manipulating "the masses on the political chessboard." Wayland believed that by keeping chaos at bay and guaranteeing religious liberty, nation-states could indirectly facilitate the gospel message. They could not, however, embody or define faith. If Christ's command to "disciple all nations" precluded any watchword but "onward" for believers, Wayland concluded, this extrapolitical agenda began and ended with "[establishing] a *spiritual* kingdom in the hearts of men."[15]

Ironically, Wayland sharpened his pietistic redressing of nationalistic excesses even as he publicly joined the sectional fray in the 1850s. In civic addresses he blasted the Kansas-Nebraska Act and urged Northern solidarity against the expansion of slavery into the territories. As the sectional crisis bled the anemic Whig coalition in the 1850s, Wayland enthusiastically cast his lot with John C. Frémont and the Republicans in the 1856 presidential bout. He "smelt a rat" amid the turmoil, however, and warned against linking a morally and socially just cause with the essentials of religion. Nor did he bestow special sanctity on his Northern compatriots. In a widely acclaimed 1853 religious jeremiad delivered before the New York Baptist Union for Ministerial Education in Rochester, New York, Wayland reminded his young colleagues that their essential mission had nothing to do with republican glory. Calling for a return to "the Apostolic ministry," he cautioned:

> To hold forth our inferences, or the inferences of other men . . . , to show the importance of religion to the temporal well-being of men, or the tendency of the religion of Christ to uphold republican institutions, and a hundred other topics of similar character, may or may not be well; but to do either or all of them certainly falls short of the idea of the apostle, when he determined to know nothing among men but Jesus Christ and him crucified.[16]

Wayland similarly dismissed Northern self-righteousness and claims that abolitionism attested to waning human depravity in his section of the country. Such boasts might seem "externally impressive," but they also acted to "undermine and subvert" the preacher, he instructed one minister. "Abolishing slavery is a good thing but it is not religion. . . . Northern men, if it were profitable, would themselves hold slaves in the present state of religion amongst us."[17] In sum, Wayland worried that religion's compromise with nationalistic and humanitarian aims ultimately distorted its critical potential and diverted popular interest from the central purposes of faith. Personal commitment to secular causes only solidified his demands for an exacting vigilance against subtle material encroachments upon the ancient faith. He told his Boston colleague Rufus Anderson that, with great peril, "we are making a difference between the times of Christ and his apostles, and our own times, which I suspect does not exist."[18]

Wayland's critical republican vision spoke broadly to the cultural usurpations of "Christendom." He also explained, in unequivocal terms, that spiritual discourse must remain fixed on a salvific message to individuals, lest it become subservient to the schemes of national collectives or republican advance. There was nothing wrong, he freely admitted, in acknowledging the salutary influence of religion on national morality or republicanism. But such results were not coequal with the primary salvific mission, and they were not endowed with eternal significance. However much religion contributed to social renovations, evangelism under the banner of such temporal purposes fatally corrupted its central purpose. So seriously did Wayland take his own critical vision that by 1860 he was denouncing his career as an erroneous departure from regular preaching of the gospel.[19]

Wayland was hardly alone in his cause. No less a figure than Charles Hodge carved equally sharp distinctions between a spiritual mission and nationalistic blustering. Princeton theologian and for forty years editor of the influential *Biblical Repertory and Princeton Review*, Hodge provided broad intellectual leadership among antebellum Protestants. By the 1860s, he had personally directed the studies of more seminary students than any other American theologian.[20] In his sermon "The Catholicity of the Gospel," published in 1859, Hodge stepped outside his role as seminary exegete and Presbyterian apologist to describe a larger Protestant mission. He warned against adopting Israel's material and temporal expectations of faith. The favored status of the ancient Jews in Jehovah's plan too often produced the "proud and self-righteous spirit which [they] manifested toward the heathen." The Christian message, he contended, overturned the old notion that the fruits of faith were rites, ceremonies, material blessings, or the enlargement of national territory and power. The Christian "revolution," Hodge boomed, promised not "worldly prosperity . . . not dominion over nations, but the forgiveness of sin, the renewal of the heart, reconciliation with God and eternal life!"[21]

Hodge insisted that "national" covenants were anachronisms, at odds with gospel "catholicity" and spiritual blessings "incapable of being monopolized" and always corrupted by a "narrow and exclusive spirit." He could not have been more specific: "That the gospel is designed and adapted for all mankind supposes the spiritual nature of Christ's Kingdom . . . that the government of that kingdom is spiritual government, and that its blessings are spiritual blessings."[22] Though the strictures of spiritual discourse precluded specific social or political analysis, his sermon quashed nationalistic and political materialism that hewed an earthly hoard from a Protestant mission bounded by spiritual purpose.

In a sermon aptly titled "Allegiance Due to Christ," Methodist bishop Davis W. Clark affirmed the reasoning of Wayland and Hodge. He insisted that man entered the kingdom of God not by "natural descent, not by "being descendants of the pious," and not by "blood." He denounced the "presumptuous trust" of those ancient Jews who "flattered themselves [as] partakers of the sure mercies of David" simply because of their Abrahamic heritage. Redirecting his fire at "presumptuous" Americans, he chided: "Are there not too many [today] who pride themselves upon having Abraham as their father?" The only claim to "citizenship in the Kingdom of Christ . . . not lighter than vanity" rested on belief "in His name," Clark warned.[23] Sermons like Clark's typically culminated in a mandate for believers to "spread the gospel to the ends of the Earth."

Themes placing the exclusive, Protestant salvific mission beyond national and republican conceits reached to the most basic levels of Protestant communication. An 1834 "circular letter" to churches of the Edgefield Baptist Association in South Carolina explicitly urged "unceasing vigilance" against the "intrusion of unworthy characters." Believers worldwide constituted the "appointed medium" of gospel expansion. This global army needed no national auxiliaries, since its active agents comprised "spiritual materials only." Nothing must be allowed to interrupt this "communion of renewed minds."[24] Anglican minister Thomas Young told a Charleston gathering of the Society for the Propagation of the Gospel in Foreign Parts that "aggression and universality" were the peculiar "properties of the Gospel" and also the exclusive preserve of the " 'kingdom of heaven'—the Church."[25] Such pronouncements offer little reinforcement to the thesis that mainstream Protestants had committed to an uncritical republican religion that made faith's progress dependent on national contingencies. And as the detailed examination of regular sermon and sermonic tract themes suggests, the largest body of spiritual discourse also remained aloof from such indiscriminate bonding.

Those ministers who sustained this critical republican vision also shared a general Protestant dread of physical isolation from the culture. They decried "monkish seclusion" as symbolic of spiritual "vanity and pride" and inconsistent with the evangelical mission. They confessed republican sentiments and national loyalties. Just as incisively they decried a confusion of political and religious values that endowed republican ideas with transcendent rather than merely temporal significance. Such a confusion, they believed, sanctified popular political cant and undermined their own exclusive claims for Protestant faith. Confusing the objectives of "time" with "eternal destiny," Wayland argued, left Christianity in bondage to "public opinion." Faith did not coincide with but transcended the democratic idea. Its principles produced lives so "diametrically opposed" to those of men living for "the present" that the two could "never coincide."[26] Such exceptionalist zeal is hardly surprising. Confronted with an emerging liberal culture that promised everexpanding liberty and diversity, Protestant critics expended more effort defending Protestant exclusivities than linking their spiritual destiny to a Republic that no longer bowed to orthodoxy.

In sum, antebellum mainline Protestantism sustained a critical republican vision that honored historic distinctions between sacred and secular aims. The clergy's civic discourse at times succumbed to the larger culture's republican boasts, but such internal acquiescence often galvanized resistance. This dissent often expanded to include broader strikes against "Christendom" and concomitant pleas for a traditional message of faith to restore the subordination of political to eternal aims. As the old republican order gave way to a culture sacralizing individualism and democratic liberty in the 1830s, the religious jeremiads provided an outlet for rethinking the relationship of orthodoxy to this expansive freedom. Clerical second thoughts about the maturing of American liberty must be included within the corpus of their critical republican vision.

A Boundless Liberty

Revolutionary ministers may have considered liberty a "sacred" component of American republicanism, but mainline Protestantism by the 1830s nurtured vigorous criticism of liberty's unpredictable turns. The disintegration of an older republican economy and the rise of Jacksonian democracy provided the political foundation for a new generation of seekers who probed cultural frontiers of personal freedom far beyond the political realm. Although politicians continued to bathe their rhetoric in the language of public virtue, Protestant critics blamed the new political order for nurturing a public conception of "virtue" contingent on personal and social utility and validated by the "popular will." By the 1840s, few clergymen doubted that fractious political and social conditions had become permanent manifestations of a new freedom, not temporary blights on the republican landscape. An Illinois Congregationalist writer admitted in 1843 that one could choose how to respond to the new factious order, but, for better or worse, democracy had become the "universal solvent," the "ruling spirit of our era." The great question, he concluded, was whether men "escaping from the extremes of credulity," would press democracy to "the extreme of skepticism."[27] Probing the religious consequences of democratic liberty became an important dimension of late-antebellum Protestant dissent.

Since Plato's critique of Periclean Athens—crystallized in *The Republic* —there have been purely political and civic reasons for opposing democracy. Mainstream Protestant leaders typically shared with secular conservatives a devotion to property rights, social order, and cultural identity. Evangelicalism has long been recognized as a conservative influence among antebellum Whigs.[28] Religious concerns unbounded by material or political agendas evoked a powerful clerical rebuke of the liberal ethos, however. Ministers believed that as political power descended, popular sentiment shifted from a religious to a political base and made faith less a matter of duty than of personal consent. One minister lamented that the new order assumed the people's "inherent virtue," flattered them as "uttering the voice of God," and anointed them as "the source of all power and right."[29] Unraveling this religious dissent from the new political order requires recognition of clerical objectives distinct from secular conservatism.

Protestant preachers who wanted to rein in liberty's innovative trek pronounced it more than a mere corollary of "free will" or a necessary process of "free inquiry." They pressed beyond its cultural liabilities to its capacity to place Christian "first principles" on a permanently unstable footing. For centuries Protestants had warned of corruption and infidelity in high places and yearned for the freedom from papal and political tyranny that the Constitution now afforded. Antebellum ministers who engaged in civic discourse continued to celebrate American liberty, but they spoke to their own interest in making liberty yield steady gospel expansion. A common operative definition appearing in regular sermons and religious jeremiads recalled New Testament admonitions to seek "that liberty by which Christ has set you free." Consequently, affirmations of personal freedom intended to strengthen the ramparts of orthodoxy became a platform for rebuking a new republican liberty that burst such constraints.

Noted Connecticut Congregationalist Samuel Harris demonstrated the critical potential of this tension in an 1847 warning to believers, shrewdly titled "The Dependence of Popular Progress upon Christianity." His objective was not to endorse the nation's political drift but to caution believers against consecrating republican liberty on cultural terms. He exhorted readers to be disabused of the "dream" that civil liberty is the "panacea of human misery" and that if "republicanism can be established it will be all the millennium the world will ever need. . . . Without religion in the heart," he argued, the spirit of liberty was the spirit of "tyranny and pure selfishness." Christianity alone could "extract the poison which the liberty tree sucks up from its roots of sin." The true patriotism that transcended shallower pursuits of national welfare and public-spiritedness derived from "religion in the soul" and devoted all "to the general welfare of mankind." The salvation of individual men, he insisted, was "grander than the destiny of states."[30]

Though religion and politics had traditionally been at odds, liberty and democracy now pushed the struggle from its lofty intellectual plane to the grass-roots level, where, as Harris observed, the "will of the people" was practically equated with the "will of God." In a nation ruled by party majorities, he argued, the opponent of the popular will could expect to be labeled an "aristocrat" and promptly "crushed beneath the foot of a giant."[31] Harris cautioned that in light of popular political power, believers must spread the gospel not only out of reverence for Christ's command to teach all nations but also "in defense of her own existence. . . . If the church do not make Christianity control this movement, it will sweep her to destruction." As the essential weapons of defense, he demanded a return to "the same old . . . doctrines of the cross."[32] Here again, the religious core of antebellum clerical anxiety updated Augustinian political fears to suit the challenge of a new political order. These spiritual concerns distinguished their views from mere political conservatism. When theologians like Harris mocked the idea of a millennium of liberty, republicanism, and "earth-born morality," they were pitting their religious agenda against secular political rhetoric that clearly championed such goals as the end of human effort.

Horace Bushnell's counsel against an aggressive and unpredictable political culture testifies to the breadth of the Protestant quarrel. Pastor of the North Congregational Church in Hartford, Connecticut, Bushnell must be counted among the most controversial of antebellum divines. Clashing cries of heresy and unstinted praise followed in the wake of almost all of his published works. As easily as he denounced old Calvinist notions of total depravity, the fiery Bushnell could blast "fallen humanity" and defend the "new birth" as the only "supernatural" hope. His controversial 1846 work *Views of Christian Nurture* countered revivalism's emphasis on flash-point conversion (what Bushnell counted as an excessive indulgence of liberal culture's individualism) with a plea for Christianity as a sometimes gradual process of spiritual transformation. Yet Bushnell established no sharp dichotomy. He was an admirer and friend of revivalist Charles Finney and cautioned that to "suppose, or even require [regeneration] to be gradual" was "an error quite as likely to confuse the mind."[33] As ardently as did his evangelical compatriots, Bushnell defended spiritual transformation as the only means of realizing true liberty and avoiding its detachment from divine authority. Bushnell's speculative discourse at times struck contemporaries as dangerously vague and spurred attacks on "heresies" that were more apparent than real. The *Puritan Recorder* summed up contemporary frustrations, styling Bushnell a " 'chartered libertine' " whose "genius procures him great indulgence in his eccentric flights and aberrations."[34] More than a century after his death, the "nebulosity of his ideas" continues to resist precise scholarly definition and the somewhat unsatisfying epithet of "transitional figure" will likely remain the historical resting place of Bushnell the speculative theologian.

A study of Bushnell "the preacher," however, offers a more productive avenue of inquiry for the purposes of this study. Within this context, Bushnell's spiritual discourse and prescriptive purposes are not overshadowed by his subsequent prominence as the great anticipator of modern religious liberalism. The central themes that issued from his pulpit suggest that the intricate weave of his theological moorings did not yield a bland neutrality at peace with American culture. Bushnell embraced the role of preacher and eschewed an academic platform. His twenty-eight-year tenure in the Hartford pulpit (illness forced his resignation in 1859) offers convincing evidence of his claims. He denounced critics who branded him an innovator and insisted that his religion looked to a primitive faith uncorrupted by the "New Light" innovations of eighteenth-century Puritanism. The "orthodoxy" claimed by his peers, Bushnell argued, was in fact of recent vintage. This penumbra of theological rigidity and exclusivity dimmed the light of spiritual unity and faith that guided the ancient community of believers. Man-made systems had subtly replaced the older simplicity of a Christocentric faith.[35] Bushnell's central purpose was not to build theological bridges between orthodoxy and Unitarian liberalism. He looked to the resurrection of an ancient faith that would indict the conflict itself as a product of cultural compromise and human arrogance.

Bushnell charged that a destructive "individualism" often grew from modern revivalism's emphasis on personal spiritual cataclysm. Interludes of religious excitement, Bushnell believed, must not supplant the believer's need for mutual nurture and chronic spiritual growth. Congregationalist divine Austin Phelps appreciated Bushnell's "apostolic mood" and the irony of the Hartford divine's belief that "he was nearer to the fountain-head of the very doctrine which his critics were trying to preserve than they were themselves."[36] In sum, the controversy that dogged Bushnell convinced him that fellow ministers had unwittingly fallen prey to the corruptions of modern democratic culture. This understanding made him a frequent critic of both.

Before Bushnell committed himself to the ministry in 1831, he received a secular baptism as associate editor of the *New York Journal of Commerce* and as a law student at Yale. Throughout his ministry, Bushnell retained evident pride in his "worldly" knowledge and counseled a "revival" of civic virtue to sustain New England's economic and political prominence. Yet his pulpit became a bulwark against selfish materialism and moralism, the stuff of human "shallowness and conceit" and the seedbed of a "destructive and vapid liberalism" that advanced "under the pretext of liberty."[37] His own civic consciousness notwithstanding, Bushnell relished the task of defending Protestantism's exclusive claims. The so-called Log Cabin presidential campaign of 1840 between William Henry Harrison and Martin Van Buren offered him ample opportunity. Whigs embellished Harrison's claims to humble backwoods origins, Democrats crowned Van Buren the genuine people's champion, and both sides anointed an American vox populi as grand marshal of countless torchlight parades. But Bushnell demurred, inveighing against national conceits on both sides and warning against the sacralization of politics and democracy:

> I have no objection to any such praises of democracy as our countrymen may choose, if they do not trespass on the sacred distinctions of truth and holiness. . . . Under any and all forms of government you will have unholy work; for man is unholy, your democracy is unholy, full of mischiefs, treacheries, cruelties, and lies. This is the doctrine of the Gospel. . . . But it is only meant, you may suspect, the *doctrine* of democracy as *the true form* of government is holy, i.e. sanctioned by Christ. But before we are deluded thus, we had better ask, where and when it was done by him? When did he condescend to tell us that ours is the true form of government? When lend himself to any such mischievous flattery as this?[38]

Bushnell's response resurrected key Augustinian tenets—that man is inherently evil, that the political world tended to ignore human corruption, and that Christianity was the only means of mitigating temporal wrongs. He declared that, when the Roman governor Pilate and the citizenry combined imperial power and popular consent to condemn Christ, they confirmed that "man is fallen and unholy everywhere," a "slave and tyrant in his nature," and worthy of trust only when Christianity renewed his heart.[39] Bushnell's rancor is less a manifestation of political concerns than a keen suspicion of a political culture that could shape religion to its own purposes. Aloofness from social responsibility was not his cure. Rather, he prescribed spiritual probity as Christianity's original essence and an essential barrier between religious belief and political arrogance.

Social consciousness did not mitigate Bushnell's sense of human sinfulness or his yearning for primitive piety; it hardened his commitment to both. His interest in eternal existence quickened in the 1840s. The death of his only son in October 1842 (and perhaps worries about his own poor health) prompted sermons on the "life of heaven." In 1848 he claimed a personal transformation from "partial seeings" to an acute sense of Christianity as the "personal discovery of Christ," possible not by "assent to any proposition" but by the "trusting of one's being to *a being*."[40] The following year, Bushnell's religious jeremiad to the New England Society of New York chided modern believers for ignoring the powerful otherworldly vision of the Puritan founders:

> They came not with any conscious or designing agency in those great political and social issues which we now look upon as the crowning distinctions of our history. Their ideal was not in these. Sometimes we smile at their simplicity, finding that the highest hope they conceived was nothing but the hope of some good issue for religion. We wonder that they could not have had some conception of the magnificent results of liberty and social order here to be revealed. We want them to be heroes, but we cannot allow them to be heroes of faith.[41]

Bushnell did not reject Christianity as a social force; he rejected the idea of religious faith validated by its material harvest. He marveled at the founders' spiritual power, sustained not by "palpable achievement" but by a supernatural trust in an "unknown future." Their genius lay in an "unconscious" yearning after divine purpose beyond the "visible life."[42] Despite his own hopes for human progress, Bushnell decided that faith in a creed of democratic liberty and human achievement was no faith at all.

One of the most revealing and ironic examples of Protestants' rethinking liberty occurred in Rhode Island. Thirty-seven churches of the Warren Baptist Association gathered in 1841 at the Third Baptist Church in Providence. The Baptist tradition of issuing a "circular letter" to member churches prompted on this occasion a communiqué trumpeting Roger Williams, Baptist freedom, and the tiny state's birthright as the wellspring of American liberty of conscience. "Long shall this glory be ours alone," the writer boasted. Then the panegyric abruptly ended, and these Baptist champions of liberty offered a collective rebuke to its disturbing and unanticipated turns. Too many misguided folks were assigning greater sanctity to "*liberty* to worship" than to "*the worship itself*," the writer warned. This confusion could nurture the fatal notion that freedom of worship also meant "*liberty to omit it*." "To believe what they please, and practice what they please, is not the liberty wherewith Christ makes his people free." A person's self-love could magnify love of individual liberty until, like "a baneful poison, it be diffused throughout his soul." The progress of liberty becomes a "cloak for sin" and, like the cars of a runaway locomotive, its bonds to religious purpose are "shattered to pieces by the speed of its flight."[43]

The Warren Association Baptists admitted fully the paradox that rendered their historic praise for American freedom increasingly anachronistic. Defining American liberty no longer required reasoning based on orthodoxy. The smug self-certainty that grounded their forebears' confidence in liberty as the mother of faith no longer obtained. For many Protestant leaders, Christ's millennial triumph seemed more securely anchored by theological moorings than by practical realities. Freedom was still to be lauded and cherished, but it was freedom that now defied definition and boundaries. Whatever the religious consequences, late-Jacksonian Americans immersed themselves in material and ideological pursuits and gave practical expression to a yearning to "believe what they pleased."

The interdenominational American Home Missionary Society pressed for liberty's containment as forcefully as did the Warren Baptists. Thirty years after its founding by Presbyterians and Congregationalists in 1826, the society instructed ministers to transcend cultural "confusion." More than ever, the society's periodical charged, popular opinion had to be shaped by a "just apprehension of the principles which constitute—and, in constituting, limit—our American liberty." The journal assisted this "absolutely essential" task by offering a second helping of pamphlet material it had already served up two months earlier. American liberty, the writer shrilled, meant "'liberty to worship God, the God of Christianity, and not any other being, real or imaginary.'" As a "Christian people," the United States had no constitutional obligation to protect the rights of those who worshiped "imposters." In short, republican liberty meant "'full personal religious liberty'" constrained within a framework of "'general Christianity.'"[44]

Consonant discords from English Congregationalist John Angell James—his publications circulated widely in the United States—suggest the transatlantic depth of Protestant anxieties. Indeed, James's evangelical zeal and regular contacts with visiting U.S. ministers made him one of the most popular of English divines among American evangelicals.[45] He decried in 1838 that "party spirit scarcely ever ran so high" and that many had "lost their religion in their political fervour. . . [neglecting] the concerns of eternity for the struggles of the times." For those drawn into the "whirlpool" of political strife, he blustered, often "nothing of piety remains but the name." Christians should not escape to the closet, but their interference should be "that of religious men."[46] In assessing the relative importance of temporal and eternal concerns, James recounted a familiar Protestant conception of patriotism:

> [Christians] . . . should watch and pray lest they . . . forget that they belong to a kingdom which is not of this world; that their citizenship is in heaven. . . . A deep sense of the infinite importance of eternal salvation and invisible realities; a due impression of the shortness of time and the uncertainty of life; together with an intelligent consideration of the great end of God in sending us into this world, would repress all undue political fervor . . . and make us feel that . . . every inferior interest should be pursued with regard to true religion. . . . "We are dressing ourselves for eternity."[47]

Contemporary struggles between Whigs and Tories, Anglicans and Dissenters spawned James's attack, but he attached his argument to historic concerns. Acknowledging his intellectual debt to seventeenth-century Puritan John Howe, James quoted him at length and stressed the continuing relevance of Howe's demand that Christians subordinate political to spiritual interests.

These transdenominational critiques reveal the breadth of Protestant concerns about liberty that defied their proscriptions. That they cited the piety of spiritually transformed believers as the anchor of security from freedom's flight testifies not to how "secular" and utilitarian the Christian message had become but rather to how otherworldly it remained in the face of change. Civic discourse continued to praise religion's incidental benefits to republicanism, but nationalistic boasts beyond that hierarchy as often incited clerical rebukes of such internal accommodation. Regular pulpit fare and religious jeremiads declared liberty's encroachments as cultural signposts of spiritual vulnerabilities, not republican peril.

Significantly, the diffusive, unpredictable character of this muscular liberty goaded Protestant dissenters as much as specific transgressions that they assigned did. This perception of an expansive, elusive freedom propelled the Protestant critical republican vision toward a much broader scan of liberal culture. In short, Protestant contestants squared off with liberal individualism, the unruly cultural offspring of political democracy.

Freedom beyond Faith

Alexis de Tocqueville first used the term "individualism" to describe the tendency of maturing democracy. Personal liberty allowed the citizen to separate self from society and act solely from a cool assessment of personal interest. He traced individualism to an excessive popular interest in democratic equality that ultimately discouraged mutual cooperation and severed human ties. Happily for Americans, Tocqueville believed, politicization at all levels of society forced compromise upon recalcitrant individuals and brought self-interest in line with social goals. Community in a democratic society, in other words, depended heavily on a material base.[48] For Protestant critics, however, such a utilitarian end run gave cultural respectability to self-interest and complex motivation, both of them at odds with "gospel simplicity" and spiritual unity of purpose.

Mainline ministers did embrace "individualism," but as they did with their republican vision, they typically embraced it on their own terms, hoping to protect evangelical frontiers from cultural confusion. Addressing an Andover audience in 1857, Congregationalist divine Austin Phelps humbled individual potential squarely at the threshold of spiritual destiny. The world too easily confused faith's "practical energy" with its spiritual purpose, he warned. Christianity was a remedy for sin addressed to individuals, "not to communities, not to nations, not to the race." It was not a system of "social civilization," a "standard of political economy," or a "manual of universal progress." Nor was its reception mandated because it was the "religion of the fathers" or the "religion of the country," or because of its "salutary bearings on organized society." These, Phelps cautioned, were the "arguments of superstition," collective diversions from a more singular fate. Phelps's vision paralleled Wayland's Baptist perspective: "In the Old Testament we find nations addressed, and the communications from God are to them. . . . In the New Testament we perceive nothing of the kind. The gospel of Jesus Christ is a communication made from God to *each individual*."[49]

Here again, internal prompts helped ignite Protestant criticism. Selfish individualism, it seemed, had penetrated the ranks in the form of denominational fragmentation. By 1860, for example, Methodists and Baptists accounted for 70 percent of Protestants, yet those two groups had splintered into seventeen separate bodies. Presbyterian bickering over revivalism and doctrinal issues produced the highly publicized heresy trials of Albert Barnes, George Duffield, and Lyman Beecher and led to the formal schism of the church into Old School and New School wings in 1837.[50] By 1846, the growing section crisis split Baptists and Methodists along North-South lines. The new Republic also became home to innumerable smaller sects, as well as larger movements like the Disciples of Christ. Brigham Young's Mormon flock escaped the bickering and incensed orthodox Protestants in 1847 by claiming a new promised land near the shores of Utah's Great Salt Lake. Hundreds of periodicals carried the sectarian rivalry to mass audiences in what one minister called a "malicious" exercise likely to drive honest seekers "not to Jerusalem, but to dreary unbelief and skepticism."[51]

Deep cultural doubts shadowed denominational cheerleading. "There are *sects enough*," a frustrated *Home Missionary* writer opined in 1856. The enervating spirit of division represented believers' collective knuckling under to selfish aggrandizement instead of obedience to the unity of Christ's spiritual kingdom. The "practical effect" was to replace spiritual pursuits with a material quest that "[identified] the Kingdom of God with the denomination." Impressed by the piece, evangelical luminary Catharine Beecher publicly concurred and appended the article to her book *Common Sense Applied to Religion*.[52]

Significantly, clerical dissent regularly tallied beyond narrow denominational costs. A Reformed pastor argued that political fragmentation was only the most visible component of an individualistic spirit penetrating the whole of American life. It signaled a rejection of religion and a new faith in political and social bases of unity. Men were practically denying their "radically ruined" nature and deceiving themselves with their confidence in unity based on "*development, progress* and *improvement* as if all this were the acquisition of new and substantial good by [their] own latent powers . . . and not a gift from without." As a spirit of "alienation and plurality," individualism threatened to "dispute the Revelation-fact itself" and "assert and maintain man's capability of self-regeneration and development."[53] Noted another Reformed, "perverted reason" and "an endless spirit of division" would eventually portray Christianity as mere "trickery" employed to "rob people of their sacred and dear rights."[54] Not surprisingly, Confessionalists often flayed the "individualistic" piety of groups like the Baptists as lamentable evidence of internal complicity.

Episcopal divine J. T. Brooke raked believers who succumbed to the "idolatry of liberalism." This idolatry, he explained, resulted from the culture's movement from a judicious acknowledgment that "all sects have equal rights," to a sacralization of individual choice that rendered the "*essential* doctrines" of Christianity vulnerable to secular processes. Individual freedom to adopt those "leading *essentials*" must not, he explained, be exchanged for an "unscriptural" acceptance of each doubting but "sincere inquirer" as "somehow just as acceptable to God." Constitutional securities must not come into "profane contact with the *veracity* of God." "Excellent" as the Constitution was, Brooke warned, it was not a product of "divine inspiration." Neither could it serve as a "rule of faith" or a "standard of responsibility to God." Liberal cries against "bigotry" and narrow-mindedness only disguised their own unbending creed—"a belief in the sufficiency of all unbelief." He admonished believers to accept orthodoxy as necessarily at odds with the liberal "expansive spirit of the age." Beware that believers "bow to an idol," Brooke cautioned, when they affirm liberalism's motto "prosperity to all religions and preference to none." Impressed with Brooke's sermon, the *Episcopal Recorder* editor printed the piece twice in 1850.[55]

In sum, critical ministers cited expressions of liberal individualism as unacceptable departures from republican liberty that hewed to a spiritual course. The individual freedom from political oppression that was supposed to secure an open road to the gospel, they believed, now led as easily to intellectual fragmentation, blurred distinctions between good and evil, and complex motivation instead of the fixed principles of spiritual unity and truth. Liberty had set the popular mind adrift in a sea of systems, Scottish evangelical writer Peter Bayne noted in 1852, and "while newspapers, and mechanic institutes, and even ragged schools exist, men will know that the mode of their parish, of their country, of their generation, is not the only conceivable mode."[56] Resistance to the intellectual diversity and complex motivation that characterized liberal individualism may be examined more closely in the work of two prominent figures—revivalist Charles Grandison Finney and Baptist writer Henry Clay Fish. Their work reveals a commitment to replace the new order's cultural lodestars with the unity and simplicity they claimed as the exclusive preserve of Protestant faith.

No American revivalist stirred more souls—or more controversy—during the 1820s and 1830s than Charles Finney. A Presbyterian malcontent who despised Princeton's Old School Calvinists, Finney borrowed such techniques as the "anxious bench" from the early Kentucky revival and ignited revivals in such western New York cities as Auburn, Utica, and Rochester before assuming a New York City pastorate in 1832. In 1834 he accepted a professorship at Oberlin College in Ohio where he also edited the strongly abolitionist *Oberlin Evangelist* newspaper. His *Lectures on Revivals* earned international recognition, explained his "new measure" evangelism, and affirmed a salvation message open to all. From 1851 to 1866 he served as president of Oberlin.

Finney's electrifying style, pragmatic approach, and mass appeal tag him in many studies as the quintessential clerical exponent of an individualistic Jacksonian spirit. He apparently told listeners that free will empowered them to "convert themselves" and bring on the millennium, perhaps within three years! His theology exacted a heavy toll from divine authority in order to exalt human potential and subsidize a democratic religion in harmony with the "liberality" of the age. Scholars have not erred in exploring the controversy surrounding his innovative "measures" and occasional bold pronouncements. It is Finney's core message to believers (in his *Lectures to Professing Christians*, for example) that represents an often neglected but revealing component of his theology. Whatever the democratic consequences of his cocksure methodology, Finney ironically told the people to declare personal war on the cultural transformations that he exploited.[57]

For Finney, liberalism foundered on the principle that man necessarily acted from complex motives and that rational self-interest could produce individual and communal harmony. Christianity was no moral code designed to "control" self-interest, he regularly insisted. True faith removed self-interest as a motive through the supernatural intervention of the Holy Spirit. Individual regeneration and personal piety, in other words, were the indispensable agents of Christian community. The sanctioning of motivational complexity—liberalism—was the real enemy of religion in Finney's spiritual vision.

In *Lectures to Professing Christians*, Finney spoke directly to believers and insisted that as "new men," they must replace complex motivation and intellectual fragmentation with a unified vision of selfless "duty" and "love" controlled by the divine will. This true freedom culminated in "entire sanctification," the believer's full commitment to pursue a life of "Christian perfection" or total conformity to Christ's purpose. The goal was nothing less than "perfect obedience to the law of God," the state in which believers "have no will of their own, but merge their own will entirely in the will of God." Finney's plan mirrored John Wesley's admonition to pursue "holiness," but, like Wesley, he confined human progress to a path of spiritual obedience. As Leonard I. Sweet has noted, Finney was ultimately less interested in claiming complete sinless perfection for himself or others than in "spurring on stubborn, lazy, and reluctant people to horizons within their grasp but beyond their reach." Any lesser aspiration implicitly limited the Holy Spirit's power over the believer. The eternal consequences of human corruption and sinfulness, not popular power or social renovation, remained the centerpiece of his message.[58]

Finney emphasized that the "Kingdom of God" grew not with expansion of the Republic but by saving souls and supplanting personal freedom with duty to God. His perfectionism revealed not inflated notions about man's ability but his belief in the Holy Spirit's unlimited power and an obsession for obliterating selfishness as an excusable motive for the believer. Finney wanted action but rejected the idea of multiplying conversions to perfect republican virtue, pursue social reform, or produce the millennium. Such earthly motives fatally contradicted the divine plan. Religious striving in pursuit of salvation from either "temporal or eternal ruin," Finney insisted, was as selfish as "any work of any devil is," a surrender to cultural endorsements of self-interest. In his sermon "False Professors," he blasted the "multitudes in the church" who by word and deed admitted that their "grand determination" was to secure earthly bliss or to "get their own souls planted on the firm battlements of the heavenly Jerusalem, and walk the golden fields of Canaan above." Such characters surely "will go to hell," Finney warned. "Their religion is pure selfishness."[59]

The political mind—thriving on pride, "self-love," and the whims of public opinion—was anathema for Finney. Only through the "new birth" could individuals embrace a "first principle in religion, *that all the world is wrong*," and seek holiness and community beyond cultural imperatives. Finney was sanguine about the external morality of society only as it reflected individual deference to a transcendent spiritual community driven by selfless devotion to God. He commissioned believers not as lieutenants of American liberty but as vessels of divine authority, completely controlled by the Holy Spirit. This complete "yielding up of our powers so perfectly to his control," Finney triumphantly proclaimed, was the only means of realizing the "liberty of the gospel."[60] His was also a path to spiritual freedom that veered sharply from the course of liberalism and an open society.

The celebrated English evangelical John Angell James gave transatlantic expression to Finney's views. When Finney toured England in 1849, James overcame his initial doubts about the pulpit star's methods and provided critical support. Like Finney, James expected a millennium but tied evangelistic enterprise to individual salvation and the building of a spiritual kingdom reserved for a "peculiar people." To deny this community's "singularity" and "accommodate it to the community by which it is surrounded is an encroachment on the authority of its head, an incipient alteration of its nature, and a frustration of its design." James urged the pursuit of "Christian perfection." Like Finney, however, he defended the cause less to affirm human power or practical possibilities than to deny believers any quarter of liberty from divine authority. Chronic spiritual striving testified to a process of absolute acquiescence.[61]

James hardened his dichotomy between Christian simplicity and cultural complexity in *An Earnest Ministry the Want of the Times* (1848). He detailed a world of exploding popular choices only to prescribe a retreat to the "apostolic ministry" of the ancients, "who never once conceived . . . that they must accommodate themselves to the philosophy or the taste of the age." As politics stirs material lusts and nations "daily become desirous of more liberty," James queried, when will such freedom "leave the soul at liberty for the affairs of a kingdom which is not of this world?" In a secular world that daily "[poured] forth streams of information," James speculated on the most "insidious" potential of the new order. The modern "guides of the popular mind" could now attack religion without "open assault" by simply ignoring it, by "[treating] the whole subject as a negative, a nonentity, a thing to be forgotten." Turning inward, he assailed materialistic and indulgent believers for "[corrupting] the simplicity that is in Christ" and inviting their own destruction.[62]

Baptist minister Henry Clay Fish shared Finney's insistence on individual responsibility to God. The Newark, New Jersey, pastor's master work, *Primitive Piety Revived* (1855), became one of the celebrated tomes of the decade and a catalyst to the revival fires that swept the nation in 1858. Less than a cogent theological treatise, its practical, popular message nevertheless went beyond "revival propaganda."[63] Critical planks redressing the culture's subtle indictment of historic faith supported Fish's restorationist yearning. Recounting the gospel's triumphal promises clashed with a harder analysis of a cultural rejection of Scriptural piety. Most egregious was the superficial faith infecting the church itself. If Fish hoped to spur revivals by inciting a "crisis" mentality, his alarms generally favored critical soundings of liberal culture over concocted phantoms.

Americans who were well schooled in the "essential individualism of *republicanism*," he argued, were losing sight of the "essential individualism of protestantism,—of *Christianity!*" Fish insisted that Christian individualism produced a "unity of purpose" based on spiritual transformation and personal commitment to propagating the gospel. Like Finney, he regarded complex motivation as an unacceptable compromise with man's naturally "selfish and depraved" spirit. His hopes centered not on a Christian commonwealth but on the spiritual community of believers galvanized from temporal threats and energized by the eternal priorities of a "primitive piety." As "pilgrims and strangers upon earth," Christians must be "neither elated by its prosperity, nor crushed by its adversity," he emphasized.[64]

Fish's sweeping analysis culled the theme of Christian "peculiarity" throughout. The essential spiritual distinctions of believers as "a *peculiar people*" could not be mollified by cultural ties, he warned. Christian individualism required believers divorced from material indulgence, wedded to personal humility and self-sacrifice, and committed to persevering in a "community by themselves." Quite the opposite, Fish thundered, characterized modern Christians too fearful of the tag "singularity." Professed followers of the "*humble, self-denying Jesus*," too often found greater solace in leading the material frenzy. "Lax accommodation," he counseled, denied the anchoring rationale of spiritual separation: "Christian countries are, in an important sense, *unchristian*."[65] He projected hopes of spiritual progress based on biblical authority, not on the fascinations of liberty that he laid upon a wayward flock.

Fish's diagnosis of cultural ills may have tapped widely shared anxieties, but the "spiritual individualism" he prescribed fit within a broader mosaic of clerical remedies. Lutherans, Episcopalians, and German Reformed, for example, hewed more closely to the Reformation ramparts of creed, church, and sacrament. German Reformed leader John Nevin rejected outright the "unhistorical, unsacramental, and unchurchly" versions of Christian community espoused by Reformation "renegades" like the Baptists. "Churchmen" like Nevin found in the stabilizing influence of traditional liturgy, creed, and episcopacy the essential compensation for the weakness of the individual will.

Wearied by both sectarian division and political disintegration at mid-century, one despairing Episcopal writer confessed that even the universal acceptance of "Wesleyanism" would be preferable to the present state of decay. He wailed that Americans had mistakenly assumed that since all religions "*may* exist under the constitution, therefore they *must* exist." To grant the evils of "established religion," he argued, must not preclude the necessity of a "national" faith. It was more necessary than ever in light of the "internecine wars" of the political world, which encouraged hostility to all "fixed principles." God's eventual triumph was certain, of course, but believers must oppose a growing liberal spirit that "eats away, and dissolves, daily, all common principles and ideas." The "grand advantage" of Episcopalians—their "absolute unity of discipline and worship"—offered the most effective Protestant contradiction to corrosive diversity.[66] Such attacks spoke to the needs of a Christian commonwealth, only to fire hotter themes at a liberal culture drifting away from orthodoxy.

Even Protestant leaders who established new movements and challenged old hierarchies did so in pursuit of stability and community that could counteract this individualistic spirit. Division was a means of expressing dissent from liberalism. The Disciples of Christ, for example, are often regarded as exuding the American democratic spirit. Springing from the frontier ministries of Alexander Campbell in western Pennsylvania and Barton W. Stone in Kentucky, the Disciples extolled religious freedom, rejected organizational hierarchy, and urged all pious Christians to abandon a corrupt European Protestant tradition. By 1860, they were the largest indigenous mainstream Protestant group in the nation. Yet the founding rationale of the Disciples centered on an avowed hatred of Christian disunity. They condemned creeds and liturgical traditions as divisive human conventions that corrupted the original unity of believers. The group hoped to reunite all believers under a banner of "primitive Christianity" and devotion to the Bible only. Significantly, Campbell embraced religious freedom only to become progressively more intolerant of diversity within the Disciple movement after a merger with Stone's group in 1832. Like other Protestant ministers, Campbell was obliged to celebrate civil and religious freedom even as democratic liberty and liberal individualism extended freedom's limits far beyond the spiritual boundaries he envisioned.[67]

The expansion of a critical republican vision to expose the corruptions of liberal individualism sharpened the dichotomy between a spiritual message of unity and simplicity in a world of complexity and diversity. The new order hailed diversity as a positive good and licensed every person to write his own script for progress, bound only by human law and personal ambition. Protestants by the 1850s believed that this was the strategy of a new Antichrist, insidiously stalking "gospel simplicity" with the lure of "faction," "double-mindedness," "man-power," and "pride." "Is there not danger of our being corrupted from it?" the *New Englander* queried in 1854. "We are tempted to think [the world's maxims] innocent, because common."[68]

Protestant praise for the Republic in the decades before the Civil War was accompanied by a countervailing "critical republican vision" that turned its focus to the secular potential of American liberty. From a determination to preach the limitations of classical virtue in the early part of the century, Protestant critics extended their reach to the new political order and to the liberal culture it nourished. Fearing the new amalgam of material ambition, political power, and intellectual freedom among the people, these doubters deployed important themes of cultural criticism among Protestants who otherwise found plenty of reasons to disagree. Confessionalists and pietists alike feared the complexity and relativism of a liberal republican order that boldly challenged Protestant conceptions of liberty and individualism.

Harangues against human sinfulness and demands for the spiritual regeneration of individuals figured prominently as restorative adjuncts to this cultural analysis. The strategy gave new relevance to historic concerns. It also sharpened the boundaries between Protestant religious exceptionalism and burgeoning republican and nationalistic vaunts. Protestant civic discourse continued to affirm the temporal benefits of faith. But even these homilies often fit Augustine's strategy of interdicting political criticism by asserting religion's salutary impact on the state. Certainly ministers shared a broader national desire to preserve the Republic, and they believed that Christianity would help sustain it. But underlying these jeremiads lay a deeper determination to keep the centrifugal energies of liberalism from jettisoning religion altogether. The Republic needed Christianity, but neither the Christian mission nor man's final destiny turned on political or material successes, however real God's providential power.

Princeton theologian Archibald Alexander urged believers not to be hoodwinked by the alluring countenance of individual freedom. "The spirit of the world is the same as formerly, but the mode of attack is changed," he warned. The old challenges of "fire and gibbets" and the "openly profane" now gave way to the subtler advance of compromisers and "false professors" who scorned piety as "illiberal, bigoted, and inimical to human happiness and to elegant improvements in society." For believers, Alexander cautioned, the new order must serve to reaffirm historic salients: "This enmity is not inoperative. The opposition which exists between the spirit of the world and the spirit of true religion must produce a conflict. . . . Victory over the world," he concluded, came only as the "fruit of regenerating grace" imparted by the "illumination of the spirit."[69] Alexander's emphasis on inevitable conflict provides a useful backdrop for examining how a Protestant critical republican vision extended to much broader probes of the new liberal order.

3

Frontiers of Spirit, Frontiers of Space

In 1848 the *Christian Observatory* unleashed a caustic rejoinder to nationalistic cant:

> We have watched with deep interest, the efforts of many in our land, to rouse our people to the destiny of the Anglo-Saxon race; a destiny, as they represent it, of conquest and universal dominion. We do not regard it as idle talk. For, let that sentiment once be impressed on the nation, and no war-cry would be half so terrible. Under its stimulus, not only Mexico, but all South America, will be trampled by invading hosts, and the star-spangled banner wave over the entire Western continent. Give to our people this impression, and you have let loose a power which will not be checked, till the end is attained. Hence, we deprecate such teachings, and would have the mind of the nation drawn to juster views.[1]

The writer called for replacing motives of greed and aggrandizement with a more "glorious destiny" as "light to the world" and a "blessing to mankind." He rejected the spiritually inert rhetoric shaping the new liberal order. Protestantism's religious mission, he contended, was necessarily the superior and separate cause.[2] In the wake of unprecedented commercial and territorial expansion in the 1840s, an outpouring of religious jeremiads bared the fears of Protestant critics that these physical probes were giving keener edge to unchecked cultural freedom. They focused on the unraveling of materialistic conceits that they believed both girded expansionist aims and further alienated their spiritual agenda from the earthbound course of emergent liberal culture. A jeremiadic scouring of missionary and evangelistic enterprises by mid-century acknowledged a concomitant need for spiritual vigilance within.

Ministers who suspected that a muscular political and material grasp controlled the new expansionism could find plenty to fret about as the nation approached 1850. John Tyler's unexpected presidency following William Henry Harrison's death consummated the nation's decades-long pursuit of Texas annexation and set the stage for James K. Polk and his expansionist allies. The Anglo-American dispute over Oregon succumbed to negotiated settlement in 1846, but not without much rhetorical ado about a third row with Great Britain. With the largest portion of Oregon pocketed, Polk abandoned pacific ways for Pacific gains in the Mexican War. American victory and the Treaty of Guadalupe Hidalgo added California, its fine harbor at San Francisco, and $200 million in gold between 1848 and 1852. California's population swelled to 250,000 by the early 1850s, and the state's petition for admittance to the Union fired sectional tensions that produced the Compromise of 1850. Steam navigation and the railroad assured the conquest of the West and fueled land speculation well ahead of actual development.[3]

Beyond California, the Tyler and Polk administrations announced the nation's expansionist aims as global and commercial. Attempts at formal diplomatic relations with Hawaii began in 1843, while in 1844 Caleb Cushing, the United States' first minister to China, successfully negotiated the Treaty of Wanghiya, opening Chinese ports to American ships. Anticipating a new age of international commerce, Boston's entrepreneurs expanded docks and deepened ports in the 1830s to accommodate larger ships. Imports tripled and foreign trade traffic doubled during the decade.[4] For merchants, entrepreneurs, fledgling industrialists, and politicians, control of one's destiny meant secure connections with an expanding, global marketplace.

With North American territorial disputes mostly settled by mid-century, Britain became more an economic competitor than a military threat to the young Republic. Her "free trade" empire hinged on cheap textile exports and iron manufactures as her economic base shifted decisively toward manufacturing between 1825 and 1850. British investors expanded port facilities worldwide to assure the supremacy of the nation's merchant fleet. Confidence in the British Empire's trade superiority brought an end to old government economic controls and signaled a commitment to the unfettered accumulation of world markets. Between 1830 and 1850, Britain repealed the Corn Laws, ended the East India Company's exclusive China trade privileges, and repealed the last of the Navigation Acts. Her economic and political dominance of India culminated in 1858 with the supplanting of East India Company rule with direct British control. Seemingly acquiescent to economic liberalism, Parliament, as Phyllis Deane notes, in fact extended a "visible hand" determined to make sure that private economic development redounded to British national interests.[5]

Neither American nor British expansionists attributed their global commercial scramble to simple greed. Many saw the quest as inevitable, necessary, and tied to higher ideological purpose. They laced the pursuit of land and markets with all sorts of ancillary justifications that did not go unnoticed by Protestant leaders. English Victorians combined confidence in the superiority of British civilization with equal certainty that the empire's indigenous populations needed to assimilate Western culture. Americans and Britons talked of "destiny" and the irrepressible march of Anglo-Saxon influence across the globe.[6]

Political apprehensions still laced with the principles of classical republicanism led some expansionists to claim empire as essential to preserving a virtuous agrarian base and interdicting American descent into the decadence of a closed, urban society. Popular presses served up the Mexican War as high adventure, a visible demonstration of republican superiority and a tribute to the nation's still-vital "spirit of '76."[7] Writers extolled a "vigorous and omnipotent" young America, driven by the inherent expansiveness of American democracy. The Rocky Mountains were useless "battlements against invasion," the *Baltimore American* bragged in 1839. American eyes fixed on the "green valleys of Oregon" inspired an "advancing wave of emigration" already "mingling its spray with the billows of the Pacific." Possessed of a national character that mandated "ample room and verge enough for safe expansion," the writer concluded, Americans needed the West as a "safety-valve" to escape the "evils of an overgrown population" and the "ill humors that might grow into sedition."[8]

It is commonplace to portray Protestant leaders as comfortably perched atop expansionist zeal. Sidney Mead put the argument simply: Democratic liberalism became more a religion than a political idea in the antebellum American mind. As an expansive, "free-enterprise," individualistic way of life, it declared its principles universally valid. By the time John O'Sullivan christened the new faith "manifest destiny" in 1845, Americans already knew the catechism. Denominational religion stood apart from this democratic faith, but lacked the resources for dissent. Complacency, providential thought, and an "amorphous" intellectual structure saddled antebellum Protestants with a critically deficient ideology. Ministers sanctified notions of expansion, mission, and destiny, Mead argued. Conflict and tension with the culture became "almost non-existent."[9]

To the extent that church leaders demanded a certain mutuality between material frontiers and the missionary enterprise, Mead's argument holds. Further, it would seem that Protestants pumping huge sums into global missions by the 1830s would have had every reason to link evangelical and material expansion. Transforming trade routes into gospel roads did fuel the enthusiasm of many a missionary. Given this attractive lure, a large contingent of ministers challenged the integrity of such links and demanded sharper discrimination of purpose. Their argument deserves closer consideration.

The roots of the dissent lay not in the idea of expansion itself but in the growing disjunction between religious theories of advancement and mushrooming alternatives fed by liberty. Critical divines rued the centrifugal tendencies of the new liberal culture. Eyeing the nation's expanding material horizons, they demanded equal vigilance in policing the machinations of secular expansionists—especially those claiming "civilization" as their mantle of legitimacy. The religious jeremiads increasingly charged that the nation's advance was driven by a cultural and commercial morality that spurned historic Protestant purpose. New York divine Joseph Thompson drew the battle lines: "The hopes of humanity are centered in the struggle between a material and a Christian civilization; between the republic of Plato and the Kingdom of Christ. . . . *Christianity must conquer and control the material civilization of the world, or she herself will be conquered.*" Presbyterian divine Willis Lord chided manipulators who transformed Christ into a mere deity of civilization and commerce. Such materialization of faith, he argued, distorted its "vast central truth." Apart from Christ "the incarnate Word," "the hope of salvation," Christianity became but "a dream."[10] Such pleas betray the anxieties of Protestant leaders questioning the security of faith from culture. More often than has been recognized, ministers unveiled their religious colors to thwart an easy union of Christian and cultural frontiers.

Destiny beyond the West

Protestant leaders looked to the American West as the most visible "foreign mission" field. The advancing frontier stood as perpetual reminder —particularly to transplanted Yankees—that the nation always hovered at the edge of "barbarism." Westerners often defended their efforts from Eastern condescension. Some advocates of Western missions—particularly clergy who needed funds for church schools—found that firming their Eastern economic base required emphasis on the "civilizing" benefits of their religious efforts. Pious Western heralds outside the ministry were more inclined to confuse sacred and secular purposes in support of broader interests. Illinois lawyer Samuel Bowman instructed fellow Methodists on the great prospects of his state and the extending West. Another century of support for economic growth, education, and religion would assure to future generations "the sublime spectacle of a 'nation's flag' and the 'banner of the cross' planted on the highest peak of the Rocky Mountains, floating over a happy and prosperous people, in the free enjoyment of civil privileges and religious virtues."[11] Critical ministers, particularly those far from the frontier's edge, typically hewed a more discriminating line, one that protected their exceptional spiritual claims from conflations like Bowman's.

In a piece urging young ministers to take up charges in rapidly developing population centers like Chicago, the *New Englander* pointed to the meteoric rise of the new city as a providential opportunity to transform internal improvements into channels of the gospel. The health of the nation and the Christian cause unavoidably united at the frontier, the writer charged, and young divines could aid God and country by forsaking comfortable Eastern pastorates and trekking West. "Vital godliness" must harness the wealth of this budding "national emporium" to the cause of the gospel. God's faithful must subdue the forces of "mammon" and "take possession of the land" for Christ in this future center of national commerce.[12]

The *New Englander*'s essay tells much about Protestant strategy in the West. The clergy acknowledged that economic rather than religious interests were the driving force behind Western development. Missionaries had to react to change by transforming that which pecuniary self-interest had created into a boon to the gospel cause. God needed ministers to "subdue" hostile forces and rein in the power of greed. Prospective preachers also had to be willing to deny their own "selfishness" by rejecting Eastern comforts for greater toil in the West. Notably absent in this writer's assessment was any notion that Western development should be stopped or that commerce, industry, or culture was intrinsically hostile to the gospel mission. He anticipated no retreat from economic growth. Since Augustine, Christian tradition had taught that God turned the "follies" of man to His benefit. Consequently, providential thought did not translate easily into a belief that cultural growth and Christian expansion were the same. Providential thinking carried a strong sense of distinction between sacred and secular motivations, though its internal logic assumed that God would eventually subdue human pretensions to His own designs. The writer offered a concise description of how secular development and the gospel mission harmonized only when a critical separation of purpose was maintained:

> The "children of this world" have volunteered to excavate the harbors, pile up the stone and mortar, and lay down the extended rail tracks; and because this rough work is all needful . . . God gratifies the laborers by giving them success. He sees how he can use every stroke of the hammer . . . to advance his cause; howbeit, they who often direct these efforts mean not so, neither do their hearts think so. It belongs to the church instrumentally to infuse the spirit of the gospel into these openings made by secular enterprise. . . . There are foundations of far greater importance to be laid than these visible outward structures."[13]

Providential thought, then, kept mainstream Protestants from becoming alienated critics willing to denounce outright all secular national development. Divines galvanized by cultural assaults on Protestantism's higher, exclusive claims were likewise ill-suited to becoming uncritical cheerleaders for westward expansion.

For example, Charles White, Presbyterian president of Wabash College in Crawfordsville, Indiana, sounded at first like a devotee of manifest destiny: "This [Anglo-Saxon] race is evidently to occupy the whole of North America," he blithely observed in 1846. "To no nation on earth, is opened so grand a career . . . so splendid an accumulation of power and usefulness." As an educator as well as a minister, White believed that bearing "civilization" to the developing West was necessarily part of a college's task. Deeper in White's thinking, however, lay a sharp hostility toward the forces driving the nation's advance. His seemingly bullish assessment evolved into heated broadsides against materialism and political immorality. White denounced popular cries of "Our country, right or wrong!" as an offense to Scriptural truth, a "fatal confounding of moral distinctions." The nation's policy of Indian removal was a criminal act, one of the more visible demonstrations of "public cupidity, selfishness . . . and destitution of probity."[14] White understood his own grand hopes for expansion of the nation's political and religious ideals as inconsistent with the patriotic and political morality he saw driving American material dreams. He sought to affirm an expansive American vision and at the same time destroy cultural assumptions that he believed the nation wrongly cherished. Though an infusion of Christian virtue could check moral corrosion in the nation, White believed, the country seemed headed toward baser aims: physical power, revenue, territory.

On a crisp, rain-soaked evening in October 1823, Baptist luminary Francis Wayland delivered the annual address to the Boston Baptist Foreign Missionary Society. Hoping to ignite evangelistic passions with his sermon—"The Moral Dignity of the Missionary Enterprise"—the youthful preacher sensed a congregational chill matched only by the weather. He was mistaken. Enthusiasts recommended publication, and the piece was picked up by the interdenominational American Tract Society. It became one of the most widely circulated sermons of the antebellum period. Wayland's religious jeremiad called for the onward march of the gospel. It also drilled a supranational theme of spiritual conquest that begged no cultural mandates.[15]

Wayland touted the exclusive supremacy of the Protestant mission and used the culture's "civilizing" agenda as an example of distorted priorities. The nation manufactured its own reasons for extending westward, Wayland contended. Its justifications subtly undermined the spiritual "dignity" of missions. Social "apathy" and open "ridicule" of the Christian cause signaled a conflict of purpose between sacred and secular expansion that believers had to openly oppose. Universal depravity was the fatal disease of humans, and misplaced faith in human effort—"civilization," "reason," "philosophy"—obscured the true gospel mission. The "cross of Christ" alone, Wayland thundered, transformed man into a "new creature" and remedied his "temporal and eternal misery." Wayland indulged millennial and heavenly hopes, provided that this simple message of spiritual salvation subsumed the "complicated and tumultuous" regenerative schemes of the larger culture.[16] By mid-century such qualifications matured into stinging rebukes, and the preeminent champion of missions also became one of the sharpest critics of the missionary enterprise. Wayland by 1850 was committed to exposing violations of his core spiritual message: "The kingdom of Christ is extended as the number of true believers is increased, and as new members are added to his spiritual body, and in no other manner."[17]

Still, it would be wrong to conclude that the Protestant community never yielded to religious nationalism. Presbyterian divine Lyman Beecher's *Plea for the West* fits the mold well and is often quoted by scholars wanting to show Protestantism's uncritical assimilation of the culture's agenda. Beecher whipped up his "plea" in order to garner construction and endowment funds for his Lane Theological Seminary in Cincinnati. In the 1830s he toted the piece to seaboard Presbyterian pulpits. His theme was simple: The fate of the nation and hopes for the millennium depended on the spiritual, political, and educational consolidation of the West. "If it is by the march of revolution and civil liberty that the way of the Lord is to be prepared," he wailed, is it not obvious that "this nation is, in the providence of God, destined to lead the way in the moral and political emancipation of the world?" Beecher further exaggerated national purpose, insisting that "all providential developments" and "all existing signs of the times" suggested that the "millennium will commence in America." He admitted that such a scenario had seemed "chimerical" to him earlier, but now he was sure of the nation's prospects. Beecher's audience confronted hyperbolic visions of national calamity, papal plots, foreign invasion, and barbarism—all of which could be replaced by millennial bliss if the East sent its riches west.[18] Unlike Charles White, who emphasized the nation's need of Christian virtue, Beecher seemed to make the Christian mission equally dependent on the nation's political ideals.

Such forays into blatant religious nationalism, however, did not go unchallenged. Riled editors of the Baptist *Christian Review*, the most important quarterly of the nation's fastest-growing denomination, pounced on Beecher's excesses. They singled out his nationalistic claims as misguided distortions of the gospel mission. That this overly "proud," "avaricious," and "criminally vain," nation is about to "convert the world . . . we have but little confidence," the *Review* charged. In demolishing Beecher's assertions that the millennium would begin in America, the writer separated Protestant "hopes" from perceptions of immediate reality. There would be a millennium, he agreed, and the gospel would one day reclaim the Earth for Christ. But pursuit of the millennium was a flimsy, selfish rationale for evangelization, one too often exploited in "asking men to contribute their money." Such "declaiming about the millennium" obscured the primary responsibility to preach salvation and "[yearn] over individual sinners."[19] The *Review* shrank from Beecher's allusions to Americans as special agents of the divine in deference to a Protestant mission that transcended visions of cultural or "national" destiny:"

We are not certain, that any Christian nation, now existing, is to advance with a regular progression, either in civil liberty or in holiness, without a reverse, till Christ shall reign over all nations—"king of saints." Much less are we certain, that "the providential developments," and "existing signs of the times," corroborate the opinion, that the "renovating power" is to go forth from America. . . . The "renovating power" is in Christ, and will, at the appointed time, go forth from him. . . . But the sun of righteousness, in America, may first be eclipsed.[20]

By mid-century Beecher's "west" had been dwarfed by frontiers extending to the Pacific rim and beyond. Ministers joined other Americans in trying to make new lands and new ideas cohere with past understanding. The Mexican War and its aftermath sharpened nationalistic zeal even as it set the stage for renewed sectional controversy. Preachers, politicians, and the popular press served up a myriad of conflicting scenarios of the American "empire's" destiny. For good or evil, most Americans expected the war and subsequent territorial expansion to be a watershed in the nation's history. Some Whig opponents warned of political and commercial overextension and a subsequent cycle of politically enervating greed and corruption. Other observers spied Machiavellian tendencies in Polk's aggressive use of executive power. Many Americans, as Robert Johannsen has recently demonstrated, viewed the conflict as a cathartic experience.[21] It provided opportunity to demonstrate personal republican zeal and the resiliency of American political institutions. But renewed sectional conflict just as surely lay ahead. While the conflict still raged, Methodist and Baptist organizations experienced irreparable splits in what has been called a dress rehearsal for later disunion.[22]

Among Protestant leaders, the Mexican War evoked nothing like the outpouring of clerical support prompted by the Revolution. Politicians emphasized Mexican atrocities and billed the conflict as a blow against a Catholic and barbarous people. Spiritual guardians saw a hydra multiplying threats to the faith by deflecting popular energies toward material and political causes instead of religion. Many New England ministers shared in their section's anxiety about eroding political clout as the nation expanded. But Protestant concerns ran deeper than Whig politics. Few ministers bought the notion of a "covenanted" people marching against the forces of Romanism and barbarism. That God could always providentially force human events to serve His own designs did not mean that national actions were thereby mandated and "holy." In an obvious slam at American political and military belligerence in 1848, the *New Englander* charged that the "divine" origins of civil government never guaranteed the sanctity of its actions. Everywhere man exists, the writer insisted, he is the "same sordid and selfish being. Free governments and despotic have been alike ambitious, grasping, and oppressive." He contended that man's ultimate happiness depended on acquiescence to the *"sole sufficiency of Christ and his Gospel."* [23]

Nearly all Congregationalists and the majority Old School within Presbyterianism openly opposed the war. The relative silence of Lutherans, Episcopalians, and German Reformed reflected not support but a historic determination to eschew political controversy. Northern Baptist support for the war was lukewarm, although Southwestern Baptist leaders, closer to the hostilities and already supporting missionaries in Texas, generated more support. [24] Even before the war began, the Connecticut-based Baptist *Christian Secretary* declared its antiwar stance. It complained that the "pagan" admonition to prepare for war during peacetime forced Americans to spend more on annually financing a single ship-of-the-line than Christians did in financing the American Board of Commissioners for Foreign Missions. [25]

New England regional anxieties over declining national influence no doubt colored some clerical opinions. But no periodical attacked the war effort with more ferocity than Charles Finney's Ohio-based *Oberlin Evangelist*. The influential Chicago Baptist newspaper *Watchman of the Prairies* sustained unwavering opposition to the conflict. The Old School periodical *Presbyterian of the West* objected to excessive attention to politics and expansion instead of the gospel. [26] The *Western Christian Advocate*, a Cincinnati-based Methodist weekly, rebuked the secular press for encouraging a "belligerent" American spirit through incessant declamations about the "coming glory of American arms." As an icon in the public mind molded from accounts of "inhumanity and barbarity," the paper contended, the war could only divert attention from "holiness among Christians," "peaceful pursuits," and national unity. [27]

Ministers North and South agreed that the Mexican War had fatally obscured their primary religious mission, and each side found the other exceptionally burdened with guilt. Southerners identified abolitionism as symptomatic of Northern materialism, greed, and ideological breakdown. If hopes of evangelical unity withered in the wake of war, an Athens, Alabama, Methodist wrote, it did so at the beck and call of Northern believers, who sacrificed the wholeness of truth for the "apple of abolitionism" and a place at the altar of "Discordia." [28] The *Tennessee Baptist* attributed declining Baptist membership in the North directly to the North's confounding of religion and abolitionism. [29]

Southern clergymen, however, could bend to the pressure of political crisis. In the thick of political debate over what would become the Compromise of 1850, an anonymous writer in the *Southern Presbyterian*

Review declared that Northern political bullying—like that of the British in 1776—represented extreme corruption that necessarily made bedfellows of religion and politics. "At certain junctures," he declared, "patriotism and religion become one and the same . . . the duties of the citizen and the duties of a Christian blend and combine." Ministers who shrank from defending Southern civilization were "recreant" in both obligations. Reasoning that Northern Christians could embrace abolitionism only as they drifted away from true religion, the writer triumphantly declared the Southern, proslavery pulpit as the true preserve of salvation truths and the slave's only hope for eternity![30] Ministers nevertheless struggled against the secular world and themselves to protect their religious cause from the political chaos threatening the nation's expanding frontiers. In the midst of the Mexican conflict, a writer in the Baptist *Christian Index* parodied wartime jingoism in order to distinguish his religious cause. Leading his audience, he decried "[leniency] to our enemies." "They must be conquered not coaxed into peace . . . [with] each last blow the heaviest." Then he chided readers for being duped by the rhetoric of "earthly, carnal warfare" and urged attention to a "more desperate war . . . to rescue captive immortal souls from everlasting peril."[31]

As American victory heralded national progress, destiny, national aggrandizement and the "march of civilization," suspicious ministers integrated the war into their larger transatlantic probe of spreading materialism and practical unbelief. Popular rhetoric contingent to the war and new expansion reinforced clerical suspicions that had been solidifying since the 1830s. Unwilling to join their Southern counterparts in attributing abolitionism to Northern greed, they could nevertheless agree that the slavery issue was part of a larger web of cultural confusion that threatened the gospel cause. In 1856, for example, Methodist circuit rider Francis Asbury Hester made a rare "political" entry in his diary to express concern over "bleeding Kansas." His disdain for "pro-slavery ruffians" made clear his "social" position on abolition, but his primary religious concerns emerged equally plainly. Politics had become "insanely exciting," he lamented. "How difficult under such circumstances to pursue a proper ministerial course, and avoid party politics." Days later in a small chapel near Jeffersonville, Indiana, Hester initiated a series of sermons not on the social evils of slavery but on "The World, in a religious point of view, without the Bible."[32]

The Congregationalist *New Englander*, equaled in its antiwar zeal by only the Unitarian press, confessed that American victory was a fait accompli and that believers must now accept the new challenge of Christianizing the territories and guard against future sanctification of belligerent, nationalistic aims. The great danger now was that the people would confuse God's providential ability to "bring out of this war a better condition of things" with the false notion that whatever was politically expedient must also be "Christian." In the future, the writer declared, "the pleasures we feel in the possession of privileges, and even in the contemplation of improvements in human affairs, is apt to reconcile us to means and measures of doubtful propriety."[33] As the nation extended its political and economic reach, in other words, material aims would eclipse spiritual purpose. Philadelphia Episcopal divine Richard Newton cited the dangers that expanding global frontiers imposed on the missionary effort: "Our piety is of the gold-leaf variety—very little of it spread over a wide surface." This "superficial piety," he warned, threatened to substitute the duties "springing out of religion, for religion itself."[34]

Americans received another open invitation to sanctify their global reach when Louis Kossuth sailed into New York harbor in December 1851. Fresh from a series of political setbacks in Europe, the Hungarian revolutionary hoped to convince Britain and then the United States that their global vision should include aid for his political struggle against Hapsburg dominion. Kossuth gained widespread recognition in 1848 for an impassioned freedom speech to the Hungarian Diet that helped set bourgeois political spirits ablaze in the revolutions of 1848. Demanding partial autonomy for the Magyars and other national groups under Hapsburg rule, he helped to topple from power aging Austrian prince Metternich—architect of the post-Napoleonic European political order—and expedite the demise of France's Louis-Philippe and the rise of the Second Empire.[35]

Kossuth initially tapped a well of popular enthusiasm in the United States. His image as an anti-Catholic, European pilgrim in the service of God and the principles of '76 played well until he added pleas for direct American economic and military aid. His American tour then fizzled, but not before some Protestant leaders had succumbed to his republican rhetoric. Kossuth earned his warmest clerical welcome from urban New School Presbyterians, particularly in New York. To no one's surprise, Henry Ward Beecher—never one to shrink from blending religious, social, and political causes—lent Kossuth the pulpit of his three-thousand-seat Plymouth Church in Brooklyn for speaking and soliciting subscriptions. But Beecher's zeal represented the extreme of an initial Protestant reaction that was generally mixed and subsequently cold. Protestant editors and clergy at a distance from Kossuth's seaboard tour, particularly those in the West, variously embraced the Hungarian's cause cautiously, ignored him altogether, or openly warned against the revolutionary's cryptic religious position.[36]

Reformed leader John Nevin, one of the most brilliant intellects of antebellum Protestantism, whose influence reached far beyond the Reformed tradition, seized upon Kossuth's visit to derail American nationalist and expansionist claims. Nevin is often studied as Protestantism's preeminent Cassandra, but his theological chords that harmonized with broader Protestant dissent can be easily established. The Scotch-Irish Princeton graduate taught at Western Theological Seminary in Pittsburgh before committing to the confessional tradition of the Reformed church in 1840. As a professor at Mercersburg Seminary in Pennsylvania, Nevin attacked the "anxious bench" revival tactics of Finney and scolded his compatriots for abandoning the sacramental, confessional standards of the Reformation. His work *The Mystical Presence* (1846) called for restored reverence for the sacraments and revival of a churchly, communal tradition. Nevin cultivated special disdain for the pietistic individualism of groups like the Baptists. Such "corruption," Nevin believed, thwarted its perpetrators good intentions, isolating believers from the Reformation anchors of Protestant community and primitive faith that they sought to preserve. Return fire blasted Nevin for unwitting complicity in a fifth column defense of Catholic tradition.[37] Yet his personal integrity and exegetical powers assured widespread and serious consideration of the "Mercersburg movement." If Nevin's theology at times struck fellow ministers as eccentric, his commitment to a separated faith responded to a Protestant cause broadly shared.

Nevin unleashed his attack in a baccalaureate address to his denomination's Franklin and Marshall College in 1853. The classic religious jeremiad bypassed theological speculation and bared the core of Nevin's framework of Christian belief and mission. His title—"Man's True Destiny"—played satirically to popular political cant in order to manifest an opposing theme. What graduates most needed to understand, he began, was that their "supernatural destiny" depended not on the march of Britain, America, or republicanism across the globe but on their entry into the "Kingdom of God" beyond the present existence. Believers, he argued, faced a practical and theoretical unbelief produced less by intellectual rejection of miraculous truth than by a positive "determination to make the present world their end and portion." That faith alone could reveal the ultimate destiny and purpose of man had become in the "liberal" public mind a revival of medieval superstition, a "treasonous" contradiction to the new "sacred cause of freedom, popular rights, political economy, and modern civilization."[38]

The "spirit of the age," Nevin continued, seemed determined to sanctify its materialistic base, demanding that religion bend to its "politico-economical" impulses and "obsequiously" bless the worldwide expansion of "republicanism," "commerce and trade," "moral reform," and "humanitarian philanthropy" as its surrogate.[39] In demolishing the nation's inflated ego as a "universal lie," Nevin sharpened his point even further:

> It is an age of progress and reform, big with the idea of its own mission to rehabilitate man in the possession of his natural rights. . . .
> Happy, as the song runs, is the young man, who enters upon life, on American soil in the middle of the nineteenth century! The genius of the age is emphatically the genius of this rising republic. . . . Never was there, however, under such plausible form, a more perfect delusion. . . . The spirit of the age is always at war with . . . the gospel and the Church; there is a necessary contradiction between this world and the Kingdom of God.[40]

The "great error," Nevin said, was to assign "natural interests and secular ends an importance which does not belong to them in fact." A case in point was the nation's brief love affair with Kossuth, yet even Kossuth's fall from grace resulted more from "material interests" and "Yankee cunning" than from a rejection of his political exploitation of Christianity. How could "undiscerning religious admirers" fail to see the rationalistic political philosophy that girded Kossuth's "rodomontade about liberty and human rights"? Or his cries for a "brotherhood of nations"? Or the "solidarity of humanity"?[41]

In both Kossuth's reception and his subsequent snubbing Nevin spied an expansive, spiritually inert political vision malleable enough to make European socialism and American republicanism allies in a war against faith. Secular causes not subordinated and controlled by "supernatural and eternal" truth, he concluded, were the "veritable *Antichrist* of the age."[42]

When mid-century ministers analyzed their own missions and examined the most basic meaning of the gospel cause, they bristled at the irony that national success could become the nemesis of spiritual faith. Nevin's admonition that people steep themselves in the hearing and reading of the "creed" and "the Word," for example, echoed wider clerical suspicions that national development and expansion bred faith in physical activity and improvement rather than Scriptural truth and a concern for spiritual salvation. The outward thrust of Christendom for nonreligious purposes must not erode a primary faith in the "Word" and a "preached gospel" as the transcendent instrumentalities of evangelism. "Status anxiety" no doubt tinged clerical dissent, but that alone is not a sufficient explanation for it.[43]

A determination to guard the integrity of their religious mission galvanized Protestants in their quarrel with the Republic even as the sectional crisis prompted many ministers to violate the pulpit integrity they so desperately wanted to protect. Four weeks before his native state initialed the secession process, the great Southern Presbyterian leader James Henley Thornwell confessed the dilemma and his personal anguish. From his Columbia, South Carolina, pulpit, Thornwell lamented that the inevitable pulpit responses to political calamity were vulnerable to monumental distortions. As he predictably drew upon Old Testament precedent in a jeremiad recounting national sins, Thornwell prescribed "sackcloth" and humility and warned against what he saw as the most threatening delusion—confounding the nation with the kingdom of God:

> I have no design . . . to intimate that there is a parallel between Jerusalem and our own Commonwealth in relation to the Covenant of God. I am far from believing that we alone, of all the people of the earth, are possessed of the true religion, and far from encouraging the narrow and exclusive spirit which . . . can complacently exclaim, the temple of the Lord, the temple of the Lord, are we. Such arrogance and bigotry are utterly inconsistent with the penitential confessions which this day has been set apart to evoke.[44]

Clerical fears that religion itself might be consumed in a blaze of expansionist zeal and sectional animosity blended easily with concerns about the ideological and material agendas shaping the nation's oceanic frontiers. Protestant leaders wanted to define these avenues as providential "highways of the gospel." The liberal economic and political order proved far more receptive to the multiple heralds of "civilization," "commerce," and "empire." By the 1840s, this secular turn sharpened the ambivalence of Protestants toward the materialism and diversity of a democratic culture they had not anticipated.

Destiny beyond Civilization, Commerce, and Empire

Protestant efforts to affirm a transatlantic, supranational mission took a practical turn in 1846 with the establishment of the Evangelical Alliance, headquartered in London. Participants aspired to a worldwide cooperative community of individual believers rather than formal denominational or "national" alliances. British, Continental, and American clergymen—the assemblage included Methodist, Baptist, German Reformed, Presbyterian, and Lutheran divines from the United States— appealed for an end to the sectarian strife that threatened to "split up and fritter away the energies of the Protestant world." The meeting produced a written "Overture for Christian Union" that acknowledged the legitimacy of denominational Christianity while demanding an overriding Christian community dedicated to evangelizing the world. The organizing committee called for unity behind a set of nine conservative doctrinal planks called the "United Protestant Confession." Only Unitarians, Roman Catholics, Quakers, and Eastern Orthodox Christians were implicitly excluded by the "evangelical, fundamentally orthodox" statement of faith.[45]

The alliance cited the preaching of a personal salvation message as the essence of the divine mission. Admitting all denominations as human creations inherently prone to "mixture and error," the United Confession affirmed the "ministry, oracles and ordinances" of Christ's Kingdom to be the collective property of individual believers and "not confined to one nation." In charter and spirit the Alliance rejected the idea that the West's cultural and material expansion marked the progress of the Kingdom.[46]

Anglo-American commercial and territorial appetites by the 1840s had simply become too aggressive, conspicuous and detached from the Protestant spiritual mission for the clergy to ignore. Railroads, steamships, clippers, and canals that channeled missionaries carried as their primary cargo merchants, speculators, developers and settlers, their respective wares and designs. This westward vision stretched beyond gold-rich California and fertile Oregon to the scramble for the Pacific trade of China, Polynesia, and the Far East. A San Francisco newspaper writer enthusiastically predicted that his city was destined to be the western equivalent of New York. Prosperous Pacific trade and the "wonders of commerce" would make links to China and Japan as important as Atlantic contacts with Europe.[47]

The notion that commerce and Western global expansion was a blessing to merchants, nations, and native populations alike had gained a wide audience. In Britain, the Anti–Corn Law League under the leadership of Richard Cobden and John Bright regularly touted free trade as the indispensable ingredient of world brotherhood. John Stuart Mill speculated in 1848 that commerce was "rapidly making war obsolete."[48] Economic benefits aside, the global thrust of the West guaranteed that primitive peoples could begin to reap the benefits of contact with Western civilization. New York senator William H. Seward told colleagues in 1850, for example, that the "commercial, social and political affinities" of the Atlantic states were destined to encircle the globe, renovating the decadent Orient. The result would be the rise of a "more perfect civilization" to "bless the earth" with "beneficent democratic institutions."[49]

Protestant leaders had no inherent objection to commerce, education, culture or civilization. Because the clergy registered no concerted opposition to commerce or the West's expanding global reach, recent scholars have stressed harmony rather than conflict and tension in religious and secular conceptions of mission. Indeed, it would be easy to conclude that because missionaries needed the transportation, communication, and supply lines that commerce afforded, they had every reason to identify the West's expansion with the growth of the kingdom. But Protestant leaders saw in expansionist rationales (such as Seward's) proof of democratic liberalism's extending challenge to spiritual religion. Justifying the West's global reach as economically and politically redemptive simply declared the spiritual mission they regarded as transcendent to be contingent, even irrelevant to the "march of civilization." Ministers mined this motivational dichotomy within the expansionist impulse and found greater polemical riches in separating the secular pretensions of "Christendom" from their own conception of sacred mission.

Daniel Wilson, Anglican bishop of Calcutta, issued an 1829 charge to the British Empire that illustrates Protestant dissent before it took a more incisive turn at mid-century. The "empire of the seas" represented a "trust," not a "reward," Wilson argued. The "national freedom" and "augmented wealth" enjoyed by Britons would wither if the nation did not "rise to its high destiny" and recognize Christian faith as the best hope of temporal blessings. Our statesmen had to recognize that "every national sin fatally contributes to the dissolution of our power." Indeed, Wilson wrote not to sanction religious nationalism but to expose the corruptions of Christianity (his essay introduced and praised the eighth edition of Wilberforce's religious jeremiad *A Practical View of the Prevail-*

ing Religious System). He demanded an "unshrinking message of Christ crucified" to the world and assigned a sacred mission not to "Britain" but to Protestants everywhere. "The simplicity of the cross of Christ," he insisted, and the "mighty power of grace" is "all that God has determined to use to the diffusion of his mercy throughout the world."[50]

Herman Melville's celebrity among twentieth-century scholars as a signal outpost of pessimism and realism in the midst of antebellum Protestants has left clerical efforts that paralleled his own work neglected.[51] In *Typee* (1846) and *Omoo* (1848), Melville gave the lie to Yankee expansionist claims of benevolent intent. He laced his romantic South Sea adventure tales with savage attacks on a base materialism that he insisted plagued merchants and missionaries alike. He described the Congregationalists' Sandwich Islands mission and a larger profiteering "dissolute foreign population" as a study in mammonism and the abuse of power. He branded "civilization" a false idol; it was not the bearer of blessings to the "heathen" but rather an "endless catalogue" of crimes that civilized man "created to mar his own felicity."[52]

Melville's novels tapped a growing popular literary thirst for romantic adventure and exotic fare. The pair of works brought him instant transatlantic fame and accounted for the bulk of the 50,000 copies of his works sold in the United States and Britain. *Typee* had become part of the "national legend" by the 1850s.[53] When Melville deleted his slings against the missionary enterprise (probably under pressure from Harper and Brothers), the *Biblical Repository* applauded the bowdlerization while citing the work as "too well known" to require further analysis (the British edition remained unaltered).[54] The editors apparently had no complaint with Melville's slams at the "dark side" of civilization and Western culture, perhaps because that theme was hardly exceptional among Protestant leaders by 1846. Indeed, in this context Melville's work is less a "corrective" to Protestant pretensions than a supplement to clerical dissent that had been developing for two decades. A contributor to the *Literary and Theological Review* in 1835 acridly summarized the frustrations that galvanized Protestant dissent over the next two decades: "Discouraging and humiliating as it may be, the great mass of people in Protestant Christendom know nothing of the Gospel; and [even those] learned in other matters have no idea of the spiritual nature and design of Christianity."[55]

As early as 1824, four years after American Congregationalists and British Wesleyans established permanent missionary beachheads in the Sandwich Islands, the "second father" of British Methodism, Jabez Bunting, struck at distended claims for the intrinsic blessings of Western culture. Bunting rejected the growing insistence of some Britons that the economic and political development of an expanding empire must first be achieved in order for missionaries to be effective. Though "civilization and refinement" did afford certain external benefits to the gospel mission, he admitted, too often they concomitantly hindered the salvation message by allowing "secular knowledge"—literature, arts, sciences, government, law—to usurp the "grand and direct instrument" of grace found only in the "Gospel, the doctrine of the Cross and the testimony of Jesus."[56]

For Bunting, the idea that culture preceded Christianity implicitly sanctified the former. He asserted the "catholicity of the gospel" and refuted the notion that Western whites owned a "peculiar" ability to understand New Testament truths. Whatever good existed in Western culture, he maintained, could be traced not to innate Anglo-Saxon superiority but to the spiritual, meliorating doctrines of Christianity. "Accidental varieties" separating nations as well as men, he argued, exempted no one from sin and left all nations equally in need of the gospel.[57] As an expression of "Protestant" uniqueness, Bunting's message reinforces religious exceptionalism. At the same time, it sharply distinguishes between Christianity and any national culture, disposing of religious nationalism as a valid expression of faith.

Anglo-American commercial expansion into Polynesia, India, and the Far East in the 1830s compelled the clergy to defend their spiritual mission first by admitting that Western culture would expand with or without religion. Eschewing fatalism or despair, ministers opened a wide avenue of dissent by contending that the commercially driven export of civilization meant tragedy for foreign populations. In 1836, for example, the House of Commons heard testimony from a select committee appointed to determine the best means of promoting civilization and religion among native populations in contact with British settlements and commercial facilities.[58] The committee's missionary contingent included Dandeson Coates, John Beecham, and most notably William Ellis of the Church, Wesleyan, and London missionary societies, respectively. Ellis's transatlantic reputation rested on his published reminiscence of missionary struggle in Polynesia, where he labored for six years in the 1820s. In his 1829 work *Polynesian Researches in the South Sea Islands*, Ellis had already insisted that the amalgamation of even laudable "civilizing" efforts with the gospel mission necessarily vitiated the spiritual mission of the gospel.[59] His insistence that natives be preserved from the machinations of "unprincipled individuals" evolved into a stinging rebuke of

Western profligacy and cultural license in the Commons report published in 1837, which garnered unqualified accolades from the American *Methodist Quarterly Review* in 1841.

Girding praise with extended excerpts of committee testimony, the *Review*'s analyst debuted the essence of Melville's complaints against "civilization" a decade before *Typee*. He praised the central themes: that expanding Christendom did not necessarily promote Christianity; that civilization apart from faith imparted unmitigated evil to indigenous populations and that Christianity "needed no auxiliary" for its dissemination. The "conclusive" testimony exposed civilized people's natural "depravity," proving that native populations were "happier and better in the darkness of heathenism" than in the hands of Europeans and Americans destitute of "true religion" and morally chained to the marketplace. Whether directed by "irreligious men" or Christians, the reviewer agreed, efforts to introduce civilization in order to "pave the way for the gospel" must meet with "uniform and signal failure."[60] His summation demanded a worldwide Protestant consensus that the connection between Christianity and civilization not degenerate into a confounding of the two:

> The experience of centuries has shown, that with the introduction of civilized foreigners into aboriginal countries the vices of civilization have been simultaneously introduced, and the unsophisticated natives have been made the victims of fraud and violence, of diseases and vices, of plunder and imposture, until their physical and moral condition has become worse and worse by their contact with a foreign population. Such have been the results, wherever and whenever attempts have been made to civilize savage men, by the mere introduction among them of a foreign population for the purposes of agriculture or commerce. . . . The gospel of the grace of God is the first, grand, and only instrumentality in the recovery of the family of man from the horrible pit into which the human race have been plunged by sin.[61]

Neither the Commons committee's testimony nor the *Review*'s analysis acknowledged cases of missionary impropriety and mistreatment of native populations such as Melville bitterly recorded. At times, Protestant leaders reluctantly echoed Melville and confessed the vulnerability of their own. Ellis noted as early as 1829 that some missionary funds were supporting what he described as worthy but ancillary causes.[62] He even suggested establishing a separate "civilization society" to distinguish

Christian from cultural concerns. Yet gentle admonishments soon yielded to sharper attacks as critical ministers found their own crusaders succumbing to the proliferating cultural rationales of secular expansionists. More important, sallies against missionary compromises sharpened Protestant dissent that was advancing along a much broader cultural front.

In 1848, for example, the *Southern Presbyterian Review* gave Southern believers a lesson in cultural "subterfuges." The title of Gaboon missionary J. L. Wilson's religious jeremiad—"The Certainty of the World's Conversion"—sounded optimistic enough. But optimism drawn from evangelical theory clashed directly with his attacks on the culture's corruption of spiritual purpose. Present realities defied the notion that "any considerable progress" toward the grand objective had as yet been made.[63] Wilson specifically assaulted cultural arrogance and millennial visions that Anglo-Saxons had shrewdly adopted to "exonerate themselves" from spiritual obligation. The culture's "overweening regard" for the "superior excellence of the white race," Wilson chided, threatened to link the missionary enterprise with the corrupted purpose of "[supplanting] every other race, and ultimately becoming sole occupants of our globe." Christianity was intended to bind believers in "common brotherhood," not to exalt "one portion of the human family at the expense of another." Adopting theories designed to "root out other races, to make room for the expansion of our own" transformed spiritual endeavor into a "career of reckless disregard for the rights and interests of others." Likewise, Wilson extended his sortie to the supposed "friends of missions" whose real interest lay in the millennial "fulfillment of their own expectations." In Wilson's view, missionary success required dependence on spiritual means and vigilance against cultural improvisations.[64]

Congregationalist divine Mark Hopkins issued a manifesto to the American Board of Commissioners for Foreign Missions (ABCFM) in 1845 that pronounced obstacles to missionary integrity a troubling extension of domestic foils. Along with the Presbyterians, Congregationalists were the soul of the American Board, and few individuals wielded more personal influence in the organization at mid-century than Hopkins. As professor of moral philosophy and president of Williams College for more than thirty years (1836–72), Hopkins sustained his institution's historic commitment to foreign missions generally, as well as the board over which he would preside by 1857. Organized in 1810, the American Board was the nation's oldest interdenominational arm of a foreign mission movement formally established at Williams in 1806. The ABCFM directed initial missionary efforts in Hawaii and served as the most active agency of Protestant overseas missions. By 1860, mission outposts included India, Polynesia, Ceylon, Syria, and Canton.[65]

Like Wayland, Hopkins elevated the ministry above education in a personal hierarchy that scholars have too easily inverted. It was Hopkins the minister who pressed the board to beware the culture's infectious reach and restore the simple message of "death and judgment and eternity" that inspired the "disciples of primitive times." Christianity's incidental influences and the material priorities of humanity were confusing "the desire to preach Christ" with attacks on "specific forms of evil" and popular enthusiasm for promoting "civilization." The board was not a "society for promoting civilization, or literature, or the arts; but for saving men," Hopkins keened. Christians, he believed, were being duped by the liberal age. "Money cannot convert a soul," he chided. Nor could he recall that Christ or His Apostles had depended on literary promotions or progressive technology. Protestant faith itself faced mounting uncertainty if believers failed "to *preach the word*" and effect a "radical" revolution within the human soul.[66]

Hopkins rebuked those who spied the "borders of the millennium" in the "liberality of the nineteenth century." Such "worship of democracy" could inspire millennial visions only among those who failed to appreciate the ideological chaos beneath the cant. Far from yielding obedience to God, democratic culture was serving up multiple enemies in the guise of a "plausible infidelity" and a "latitudinarian charity." Hopkins held fast to his millennial faith but insisted that hard realities made it a distant hope. Believers must clutch more immediately to eternal promises as the bedrock of evangelism. Here again is the sharp authoritarian bias— a point that Jon Butler emphasizes in his recent work—that united with self-doubt and helped sustain Protestant dissent. Democracy was well and good, Hopkins admitted, provided "every man should obey God, and love his neighbor as himself." The triumph of a liberal and purely secular democratic culture, he predicted, would turn against historic faith and provide the most perfect expression of "hell upon earth."[67] Ironically, a sermon to sustain the spiritual integrity of foreign missions ultimately pressed Hopkins to chart a more hazardous domestic terrain—acquisitive materialism, self-interested freedom, and a popular "spirit of infidelity."

Clerical reassessments of foreign missions that served a broader critique of emergent liberal culture gained particular prominence in the mid-1850s, before the prospect of disunion and war redirected critical energies to the domestic crisis. Hopkins and compatriots like ABCFM secretary Rufus Anderson could take solace in fellow champions if not in cultural transformations, which now seemed to demand even stronger rebukes.[68] In one bare-knuckled 1854 confrontation, New York Methodist bishop Levi Scott pummeled the duplicity of "missionary-traders"— "merciful God, what an association!"—and demanded full support for continuing investigations to expose and punish the offenders. Reporting on his personal inspection of the Methodists' African missions, Scott gave full vent to the embarrassing facts at the annual conference of the Methodist Missionary Society. These ordained entrepreneurs had been assessing the wants of native populations, using their annual stipends to secure wholesale monopolies, and finally obliging the local poor to buy the essential commodities at grossly inflated prices. Scott expressed satisfaction at growing popular outrage and the success of recent purges but not before admitting that "several of our preachers" had been "pretty deeply involved." Still, he pointed out that such victims of commercial lusts could be successfully assaulted because they were not typical. In fact, Hawaiian missionaries often met more opposition from Anglo-American commercial populations than from natives themselves. One scholar of Yankee influence in Hawaii suggests that traders and missionaries both upset the delicate web of Polynesian culture. The more "disastrous" scenario, however, would have been unfettered exploitation by whalers and traders.[69]

The American Baptist Missionary Union demanded a reassessment of fundamental principles in 1853. A special committee employed Francis Wayland's critical talents to evaluate the role of foreign missionaries as American cultural ambassadors. Wayland, seizing the moment to air personal frustrations with secular pursuits and lobby against cultural conceits, dished up a stinging rebuke to the vendors of civilization. He granted the worthiness of charitable enterprise and educational endeavor but declared philanthropy to be a cause in which believers and "strangers to renewing grace" regularly united. The missionary, he insisted, must harness the exceptional and exclusive power of Christian faith to the primary purpose of saving souls. Wayland dismissed one missionary's suggestion that Christian civilization must use its cultural might to destroy heathenism before the work of evangelism could begin. The great educator insisted that education and cultural transfer were more likely to galvanize native populations against the faith. The missionary's peculiar and efficient weaponry was "preaching . . . the oral communication of divine truth by man to man." The minister of the gospel, Wayland concluded, was charged as neither a minister nor a facilitator of civilization. Whatever the merits of the latter cause, they were to be "in subordination" and "separate from the other."[70]

In an emphatic diatribe, Wayland warned missionaries *and* educators that insensitivity to cultural differences contradicted the religious mission. Americans must eschew any attempt to "transform the Oriental into the European character." Dogged insistence on the superiority of English and the education of a foreign elite would only create a new caste structure and transform the vernacular "into the language of serfs and peasants." "Nothing could be more disastrous," Wayland insisted, "than to confine knowledge to a few and teach men to despise their native language." He also prescribed an aggressive transfer of the burdens of evangelism to native leaders as superior to a continual increase in the numbers of Western missionaries.[71]

Wayland and his Baptist allies must have nodded with satisfaction a few months later when the American Board of Commissioners joined the assault and made it a thoroughly interdenominational crusade. In conjunction with its annual business meeting, the board issued a special report demanding a clear distinction between Protestantism's global mission and the false "idols" of secular expansionists. The report resurrected Hopkins's 1845 strictures against cultural accommodation and testified to the power and influence that would make him board president by 1857. It also must have troubled the man who had already lectured his peers on the culture's disruptive capacities. The committee charged those who supported missions as cultural ambassadors with misconstruing the "true mission of the gospel." "Civilization is not conversion," they resounded.[72]

In language as forceful as Melville's, the committee pronounced "iron rails, steam engines, electric wires, power looms, and power presses" as "no part of Christianity." More remarkable than censures of commerce and technology were the committee's indictments of seminaries, schools, books, tracts, "denunciations of existing superstition," and "persecuting edicts" as equally futile agencies for bringing people into "subjection to Christ." Bringing people together for the "preaching of the gospel . . . [was] one thing," the committee chided, while "literary, scientific, and moral training" was "quite another." And the "latter . . . by no means of necessity involved the former." Burgeoning physical resources did not excuse the substitution of "ineffectual human devices . . . external forms, outward moralities, secular humanities, or aesthetical delectations" for the "preaching of *Christ and Him crucified*." The report responded to a complex web of concerns, not a single villain. The committee targeted what they believed was an encroaching confidence in physical and intellectual resources that threatened to "subvert the true order of things."[73]

Two months later, the *New Englander* registered unstinted praise for the American Board's report. The response, penned by Massachusetts clergyman Sereno Clark, cited the report's applicability to the domestic pulpit as well as to the missionary field. Not more publishing of apologetics but the preaching of the "simple gospel" must cap the Protestant agenda, Clark argued. A renewed commitment to preaching must counteract a popular communication boom that made politics and social reform the "chief intellectual food of the millions." Social and political reformers' calculated exploitation of "popular movements, mass meetings, and public lectures" testified that the spiritually regenerated speaker alone was the divinely appointed agent of the gospel. "Public, oral communication," as used by Christ in the New Testament, Clark insisted, remained the unchallenged instrument of the gospel mission. Believers had to recognize themselves as messengers "not of this world" but of a "kingdom within a kingdom."[74] His message recognized but rejected a nationalistic inversion of religion's temporal and eternal applications:

> Christ did not come to inculcate directly external morality, nor to promote immediately any worldly advantage, to encourage agriculture, manufactures, or commerce, nor to establish schools [or] civil institutions, nor to devise and carry forward any political measures for the melioration of society. . . . The Church is not a combination for mutual aid in prosecuting the objects of wealth, or honor, or the securing of domestic peace. The empire where she holds sway is the conscience and will. . . . The salvation of the soul, the spiritual interest of the world . . . is the peculiar, appropriate mission of the gospel minister.[75]

Clark's and the American Board's exhortations were hardly exceptional. New York City Presbyterian pastor Joseph P. Thompson—usually recognized as a leading Protestant antislavery figure—carried his message of Christianity over culture to the missionary societies of Bangor Theological Seminary, Brown and Rochester universities, and Williams College. Pleading his case in 1856, the same year that he published his *Teachings of the New Testament on Slavery*, Thompson's religious jeremiad reveals the specific spiritual concerns that pervaded Protestant thought even as the nation's sectional crisis boiled over.[76]

Irritated by the praise of the British *Westminster Review* for Unitarian missionaries who replaced the "'gibberish of essential doctrines'" with more practical humanitarian efforts, Thompson pronounced the mixing of "civilization" with "Christianization" as a threat to the faith. He railed against the "benevolent" motivational claims offered by Anglo-American expansionists. The "natural" spread of civilization, he pointed out, occurred incidentally to the selfish, national pursuit of colonies and commerce, not from any Anglo-Saxon desire to "benefit mankind." If commerce at times promoted peace among the nations, it did so from the "selfish calculation of the gains of peace." "The good will that commerce bears to the nations has the ledger for its text-book and prices current for its commentary; and the pages of this gospel are written alternately in letters of gold and in letters of blood." British promises of an impending "Millennium of commerce and of peace," had swelled London's Crystal Palace during the Great Exhibition in 1851; war in Crimea three years later proved the shallowness and impotence of such claims.[77]

American civilization apart from Christianity was equally "depraved," Thompson continued. Not philanthropic or religious motives but "eagerness to augment the resources and extend the area of commerce" drove Indian tribes westward, robbed Mexico of Texas and California, carried opium and liquor to Asia, and continued the slave trade. Thompson expanded his assault. None of the components of nineteenth-century civilization—philosophy, science, literature, social and political institutions, cultural refinement—had any intrinsic capacity to help mankind. He found it destructive to equate the expanding political and economic influence of Christendom with the extension of the kingdom of God: "The advancement of civilization is incidental to its own schemes of aggrandizement; not primal for the interests of humanity. It is a state to be realized by accidental combinations of events, not a beatific kingdom to be extended by the labors of its servants. . . . Christianization is . . . to make men disciples of this religion, disciples of Christ himself, by publishing his Gospel to all mankind . . . for which every disciple holds a commission directly from the Lord."[78]

Although Thompson took specific issue with Melville's attacks on the Sandwich Islands mission, his own message largely complemented the *Typee* author's claim that a missionary enterprise devoted to "civilization" was no missionary effort at all. Like Melville, Thompson demanded missionaries steeped in piety, cognizant of the evils intrinsic to both Western and "heathen" nations, and committed to the idea that social reform is incidental and secondary to the individual spiritual regeneration of men—Christ's "sublime philosophy of reform."[79] Thompson's address reveals a determination to blend cultural criticism and Protestant exceptionalism. Against what he viewed as the culture's economic and political material redefinition of "mission," he defended Protestant Christianity alone as divinely sanctioned in its global vision of spiritual conquest.

Ohio New School Presbyterian divine Samuel Fisher demonstrated how Protestant dissent infused even messages gushing with millennial poetry about the "glorious destiny," the Christian paradise that lay ahead. In his 1850 essay "Secular and Christian Civilization," Fisher's millennial portrait assumed a twofold purpose. First, he congratulated man's legitimate hopes for a better society, only then to deny human "schemes of development" and the temporal means of creating them. Second, he attacked those who denied faith's eternal verities in order to make Christianity compatible with other "moral" efforts to "better man's condition here." His carefully constructed argument admitted parallels between his millennial hopes and secular visions of dissolving national rivalries and gaining peace through commerce and technology. Disintegrating communication barriers presaged a coming civilization and improvements perhaps grander than "history has yet recorded," Fisher predicted. The fatal flaw, he argued, was to identify the "purpose of God in their permission."[80] The accomplishments of man would pave the way for the gospel not through success but through ultimate failure that would confirm the ascendancy of the gospel.

Fisher offered a concise interpretation of the antebellum Protestant understanding of temporal and eternal hopes. Though all earthly history fit within God's inscrutable providential designs, man's hopes rested on admitting his impotence and depravity within time. "Christianity [aims] primarily at our preparation for heaven; secondly, only at our elevation on earth." Here Fisher denied the millennium, however splendid, as primal in the Christian purpose. Indeed, he combined visions of future millennial bliss with warnings that believers could check its advance by dwelling on it. Man's power source, the "Word" and the "Spirit," as well as his ultimate destiny and mission, transcended the providential kingdom. "The kingdom of Christ is not properly of this world," Fisher cautioned. "He who views the Christian scheme as having respect chiefly to time, strips it of the force essential to its success in time. . . . Its power as a civilizer of the [human] race is derived almost wholly from its connection with the forces of eternity."[81] Fisher indulged utopian aspirations of peace and brotherhood only to "correctly" locate them within the Christian millennium. His central purpose, however, was to defend the faith by denying place to nationalistic and cultural pretensions of peace through global interaction and eventual cultural unity. Like the messages of his fellow clergy, Fisher's proclaimed the exclusive powers of Protestant faith in response to a rising message of popular material redemption that had nothing to do with religion.

Separate from the World

The religious jeremiads, then, directly refuted the culture's appeals to sanctify its expanding political and economic reach. They demanded "home" and "foreign" missions that stressed the oral communication of the faith as its chief instrumentality. This Protestant exceptionalism contradicted religious nationalism by identifying man's uniqueness and potential with Protestant faith rather than with the Commonwealth or an expanding commercial and territorial empire. The jeremiads gained added support from the regular pulpit in homilies stressing "Christ as separate from the world." A thematic mainstay of the antebellum pulpit, the notion of separateness in these sermons drew from clerical apprehensions about eroding distinctions between Christianity and culture. The Anglo-American global reach for material power and wealth—a collective physical manifestation of the liberalism that they feared—accounted for no small part of their concerns. Sermons by Horace Bushnell, Vermont Baptist minister Cyrus Hodges, and Indiana Presbyterian divine Samuel Thompson establish the links between routine Sunday sermons and religious jeremiads.

With the publication of *Sermons for the New Life* in 1858, Horace Bushnell achieved a personal and public triumph over the clerical watchdogs who suspected deep heresies beneath the Hartford divine's criticisms of New England orthodoxy. Thematically, the sermons reaffirmed the revelatory experience that had ignited his passion for the inward spiritual life a decade earlier. Bushnell consciously chose homilies stripped of the speculative edge and nebulous language that baited his opponents. Drawing from early and recent works, he no doubt wanted to demonstrate a simple, Christocentric core that had reigned in his ministry from the beginning. Critics sighed in relief, and the public flocked to this straight-shooting, "comprehensible" Bushnell. In response to the accolades for his return to "orthodoxy," however, Bushnell predictably defended his "outsider" status: "I believe nothing in orthodoxy, but all in the Lord Jesus Christ."[82] His most widely read publication entered its seventh printing in 1867.

In the sermon entry "Christ as Separate from the World," Bushnell employed his classic theme to rebuke popular enthusiasm for Christ's "humanness" that obscured His spiritual separateness. To deny the unique, otherworldly power of Christ and faith he identified as the "great and desolating error of our times." Christianity had no "regenerative power" at all except in its "separated character, as a revelation." He re-

buked those who exploited the "social" character of Christ's ministry
to justify predictions of an evolving, "nearly paradisaic" state through
cooperative philanthropy. Such confidence in human effort wrongly assumed a natural "feasibility to good in man." Bushnell's attacks on notions
of a "political millennium," "self-culture," and "self-activity" tapped the
same arguments that ministers like Thompson used to plead the distinction between Christianization and civilization. "Come ye reformers
and philanthropic regenerators of the world," Bushnell shrilled. "Bring
out your paper coaches"—(Bushnell is metaphorically denouncing misplaced popular faith in planned social development, social contracts, and
written constitutions)—"and bid the sorrow stricken peoples ride forth,
down the new millennium you promise without prophecy; . . . then see
what your toy-shop apparatus signifies!"[83]

Bushnell demanded no "ascetics" or "prescribed denials" to counteract
the spreading "liberal piety" that he charged with eroding the supernatural, separate character of faith. That would have contradicted Protestantism's historic denial of "monkish seclusion" as inconsistent with
the gospel mission. But he admonished believers against trying to "beat
the world in its own way," implicitly asking its approbation. Echoing the
American Board's emphasis on the spiritual component of missionary
effort, Bushnell contended that satisfying man's temporal wants, however important, added nothing to the "living impression of the gospel."
Only devotion to that separated kingdom available through the "radical,"
regenerative power of Christ could sustain the uniqueness of faith in a
world that practically contradicted it.[84] Bushnell cataloged and localized
for his own congregation the same secular "demons" that clerics making
a broader sweep saw maturing on the expanding, transatlantic horizons
of Christendom.

Taken together, his collected sermons mark "orthodoxy" and cultural
accommodation as the false idols of a generation losing touch with the
transformative power of the ancient faith. Doctrinal controversies grated
Bushnell's sensitivity to the disintegrative power of democratic culture
and aggravated the illness that forced him to resign his Hartford pulpit
in 1859. Although he at times seems suited to the role of bridge builder,
his theological spans were anchored more firmly in the spiritual certitudes of the Christian past than in the cultural flux of his own time. Only
by restoring the radical, Christocentric faith of apostolic times, Bushnell asserted, could believers survive the struggle between dogma and
diversity.

Vermont Baptist pastor Cyrus Hodges shared Bushnell's belief that "outward circumstances" could neither indicate nor produce the spiritual separateness mandated by Christ. The material vicissitudes and inequalities of life served purposes "beyond the scope" of human understanding. As those who waded "the deepest waters of affliction" were not to be regarded as "objects of heaven's displeasure," so those who were too prosperous were not God's "peculiar favorites."[85] Reliance on "outward reformation," the "social duties of religion," or a "general belief" in Christian doctrines created only the illusion of separation, not that substantive distinctness available only through the "regeneration and renewing of the Holy Ghost."

Acknowledging the worldwide mission of the faith, Hodges praised missionary efforts "exclusively devoted to the preaching of the gospel" as sustaining the essential uniqueness of Christianity. Though Christian faith mandated benevolence toward man, Hodges concluded, the Christian's hope lay in a spiritual, eternal dimension not defined by "temporal circumstances" or "confined to the things of time."[86] The sermons of Hodges and Bushnell demonstrate one way that Protestant clergy practically implemented occasional diagnostic pleas for separating Christianity and culture at the most basic level of everyday congregational preaching.

Indiana Presbyterian minister Samuel Thompson developed the theme of separateness by distinguishing the "wicked" who lived for "time" from the "righteous" who lived for eternity. Death, Thompson insisted, was the great equalizer that demolished artificial earthly distinctions of wealth, power, and influence. The "spirit of the world," he concluded, is invariably at war "in theory and in practice with the meek precepts of Jesus." Conformity of Christians to the world and the world's mimicry of Christian principles, he cautioned, too often blurred the distinction. Only at the "bar of Jesus" would all earthly confusions be finally "swept away" and the eternal separation of saints and sinners established.[87] Thompson's piece was a classic individualized example of the religious jeremiad that acknowledged Protestant frustration with the confusion of Christianity and culture.

These spiritual discourses suggest that the nationalistic excesses that could infect Protestant civic messages largely evaporated in religious jeremiads attacking the exploitative, commercial thrust of Anglo-American expansionism at mid-century. To strike at this material expression of the new liberalism, ministers baldly denounced the confounding of civilization and Christianity as an attack upon religion itself. They urged transatlantic devotion to a supernatural, supranational conception of faith, mission, and the "Kingdom of God." They attacked the sanctifiers of Western civilization as sirens of a self-interested, secularized gospel. Masking the raw, materialist edge of cultural expansion, critics insisted, threatened to sever ordinary people from the instrumentality of a "simple preached gospel."

Strategic emphasis on supernatural remedies, as well as regular clerical scrutiny of new intellectual and physical frontiers, compel a reconsideration of whether the clergy generally identified the nation's cultural and material expansion with the advancement of Christianity. Likewise, if their message did contain a "chauvinistic" component, it drew stronger nourishment from religious anxieties than from provincial boasts or cultural enthusiasm. Frontiers of space, however, were not the only liberal thresholds pressing upon Protestant claims. With equally chaotic energy, American liberty expanded the boundaries of intellectual freedom and encouraged innovative links between moral and material progress. This source of Protestant dissent—a complex expression of liberal culture that struck clerical assailants as nothing less than a transatlantic "revolution in infidelity"—proved equally important.

4

The "New Infidelity": Redemption as Secular Progress

By the 1840s, any patron of the popular press would have recognized the word "progress" as the omnipresent rhetorical icon of the young Republic. "This glorious nineteenth century is so frequent a topic of eulogistic declamation as to become not only commonplace but disgusting," Presbyterian divine Nicholas Murray declared in 1838.[1] To question that it was an "age of improvement," a Baptist writer lamented in 1840, was to declare oneself "ignorant and bigoted . . . unfit for the companionship of the reformers of the age."[2] Popular politics and the nation's commercial and territorial thrust were only two prongs of a democratic culture probing the limits of human potential. Popular liberty also spun a complex web of social, economic, and intellectual changes that left Protestant hopes of controlling the idea of progress in shambles. Liberalism pressed individuals to reap the promises of this earth using their own ambitions and creative power.

Writing at mid-century, a Congregationalist critic recited the maddening confusion that threatened Protestant hopes: "The mind of the age utters itself through this word [progress] more frequently than through any other," he admitted. It was "vague enough" to suit the "most misty and nebulous intellects." It served as a "convenient substitute" for modern cant—"Fourierism, Rationalism, Mysticism, Land-Reform"—when precise definition would be "imprudent or suicidal." Ministers, he cautioned, were charged with preserving its "safe and Christian sense." Inevitable progress did not point inevitably to holiness, he warned: "It is very plain that men may be advancing in sin and error, rather than truth and goodness. . . . Progress must be of the right kind. . . . It cannot itself be the measure and test of right, and truth and duty."[3]

Probing the intellectual turmoil underlying a popular transatlantic yearning for progress assumed all the urgency of a crusade for many Protestant defenders by the 1840s. Multiplying individualistic and collectivist schemes for human improvement, their religious jeremiads warned, either ignored Christianity or, worse yet, championed its demise as progress in itself, the inevitable triumph of secular process over spiritual faith in humanity's onward march. American liberty, that supposed bulwark of Protestant freedom, now seemed equally capable of endorsing schemes of popular progress fixed upon humankind's redemption from both this life's miseries and the orthodox spiritual agendas that bound humanity to a more celestial path.

The ways in which Protestant defenders resisted the cultural forces driving secular redemptive schemes between 1840 and 1860 bear close examination. Acquisitive materialism, an information explosion, and growing cultural and intellectual diversity provided the domestic staples of their critical tillage. (How else to account for the dearth of revivals at mid-century?) To these homegrown tares, ministers added the diverse, transatlantic yields of Continental positivism and idealism, the foundation of what Auguste Comte heralded as a "new religion of humanity." They insisted that new European skeptics echoed neither the airy and elitist utopian designs of Plato or James Harrington nor the redundant salvos against Christian supernaturalism that had earlier issued from Enlightenment savants. Choosing compassion over confrontation, young post-Hegelian freethinkers such as David Strauss, Ludwig Feuerbach, and Bruno Bauer urged progress beyond faith as the key to popular redemption from injustice, material want, and the encumbrances of spiritual striving. Congregational luminary Noah Porter gathered these fresh material challenges under the banner not of a "new religion" but of a "new infidelity." Indeed, by mid-century, Protestant critics commonly excoriated the "modern," "novel," and "entirely changed" focus of unbelief.[4]

Announcements of a "new" infidelity at mid-century give sharp relief to the irony of this Protestant quarrel. The religious jeremiads regularly blasted an unholy (and unanticipated) alliance of practical materialism and unbelief with ideas of liberty and progress that were supposed to remain deferential to evangelical designs. Worried ministers argued that peddlers of infidelity had historically preferred an open pitch to the cover of a popular, progressive cast. The new vendors cloaked spiritual indifference and skepticism in the diverse language of human freedom, popular empowerment, and concomitant progress. In the Protestant scheme, democratic discourse or the process of "free inquiry" was supposed to unmask evil and give greater sway to the spiritual demands of Protestant faith. The new infidelity worried ministers precisely because it exploded this prescriptive model. Expansive liberty now gilded plausible material alternatives to spiritual redemption with a moral, humanitarian edge that proved more difficult to attack, not less.

A few examples at this point illustrate clerical alarms. Presbyterian Thomas Moore informed his American Bible Society associates in 1850 that "the infidelity of the present day is not the infidelity of the past." Shedding its older tendency to "disgust and alarm," infidelity now attempted to "seduce and persuade," masked its true character as the "enemy of religion," and promised a "reformation and perfection" superior to faith.

In an 1852 sequel delivered to Southern Methodists, Moore traced the change to its transatlantic roots: "Theories of freedom and rights, that were applicable only to man in his relation to the human, were applied to man in his relation to the Divine."[5] English Congregational divine John Angell James, widely read on both sides of the Atlantic, called this new infidelity *the* danger of the age" and warned believers of its "subtle and insidious" democratic garb. It indulges your *"love of freedom* . . . invites you to throw off the yoke of authority," and offers redemption from the constraints of spiritual faith through the "irresistible power of free inquiry," he cautioned. No longer the "vulgar ribaldry of Paine" or the "half-concealed sneers of Gibbon," this new, "more *artful"* infidelity was at once "specious, plausible, persuasive."[6] Leading Protestant sentinel Samuel Harris bemoaned the new infidelity as unrecognizable to those familiar only with the "shallow and vulgar skepticism of the last century." Unbelief, he warned, now "[made] itself popular" through alliance with "liberty, progress, and social reorganization" and claimed to be "the highest development of man."[7]

Scholars have paid scant attention to this war on a "new infidelity" that raged between 1840 and 1860. Its potential for explaining late antebellum Protestant cultural dissent has been overshadowed by studies exploring the nationalistic, millennial, and ideological sources of Protestant motivation. Ronald Cashdollar recently filled an important gap by explaining the central role of Comte's positivism in shaping theological understanding, especially after the Civil War. Rudimentary awareness and understanding of Comte's ideas limited his impact before 1860.[8] Yet that imprecision resulted in part from the distractive power of a broader materialist challenge. For the antebellum era, Protestant anxieties did not grow solely in response to a maturing understanding of Comte's philosophy. Indeed, Comte's ideas were threatening precisely because the clergy placed him within a more ominous constellation of foreign and domestic materialist adversaries.[9] Less urgent than particular accommodation of Comte in cloistered theological debates was exposing materialism's "thousand points of light," now beamed at the very foundation of popular culture. It was a defense fashioned less out of philosophical ignorance or incomprehension than from worries tuned to broader cultural transformation.

Clerical ranting against infidelity has also been dismissed as a lamentable legacy of Puritan bigotry needing rebuke but not in-depth analysis. Indeed, one scholar argues that ministers attacked the "infidel" with all the bullish self-confidence of a complacent Protestant establishment. Ministers concocted the image of the infidel merely as a convenient "bogey" to rally church defenders of the Standing Order.[10] Once they renounced a sprinkling of outspoken doubters—socialist Robert Owen, labor leader Francis Wright, transcendentalist Ralph Waldo Emerson—it might seem that the clergy would have had real trouble scaring up a flesh-and-blood phalanx of "infidels" with whom to do battle. But by the 1840s, these dissenters saw celebrity skeptics as threatening precisely because they masked the "insidious" encroachment of an amorphous infidelity. Imposing tomes against Christian supernaturalism, even the perennial "Catholic menace," struck many ministers as the easy targets of an older struggle.

Significantly, worried clergy tagged the diversity and chameleonlike qualities of the new unbelief as a key to its potential. Redemptive agendas tied variously to individual economic success, social freedom, utilitarian morality, and a rational humanitarianism could mix easily and unnoticed in the shifting secular currents of emergent liberal culture. Swelling immigration, especially German in the late 1840s, hardened links with Continental thought. The cheap press and freewheeling public discourse encouraged by the lyceum movement accelerated the exchange of new ideas. Political liberty steadily pressed Americans to embrace this intellectual freedom from traditional thought as part of their constitutional birthright. Unprecedented economic opportunity and freedom churned out what one minister blasted as an endless parade of "money-making machines." It seemed that as their material ambitions numbed their spiritual sensibilities Americans only widened the channels of unbelief. An Oxford, Georgia, writer argued that the philosophic and aesthetic extremes undermining European faith would be reshaped and complemented by the "accelerating progress . . . [of] materialism and sensualism" in the United States. In America, Thomas Moore declared, "a soil is preparing" for what is "magniloquently termed the Church of the future." [11]

Few mainstream critics predicted a nation of confessing transcendentalists. Americans, they reasoned, were an impatient and practical lot, unlikely disciples of any particular theorist. The more likely domestic fruit of the new infidelity was an eclectic, "pantheistic" blessing of popular material lusts. Liberty might erode ideological precision, but the shifting mosaic would be more dangerous than coherent theory. "Opposition has put on a friendly seeming," a Methodist writer cautioned, but only to "deal a blow more deadly, because unexpected." [12] Invoking similar frustrations in 1849, the *Lutheran Observer* cited the new intellectual tide as a dark vista on the Protestant horizon and charted a strategic response: "The battle now is not so much with the bald atheism of the French Revolution as with an ethical theism, allied with all the trappings of philosophy and taste, which can only be met by showing that . . . [it] does not meet the needs of humanity." [13] In short, cultural change had dimmed older visions of liberty that leaned inevitably toward faith. New vanguards of progress embraced human freedom and opportunity while marching against a historic cadence of sin, salvation, and final judgment.

An examination of the hostility of Protestant leaders to the ideological diversity building beneath the idea of progress shows how historic religious concerns still shaped their understanding of immediate realities. The religious jeremiads reveal that the clergy's own plea for "progress" was less an easy accommodation of burgeoning materialism than a strategic countermove to keep practical and theoretical alternatives to spiritual redemption from eclipsing Christianity altogether. Better understanding of this cultural dissent first requires consideration of clerical broadsides against Americans hewing their own economic and social paths to material bliss.

A Search for Economic Redemption

Jacksonian Americans suspected that the nation possessed an almost limitless capacity to generate wealth. The popular press spread the economic gospel daily. Financial panic in 1837 elicited cautions, but Americans had seized an acquisitive mentality that resisted limits and looked confidently beyond temporary setbacks. Locating a precise niche for the clergy amid this mania is no easy task. Charles Cole notes that Northern evangelicals settled for a polyglot relationship with money, alternately "despising it, embracing it, and putting it to use." They often claimed that Christianity was the "means of national prosperity."[14] Further, ministers knew the connection between prosperity and a congregation that could support the missionary enterprise and pay its pastor on time. Baptists leaders often complained that inconsistent support accounted for the vacant pulpits and clerical moonlighting that plagued their associations at mid-century.[15] John Wesley's dictum rang true beyond Methodist ranks: "Make all you can, save all you can, give all you can."

Not much room so far for serious dissent. Ministers, it would seem, took the capitalist plunge, coming up for spiritual air only to collect tithes and raise traditional standards against greed and rapaciousness. Scholars following Max Weber and R. H. Tawney find Protestants offering precious little opposition to the "spirit of capitalism."[16] Keith Stavely, for example, concludes that evangelicals "strove to convince themselves that economic change was leading to moral and spiritual betterment."[17] The argument draws strength from the fact that orthodox ministers defended private property, opposed the political redistribution of wealth, and remained susceptible to the notion that prosperity could be a sign of divine favor. Some even joined the economic fray. Henry Ward Beecher, for example, made a bundle (more than $90,000 by one estimate) on the lecture circuit and even hired an agent in the 1850s to pump his fees higher.[18] Even excepting Beecher's indulgences, there can be little doubt that the clergy viewed economic progress and faith as potentially compatible.

James Turner explains Protestant economic accommodation as symptomatic of a broader "moralization of belief." Turner correctly notes that as religion becomes "a matter of morality," it fixes its gaze on the "here-and-now." He also synthesizes a generation of scholarship in concluding that progressivism and humanitarianism blended so neatly with evangelical millennialism that mainstream Protestant leaders themselves (not theists or Unitarians) became the leading champions of an innocuous morality that shattered older distinctions and explained the will of God as the will of man. This intellectual transformation was certainly in process. The conclusion that ensuing clerical anxieties remained inarticulate or that dissent found expression mainly in bungled attempts to accommodate rationalism deserves closer scrutiny, however.[19]

In fact, the "moral" revolution and its concomitant threat to orthodoxy received explicit analysis and criticism in the religious jeremiads. Protestant dissenters remained aloof from practical economic alternatives to liberal capitalism, but they did so largely in deference to criticisms and restoratives that addressed primary spiritual concerns. However inadequate their remedies would seem to a later generation, these early witnesses of the American industrial and commercial colossus issued religious complaints that challenged the ethos of the new order and played to a broader quarrel with the Republic. In defense of an exclusive spiritual terrain, these divines attacked a protean materialism and humanitarianism in language far afield from that of liberal imperatives. It marked one of the sharpest exchanges between religion and culture that the tumultuous century produced.

It is helpful to view ministers' talk of "prosperity" within their larger hierarchy of religious purpose. Most of them remained loyal to an older, moral economy, replete with notions of the "just price," personal "frugality," and honesty driven by Christian virtue, not economic expediency. Such an understanding dovetailed in many ways with classical republican ideals, but antebellum ministers resisted an easy accommodation of secular moralism. Their hopes for moral economic ends remained at odds with "moralistic" means. A New York Baptist writer offered typical advice. In praising believers as "superior to every other organization upon the Earth," he dismissed external efforts to "prune" human vice, prescribing faith as the only means of making "men radically and permanently better."[20] Moreover, ministers looked askance at risk-taking, a capitalist dynamo far more important than Protestant conceptions of personal industry, calling, and frugality, as Thomas Doerflinger has recently made plain.[21] These preconceptions enabled ministers still to bless the potential alignment of prosperity and faith. At the same time they provided spiritual grounds for attacking the new economy's place in a broader materialistic faith. The results of this dynamic tension between hope and reality must be examined.

An 1855 Newark Tract Society report expressed this tension by acknowledging that although material improvement in God's providential, earthly kingdom was "subsidiary to the spreading of his spiritual kingdom," the "leavening" power of Christianity was such that "science, art, and mechanical skill" could become the "scaffolding of [Christ's] temple" and "instruments of the universal sway of Jesus."[22] In a frequently noted sermon, Horace Bushnell challenged Hartford residents to accept prosperity as a communal "duty." Given his first career as associate editor of the *New York Journal of Commerce*, Bushnell's eagerness to explain Christianity's relationship to the economic order is hardly surprising. Spiritual responsibilities did not preclude Christian involvement, he argued. He rebuked Hartford residents who passively accepted economic decline as railroad construction redirected growth. Any community could prosper that would "do its duty," he insisted. Economic deterioration worked "a moral prostration in every way correspondent" so Christians could not stand aloof.[23]

Bushnell's declamation, like that of the Newark Tract Society, drew from historic Protestant rejection of Platonic dualism and monastic asceticism as inconsistent with Christ's command to spread the gospel. Those who withdrew from the material world to achieve spirituality falsely located evil in matter itself rather than in human sinfulness. Protestant confidence in radical spiritual transformation, in other words, branded redemptive strategies based on poverty, riches, or the "middle road" of frugality as equally chimerical. The last option remained preferable only because either extreme produced a "false" foundation of spiritual security. In short, ministers' economic hopes designated neither wealth nor poverty as redemptive path or spiritual marker. When it came to defending historic faith, ministers were prepared to attack socialism and capitalism as part of a generally distractive "material" faith.

The same Horace Bushnell, for example, who rallied Hartford residents to the economic fray in 1847 ended his pastorate there questioning the future of people secure in their "modern liberties" and "awash in a tide of economic progress." The confluence of individual liberty and material wealth, he feared, had trapped society in a series of irreconcilable conflicts—riches versus piety, power versus humility, indulgence versus Christian simplicity. "It is yet to be seen whether even the lowly-minded, self-renouncing religion of Jesus can save a prospering age from this folly," he chided. Could those who had "mastered all prosperity" still know the "world diminishing glory of Jesus in the heart?"[24]

For Bushnell, the hope that piety could check the emergence of a purely utilitarian economic morality seemed increasingly remote. His assault penetrated deeper than traditional clerical attacks on excessive greed. He saw the expansive potential for gain in the country becoming a pervasive materialistic mentality not necessarily contingent on the actual possession of things. Not just rich but middling and even poor people seemed to be driven by the new ethos. Such dissent, however, did not push Bushnell or most mainstream Protestant leaders toward socialism as a logical solution. Ministers could attack collectivist and capitalist conceptions of economic progress with equal fury when they detected the materialism intrinsic to both ideologies contributing to the new infidelity.

Quipped one Episcopal writer, socialists did well in demanding a wisdom that defined the "wealth of nations" as something beyond the private "accumulation of capital." They fatally erred in declaring their human idealism "the redeemer of the age."[25] Humanity labored to perfect economic and political structures in a flawed pursuit of happiness, Congregationalist divine and popular American Tract Society author Jacob Abbott warned. They forgot that "human institutions," democratic or despotic, gained "all their efficiency in evil" from human depravity. The "Christian community" did its proper work not by indulging the pretensions of system builders but by allowing Christianity to regenerate the human heart and thereby "root out depravity." Once that is accomplished, almost any system "will work well," he concluded.[26]

What most disturbed critical ministers about the new economy, however, was that it infected the population with more than a damnable penchant for money. Following a kind of "trickle-down" logic, ministers saw speculation and economic risk-taking as part of a popular ideological transformation that threatened religion more than it did society or the Republic. It was a small intellectual leap, in other words, from economic speculation to unbridled "spiritual speculation," a perversion of the spirit of "free inquiry" and liberty of conscience which Protestants had supposed would make freedom the engine of religious faith. A writer in the *Oberlin Evangelist* warned that the laudable "spirit of inquiry" that had eroded "priest-craft" and demolished "ex cathedra authority" had concurrently fostered "speculative habits," a "disorganizing tendency," and the "furious impulses of a heady independence." He insisted that human efforts to stem the tide—benevolent societies, politics, economic innovation, ethics, civil authority—had proved impotent. The ministry, he argued, must depend on the "mere preaching" of "Jesus Christ and him crucified."[27]

Critics of the capitalist bias of Protestantism insist that the Protestant message historically linked material success with spirituality. Yet as the drive for personal gain became the heart of a new economic morality, frugality and virtue seemed increasingly at odds with financial success, and the linkage broke down. Between 1840 and 1860 religious jeremiads attacking the capitalistic ethos and unprecedented national and individual accumulation of wealth far outweighed messages citing individual and national wealth as signposts of spiritual regeneration or religious commitment. "We cannot bear prosperity," minister Rufus Clark lamented in 1845. "Experience proves that as Christians are successful in their worldly interest . . . they think less of the claims of God and religion."[28]

The secular press aggravated Protestant suspicions. New York's *Demo-*

cratic Review in 1838 doubted Alexis de Tocqueville's suggestion that religious belief was a direct support of republican government. Whatever its benefits, the *Review*'s critic responded, religion was subsidiary to "enterprise" and "industry" in sustaining the nation and the morality of the people. Its present office was "to cooperate with our excellent institutions." Carrying his analysis further, the writer cited not religion but the liberal order itself—the "unlimited scope . . . of individual activity" secured by liberty—as the source of a morally salutary spirit of enterprise.[29] Ministers had no objections to economic initiative or "diligence in business"—provided their vision of spiritual containment prevailed. Rather, they worried that economic opportunity and liberty could strengthen a larger web of secular moral directives and critically invert Protestant hierarchies. Christians themselves, New York divine James Alexander cautioned, were too easily lured by causes "external, economical, patriotic, literary, or simply moral." Purposes worthy "when subordinated to the gospel" became "usurpations malign and dangerous" as they replaced the transcendent mission of the "family of true believers."[30]

In blunt, unsophisticated style, evangelist Charles Grandison Finney attacked the hardening grip of liberal capitalism on the popular mind. Charles Sellers, however, argues that Finney made religion a bulwark of marketplace hegemony, promising businessmen acting upon right principles a forward position in the millennial army. Their moral rectitude and material largesse would help bring on the earthly paradise "by converting individuals to discipline and benevolence." This analysis deserves closer scrutiny in light of Finney's spiritual discourse. Of particular interest is a determination of whether his desire to purge the marketplace stemmed from a wish to harness its millennial potential or a wish to *control* material principles hostile to the fundamentals of his spiritual agenda. Significantly, the corpus of Finney's work suggests that his "hegemonic" designs had less to do with co-opting market culture than with choking its capacity to undermine his exclusive spiritual goals. If the money changers found his sermons an easy mark for equating "capitalist asceticism" and "repressive moralism" with "Christian virtue," it is perhaps better testimony to liberal culture's creative edge than to the accommodative tendencies of Finney's preaching.[31]

Finney's evangelical faith drew partially from John Wesley's emphasis on "holiness" and "Christian perfection" and centered on the obliteration of selfishness, his one-word synonym for sin.[32] Far from being a financial nitwit, as one scholar implies, Finney understood only too well that the new economy threatened to undermine his war on "selfishness." In his frequently published sermon "Love of the World," he gave no quarter to those who insisted that business ethics need not reflect spiritual values. To make money "for His glory" using business principles "inconsistent with your own spirituality," Finney chided, was as preposterous as "talk of getting drunk or swearing for the glory of God." Modern commerce sanctified "principles of supreme selfishness . . . without even the pretence of conformity to the law of love," he argued. "Can a man love God supremely . . . who daily and habitually transacts business upon the principles of commercial justice, founded, as they are, in that which is the direct opposite of the requirement of God?"[33] Finney's remedy—the supplanting of liberal with "Christian" principles of doing business—revealed more than a yearning for the old economy or a desire to act as a financial adviser for believers. His whole conception of Christian "progress" and "holiness" hinged on the subjugation of material desires to the will of God. Consequently, even taming the capitalist leviathan remained a temporally useful act, collateral to a spiritual quest beyond the material antipodes of asceticism and indulgence.

Finney's admonition to do business according to the "law of Christian love" was hopelessly idealistic, and it harbored no personal interest in politically engineered redistribution of wealth. It did, however, show his antipathy for any economic system that provided outlet and ideological sanction for selfish motivation. Finney, like most of his peers, could conceive of social reform only from the bottom up. Apart from the supernatural regeneration of individuals, in other words, all "systems" foundered. Whatever the impersonal social forces acting on individuals, human sinfulness was the great roadblock to human progress. Since sin persisted as the dominant reality for Protestant leaders, its transcendence through individual spiritual regeneration and devotion to Christ remained their standard prescription for progress and the intellectual base from which they attacked the "folly" of equating economic success and holiness.

Finney demanded a "Christian economy" but offered no linkage between redemption and material success. Right action, he claimed repeatedly in his spiritual discourse, could never produce or define Christian virtue. In "The Way of Salvation," he made his position clear: "Our own holiness does not enter at all into the ground or reason for our acceptance and salvation. . . . We are not going to be indebted to Christ for a while, until we are sanctified, and all the rest of the time stand in our own righteousness. . . . Jesus Christ will forever be the sole reason in the universe why we are not in hell."[34]

Arriving at the same stark conclusion in "Christian Perfection," Finney asked: "How many are seeking sanctification by their own resolutions and works, their fasting and prayers, their endeavors and activity, instead of taking right hold of Christ by faith. . . . It is all work, work, work, when it should be by faith."[35] As society drifted away from his own conception of spiritual progress, Finney brusquely condemned the pursuit of holiness through material means.

Ministers could lash out at the smug complacency of believers under the spell of materialism. "The church is to be plainly and faithfully told that her great danger, at the present day, is from worldly prosperity," a Presbyterian writer concluded in 1837. "Employed to minister to the pride of life," he argued, wealth must inevitably "consume the vitals of her piety, and bring on spiritual imbecility, formalism, and death."[36] However flawed the secular theoretical assumptions of classical republican practice, the older economic ethos seemed far less threatening than a culture in pursuit of the main chance. When the credit system collapsed in 1837, ministers leaped at the opportunity to reassert God's providential authority and his willingness to distribute temporal justice to men and nations. "Attribute this distress to whatever political or financial causes you may," the *Christian Spectator* warned, but it is "the sins of the people" which have brought this "visitation of a retributive providence." Rampant speculation, the "hope of acquiring wealth without helping to create it," and "luxurious and profligate habits" were the new trademarks of a people "gone mad with sudden prosperity." Like Finney, the writer excoriated those of "high religious professions" who justified their speculative ways as a "means of great usefulness . . . for the kingdom of Christ."[37]

Forty years earlier William Wilberforce had argued that as British commercial expansion augmented middle-class wealth, corruption traditionally restricted to the "higher orders" would gradually suffuse the whole society.[38] Now the American clergy saw for themselves the truth of Wilberforce's insights. His text continued to circulate widely in the United States into the 1850s. New York Lutheran pastor A. L. Bridgman declared in 1856 that Americans had lost sight of the highest meaning of "prosperity." Not a few "professing godliness," he lamented, had more concern for the "state of the market" and the material welfare of the country than for the salvation of men and the "prosperity of Zion."[39]

In the South, Virginia Presbyterian divine Robert L. Dabney rebuked the "fashionable Christianity" that he saw advancing in tandem with the "progress of genteel society." Dabney was a Southern patriot (he would serve the Confederacy as chaplain and chief of staff for Stonewall Jackson) in one of the South's wealthiest denominations. His 1852 offensive appeared in the *Southern Presbyterian Review* during the final year of his pastorate at Tinkling Spring Church near Richmond. Already a prominent voice among Southern Presbyterians, Dabney was about to begin a thirty-year tenure on the faculty of Union Theological Seminary in Richmond. His religious jeremiad went far beyond innocuous cautions against "aristocratic excess." Dabney carried his offensive to the heart of a materialist ethos that united North and South.[40]

Dabney was worried about more than the eternal fate of a few profligate souls. His comprehensive vision focused on church materialism that could render religion a "sham" in American culture. Gone was the time when classical virtue, its vacuous spirituality notwithstanding, made common cause with Christianity against the evils of unchecked consumption. What hope was there for evangelism, Dabney asked, when the "unrenewed" could witness believers acting on the "same selfish and groveling principles with themselves"? Boasts of a "radical," spiritual separateness merely validated the "practical skepticism" of a world that shrewdly "believes our conduct and not our words."[41]

Dabney prescribed a social order in which a universal "Spartan simplicity" eliminated wealth as the basis of social distinctions. All material possessions should be subservient to the evangelical mission. In a volley that caught fellow ministers, he demanded an end to the "accommodating exegesis" that buttressed consumer culture. Dabney accepted a society built on "proper distinctions," but he dismissed an "unrighteous standard of admission" that omitted "humble worth . . . because united with poverty." Unbending loyalty to the Southern cause stopped him short of attacking an "unrighteous standard" blanketing the "humble worth" of enslaved African Americans. Still, his central theme survived the real limitations of his argument: Believers must embrace the transcendent purposes of faith or succumb to unchecked materialism that gave "the lie" to "assertions of nobler principles."[42]

As forcefully as did Dabney, Francis Wayland unleashed his anger in the wake of the panic of 1857. Dispensing with the polite restraint that characterized his 1837 critique, he bared a thorough contempt for "economic man's" influence on the faith. In one religious jeremiad from his *Sermons to the Churches*, Wayland asked why the "plain-spoken friend of publicans and sinners" no longer appeared "fit" for "selecter circles of intellectual, well-bred, and thoroughly respectable Christianity."[43] He summarized new realities behind the age-old "perils of riches." Prosperity led believers to confuse the responsibility for individual Christian evangelism with the maintenance of legal codes, civil authority, and the financial support of reform societies. Urban congregations raised churches that were barriers, not ambassadors, to the poor. The "perfect freedom of individual action" and the "boundless extent of our national domain" compounded the corrosive effects of wealth.[44] "Can the disease be cured," he queried, "by the erection of magnificent temples to Jesus of Nazareth from which the poor, to whom he preached the gospel, are virtually excluded? . . . The poor cannot and will not enter them. . . . Will the cure be effected by a few ministers of the word, whose power is exhausted in the attempt to render the teachings of Jesus acceptable to the intelligent and refined, the opulent and the fastidious?"[45]

When Wayland questioned the fate of "intellects quickened and passions inflamed by the progress of civilization," he acknowledged that Christian lethargy allowed others to claim the mantle of progress. He made no pleas, however, for a "social gospel" to supplant the spiritual priorities of faith. Indeed, he stated his position unequivocally: "The New Testament is a message from God addressed not to nations, or societies, or masses, or to any ecclesiastical caste but to every individual."[46] Wayland took aim at Christians who assumed that financial contributions to benevolent societies somehow fulfilled their evangelistic obligations to the poor. "We employ an agent to distribute these little offerings, and never come into personal contact with poverty, wretchedness, and crime. . . . In all this, do we keep or break the commandment of the Redeemer?" he asked.[47]

Wayland did not brand wealth as intrinsically sinful, but he raked capitalists glued to a treadmill of accumulation. "Rich Christians," he concluded, were most often "obstacles to the progress of the gospel." Success in providing for "every reasonable want," should convince people that they "have no right to devote the rest of their lives to the purpose of accumulation." Impersonal, meager donations to charity constituted "not the shadow of a sacrifice." Evangelization, aid to the destitute, assistance to education, all required the direct intervention of believers, not attendance at church services "conducted, for the rich." "Poverty, squalid and despairing, the cause and the result of vice," was not to be subdued by "Maine laws and vagrant acts," "prisons and jails," "houses of reformation" or other such efforts to "arrest the progress of evil."[48] To be sure, Wayland was no socialist; he advocated a collectivism centered on the spiritual regeneration of individuals as the core of the Christian mission and the centerpiece of social reform. He supported the individual's right to earn and use private wealth as desired. But Wayland's religious vision both interdicted and transcended easy sanctification of any economic system. Economic "right" was merely one more material liberty that believers must subordinate to divine authority and spiritual obligation.

Wayland's assaults blended with a larger Protestant yearning for traditional faith to offset the materialism of the age. Baptist leader Henry Clay Fish decried the corrupted piety he saw growing out of an American materialistic ethos that confounded spiritual and earthly progress. He warned that the church had become "extensively secularized," that the material progress that could become the "scaffolding" of Christ's temple was itself becoming the object of idolatry. The church and the world almost seemed "blended into one." However impressive the accomplishments of the age, Fish contended, "love of money, not zeal for God, digs canals, lays railroads, runs steamboats and packets." He indicted the new economy as pressing people toward a future inconsistent with the old piety. "What will this nation become," Fish queried, when "all branches of trade and pursuit are thrown open to the most unrestricted competition" and people continue to face an "unprecedented progress in the accumulation of property?"[49]

Fish implored believers to return to the "piety of the fathers"—Richard Baxter, John Bunyan, Jonathan Edwards—and to "gospel simplicity." Only an unprecedented commitment to personal faith and an aggressive evangelical effort could reaffirm the historic Christian mission and interdict the forces of modernity that were corrupting the church. Outward benevolence was useless, he concluded, apart from a "*deep-seated, vigorous piety within.*"[50]

Redemptive Striving and the Social Order

Clerical worries about the speculative spirit and selfish individualism spawned by the new economy were compounded by the emergence of a democratic social structure that ministers found equally troubling. Democratic culture extended and strengthened liberalism's grip by giving wider audience and social power to new ideas. It was an essential catalyst to clerical assaults on a new infidelity.

Technology, American liberty, and cultural diversity had combined to create this new democratic milieu in which intellectual speculation could thrive. Francis Wayland explained the unpredictable power inherent in the new matrix. Increasing popular power, wide property distribution, a

high literacy rate, and rapid communication made Old World rules obsolete, Wayland argued. In other large countries, "agitation at the center
has commonly died away before its wave has reached the circumference."
But here, "the whole surface, from center to circumference, is in motion
at once." The Constitution, he speculated, intended for "abasing false-
hood and annihilating folly" could "become the direct enemy of truth."
Wayland made plain that he worried most about the effect of new democratic political and social principles on faith. "Ceaseless agitation," he
argued, meant that Christianity's real social utility could be either pros-
tituted to secular causes by designing politicians or confused with the
doctrinal core of the faith. As democracy created a new "doctrine of expediency," popular power could encourage ministers to be "'all things to
all people'" and to preach Christianity not as a spiritual end in itself but
as a mere instrument of social policy.[51]

Wayland's apprehensions reinforced a larger clerical ambivalence toward the clash of a literate population with an information explosion.
Religious concerns tempered the clerical embrace of a free press. Baptist
preacher Daniel Corey told his father that in what was "pre-eminently a
reading age" the boundless yield of pen and press blanketed the country
"like the leaves of autumn," soliciting "thousands of hearts and minds"
with unprecedented speed. He prescribed no political restrictions but
cautioned that the nation had "fallen on perilous times."[52] One dis-
gruntled Reformed divine lamented that even the religious press had so
absorbed the divisive spirit of the age that it was more likely to drive
readers to "dreary unbelief and skepticism" than to regeneration.[53]

Church pastors did, in fact, confront a literate public, who had a voracious appetite for information. Illiteracy in the North was only 5 percent
among whites by 1840, down from about 25 percent in 1800. Only one
of every 574 Connecticut residents could not read in 1840. Even among
Rhode Islanders, the least-educated New Englanders, the ratio was only
one to 65.[54] Literacy rates were lower in the South and West, but the
trans-sectional intellectual curiosity of Americans impressed Alexis de
Tocqueville. However harsh the physical environment, the West was no
bastion of "rudeness and ignorance," he recorded. "It is difficult to imag-
ine the incredible rapidity with which thought circulates in the midst of
these deserts." He concluded that the nation's "civilized" backwoodsmen
sustained as much or more "intellectual curiosity [than] exists in the most
enlightened and populous districts of France."[55]

Indeed, newspaper publication exploded between 1830 and 1840 in
the West as well as the East. Protestants struggled to harness the new

medium, increasing the circulation of weekly and biweekly religious newspapers 35 percent, to 115,000. From Cincinnati, the literary nerve center of the old Northwest, issued a flood of secular religious periodicals, as well as new presses and printing supplies. By 1840 steam presses pushed daily production capability to 55,000 and drove newspaper prices down to a penny per copy. Foreign-language publications, particularly German and Scandinavian, flourished as editors labored to instruct a burgeoning immigrant population in the ways of American life.[56] Pennsylvania Lutheran divine John Ulrich drew appropriately from William Cowper's poem "The Progress of Error" to capture Protestant ambivalence toward a free press and the democratization of public discourse:

> By thee religion, liberty and laws,
> Exert their influence and advocate their cause:
> By thee, worse plagues than Pharaoh's land befell,
> Diffused, make earth the vestibule of hell;
> Thou fountain, at which drink the good and wise,
> Thou ever bubbling spring of endless lies:
> Like Eden's dread probation tree,
> Knowledge of good and evil, springs from thee.[57]

The transatlantic scope of this information explosion provided spiritual leaders with ample sources of anxiety. Note, for example, Emerson's role not only as New England's celebrated dissenter and intellectual but also as American advocate of Thomas Carlyle's Anglicized version of German transcendentalism. Carlyle first published *Sartor Resartus*, his autobiographical break with orthodoxy, in the United States instead of in England, and he did so with Emerson's help. All five hundred first-edition copies of the work, praised by Emerson for its "purity of moral sentiment," sold within months in 1836, and the book went into a second printing in 1837.[58]

Ministers worried that liberty and a cheap press made the nation a marketplace for such heterodox volumes. Emerson himself shared their perception of an information society out of control. He had his own quarrel with a print-hungry nation that threatened his property rights. Technology and economic opportunity made the pirating and reprinting of texts profitable and commonplace by the 1840s, irritating Emerson, who wanted hard cash for his ideas. Writing in 1843, he warned Carlyle of abuses of liberty that signaled new literary perils in "freebooting America." The cheap press had "worked a total change" in American book markets, he wailed. New York and Philadelphia publishing houses converted popular works into newspapers and pamphlets "hawked by a hundred boys in the streets of all our cities."[59] The transformation was bittersweet irony for anxious evangelicals. The cheap press showered the land with religious tracts, but it also gave the new infidelity limitless and maddeningly elusive outlets.

One minister commended "Romanism" for at least being a "bold and boastful" adversary. The new unbelief's "wonderful plastic energy" exploited the more cowardly and dangerous ploys of subtlety and subterfuge. This "invisible" power made it infinitely more "fearful," as it "[worked] beneath the surface" in essays, poems, novels, and periodicals that appealed to all social ranks. The popular press, divinely ordained to spread "truth and goodness," had now "strangely turned to work their overthrow." Catholicism, of course, was still a threat, he cautioned, but its agents were evidently in retreat. The "chief danger" now lay in the spread of a "subtle unbelief."[60]

The lyceum movement, oral counterpart of the cheap press, began its meteoric rise in the 1820s and compounded clerical concerns. As one of its founders, Josiah Holbrook, explained, the lyceum was to disseminate "rational and useful" information throughout the community.[61] From the start, Unitarians played a more active role in the lyceums than did mainstream orthodox divines. Financially pressed ministers often found the rostrum a useful means of supplementing their meager incomes.

The lyceum bowed to popular demands by the 1840s and shed much of its utilitarian focus. The speaker's platform became as much a source of entertainment and speculative discourse for a widening audience. Topics from phrenology to radical labor ideology rained from the new public forum and orthodox clerical support for the institution eroded. Local lyceum groups regularly solicited and paid premiums for well-known, crowd-pleasing speakers. The podium became the public haunt of such nationally known celebrities as Emerson, Henry David Thoreau, Henry Ward Beecher, and Oliver Wendell Holmes. Speakers' fees rose from little more than $10 or $15 expense money to between $25 and $75. Lectures often gained an extended life through local newspaper reviews. Emerson used the lecture circuit as a testing ground to shape and rethink what would become nearly three-fourths of his published essays. As the popular lecture became an important source of family entertainment, dozens of free-lance lecturers roamed the countryside, advertising their specialties in newspapers and garnering whatever receipts they could from one-night stands.[62] Not surprisingly, appeals for the "progress of humanity" were a popular unifying theme amid this lyceum diversity.

Thanks to sprawling railroad lines, the lecture circuit burst the confines of urban centers. Enterprising Westerners like Chicagoan Samuel Ward lured seaboard stars like Emerson, Horace Mann, and adventurer Bayard Taylor by promising a series of speaking engagements in smaller towns. Lecturers typically offered the same manuscript over and over again at cross-country one-night engagements. In rural areas, the lyceum slaked community leaders' thirst for civilization and respectability. Moral lectures drilling young men on the evils of drinking, gambling, and "frivolous amusement" typified the fare. Since religion and politics were taboo subjects, the system compelled clerical speakers to move toward practical moral themes and away from spiritual topics.[63]

Luminaries like Beecher and Unitarian-Universalist divines relished the freedom of the lecture podium as opposed to the strictures of the pulpit. Orthodox ministers overhauled earlier sympathies and rebuked what they now saw as a developing democratic cultural alternative to spiritual community and religious discourse. The lecture itself seemed less a "practical" supplement to the Christian message than a secular substitute for the sermon. Emerson endorsed the challenge: "Lyceums— so that people will let you say what you think—are as good a pulpit as any other. [They] make other pulpits tame and ineffectual."[64] It was not that Protestants worried about a wholesale public embrace of Emerson's version of German transcendentalism. Reviewers often complained that Emerson rendered his "transcendental metaphysic" incomprehensible anyway. Rather they feared the visual demonstration of how the lecture system, a cheap press, and a voracious popular appetite for information provided the new infidelity with a democratic social infrastructure easily allied to an anti-orthodox agenda.

As early as 1833, the Congregationalist *Spirit of the Pilgrims* recounted how a free society empowered men like Scottish socialist Robert Owen. The article related that in 1824 and 1825, experimental communities based on Owen's principles had been established at Jackson River, New York, Nashoba, Tennessee, and New Harmony, Indiana. In 1828 the socialist *Free Enquirer* began publishing in New York, and during the next four years Owen's view influenced more than twenty different periodicals. "Infidel clubs" had formed in many cities, while Owen's New York Hall of Science hosted a deist Sunday School, sponsored regular lectures by the utopian socialist and labor leader Frances Wright, and distributed radical antichristian literature. The writer exhorted Christian readers to counter Owen's example with a propaganda campaign that could incite believers "to imitation in a better cause."[65]

Owen's fire targeted not simply insensitive authoritarian church structures but also the idea of religion itself. He called it "childish folly," the source of all the world's evils, the last great obstacle to human progress. Alexander Campbell debated Owen publicly for eight days in Cincinnati, confessing doubts that a "wavering, doubting and unsettled public" could resist the "flood which the dragon [had] poured out of his mouth." Clergymen in the 1830s hoped that Owen was a passing flicker of extremism. When Owen and Fanny Wright left the city and sold the Hall of Science to satisfy creditors, the Presbyterian *New York Evangelist* expressed hope that their failure demonstrated the impotence of reform efforts grounded in open contempt for religion.[66]

Owen's heresies, however, seemed only the tip of the iceberg to ministers by mid-century. Democratic culture unveiled seemed to affirm a limitless capacity to enfranchise new ideas. Thomas Moore confessed in 1850 that "lectures, reviews, and newspapers" now touted in "popularised forms to every class of minds" a new order of philanthropy "more pure and all-embracing than that of Jesus Christ."[67] Diffused "in every conceivable form," its influence "[was] secretly reaching the Church herself." A Lutheran minister lamented the intellectual fragmentation: "We now have systems, and rules, and dogmas and doctrines, good and bad, rational and absurd, *multiplied ad infinitum* till surely the wildest fanatic can be accommodated."[68] Congregationalist Noah Porter predicted that the "new infidelity" would "penetrate every hamlet." An "agreeable" countenance of "honest aims and forcible statements" masked its "vague and indistinct" nature and eased its entry into newspapers, lyceum lectures, and popular journals.[69]

Concerns about democratic public discourse as an outlet for heterodoxy could incite whole groups to seek shelter in a traditional message. An 1851 circular letter issued to churches by leaders of the Ontario Baptist Association in upstate New York, for example, admonished area ministers to "*preach* only the *truth*, the *word*, [and] the *Gospel*," and warned believers "to *hear* only the *truth*, the *word*, and the *Gospel*." To attend lectures "for *investigation*," to hear "*both sides*," or to satisfy the "curiosity" of a "*restless mind*," lent credibility to "*false teachers*," and indulged "the views of the newly illuminated lecturer." The real threat, the writer argued, was that the explosion of speculative popular discourse contradicted the biblical injunction to "pre-occupy the mind with truth." It afforded lecturers opportunity to subtly undermine fundamental doctrines under the "guise of friendship" and the "pretext of exploding the dogmas of superstition." "*Hear*," the writer commanded, "but hear *God's ministers only*."[70]

More than a nimble maneuver to defend clerical authority, the jeremiad sought to parry a liberal culture ill-suited to the demands of the Ontario Baptists for spiritual coherence.

The incipient women's movement provided a key arena of conflict in the Protestant quarrel, one that offers an excellent window into the complex but profoundly religious character of dissent. By the 1830s, women were aggressively pursuing leadership opportunities amid a spate of reform movements. This struggle to expand the "women's sphere" gained immeasurably from the new openness of the speaker's platform. Female reformers such as Sarah and Angelina Grimké, for example, boldly donned the mantle of abolitionism and assumed the role of public lecturers. These offspring of Southern orthodoxy found greater personal freedom among the Society of Friends in Pennsylvania and gradually embraced women's rights as a logical extension of Quaker liberty and the antislavery movement. The pair became fast friends of abolitionist William Lloyd Garrison, a radical spirit who also gave sympathetic vent to the plight of women. Angelina married antislavery advocate Theodore Dwight Weld in 1838, one year after publishing her controversial pamphlet "Appeal to the Christian Women of the South."

Despite a rising antislavery tide and the support of many male abolitionists, the sisters' open challenge to traditional strictures against women "preachers" invited clerical wrath. In an 1838 "Pastoral Letter," Congregationalist ministers issued a collective blast against women lecturing to "promiscuous assemblies" and sparked an acerbic counterattack from the Grimkés. Congregationalist minister and successful antislavery lecturer Amos Phelps gingerly suggested to his friends that they avoid controversy and confine their public speaking to women's groups. The pair shot back a reply urging Phelps to *"examine the subject"* on his own and not under the unjust duress of the "Pastoral Letter."[71] In a letter to John Greenleaf Whittier, Angelina offered an explicit sounding of clerical maneuvers: "The ministers seemed panic struck at once and commenced a most violent attack upon us. I do not say *absurd* for in truth if it can be fairly established that women *can lecture*, then why may they not preach and if *they* can preach, then woe! woe be unto that Clerical Domination which now rules the world under the various names of Gen'l Assemblies, Congregational Associations, etc."[72]

In exposing this social conflict, the sisters recognized one component of their struggle—but only one. Their just cause and ministers' countermoves were symptomatic of religious concerns beyond the issues of slavery or male dominance. The Grimkés insisted that recalcitrant clergymen isolated women and thwarted the "wholeness" of the Christian mission. Their orthodox opponents cited female lecturing as one more example of how democratic discourse could confound social and spiritual quests. This larger religious issue shadowed Protestant efforts to sustain traditional gender roles and gained powerful expression in the dissent of Catharine Beecher. Beecher's role as the leading antebellum advocate of women in the teaching profession is well known. After establishing female seminaries in Hartford, Connecticut, and Cincinnati, Ohio, Beecher championed common schools through her Ladies Society for Promoting Education in the West. Her evangelical counterpoise to more politically centered rationales for women's rights and gender equality sparked conflict with more radical spirits like the Grimkés. Beecher shared in father Lyman's Western labors and reflected his confidence in the power of religion to improve the social order. She was, however, no mere aide-de-camp. Her personal independence and aggressive social vision dovetailed with sharp criticism of the culture and a concomitant demand that women become the creative epicenter for revitalizing evangelical strategies in the new order. Her forceful challenge to clerical power addressed the cultural oppression of her own sex. At the same time it reinforced a broader spiritual vision and revealed religious anxieties that transcended gender categories.[73]

The independent Beecher delighted in sparring with her more political compatriots, but not out of deference to the clerical establishment. Public bouts with reformers like the Grimkés (her 1837 essay "Thoughts on Slavery and Abolition" rejected their strategy) and her advocacy of public education as the divinely sanctioned cordon of female leadership testify to an independence of thought that invited confrontation. Her aggressive spirit was animated by a creative approach to orthodoxy. Willing to defend male dominance of the pulpit, she nevertheless pronounced women the foundation of childhood religious training and the key to preserving a receptive audience for the gospel. Ministers who refused to acknowledge this peculiar and superior role of woman, she believed, only empowered democratic culture to steal the attentions of the people and thereby consume the eternal vitals of the old faith. "Spiritual training," Beecher reasoned, was the preeminent practical expression of spiritual power and the surest guide to the "new birth." Woman could "go to her minister for aid," but, at bottom, *"she must decide for herself"* how to lead new generations to the *"life of the soul,* and for ETERNITY!"[74]

Here was the central dynamic that defined Beecher's personal crusade. A common religious wellspring aligned her purposes with those of the clergy. She rejected the incipient women's rights movement because she believed that its secular underpinnings weakened the foundations of faith, especially among ordinary folks. Ironically, Beecher shared with her more radical counterparts the conviction that the new liberal order catapulted women into a position of unprecedented power and importance. Her disagreement with them centered on whether women should be the leading bulwarks of the faith against the democratic tide or champions of a rights movement that tapped proliferating secular choices as the means of redeeming female liberty.

Cultural change strained Beecher's millennial hopes by mid-century. In 1851, she compared earlier anticipations of a "gradual gaining of light upon darkness" to the more immediate possibility of a plunge into the abyss of spiritual darkness. "My present prevailing apprehension is, that *this last* is the destiny before us," she lamented in *The True Remedy for the Wrongs of Woman*. "And my hope of escape rests mainly on the influence and agency of American women." Men had been diverted from faith by politics and the capitalist colossus. As the "boundaries between the church and the world [faded] away," benevolent organizations claimed power and legitimacy once acknowledged as the "peculiar" preserve of religion. Against the powers of sin and worldliness, Beecher called for preemptive strikes beginning in earliest childhood. Women were now the great "preventive" agency that could inoculate the "common people" against the lure of multiplying choices beyond faith.[75]

Beecher placed little hope in revivalism or reinvigorated clerical piety. The times demanded sustained contact with eternal biblical truth made sensible to ordinary people. The "practical truths" of the Bible, by contrast, had become so secularized and widely distributed beyond the community of true believers that acts of morality and benevolence no longer served as sure markers of eternal truth. The "press and public lectures" had replaced the pulpit in a new marketplace of morals. Beecher pronounced traditional Calvinist theology moribund because its offensive determinism and intricate morphology led modern seekers away from the "awful views of the *eternal loss of the soul*." In simpler times, she explained, Bible truths may have been conveniently ensconced in unchallenged theological tradition, authority, and reverence,but liberty had destroyed those bonds and safeguards and rendered the rigid theological constructs of the past insensible to modern seekers. Scriptural vitals were best preserved by distance from ossified methodologies.[76]

Beecher's salvific strategy linking sin and its consequences to the "wrongly educated mind," aggravated by childhood "spiritual neglect," no doubt panicked Old Schoolers. But marking her creative cultural strategies as a free-fall toward secularism obscures the otherworldly foundation of her faith. Human instrumentality notwithstanding, she announced in 1857, all means of advancing human redemption apart from the "supernatural aid of the Holy Spirit" were "hopeless." Her quarrel was not with the "fact" of humanity's depraved behavior but with an untenable "philosophy" of the fact, she exclaimed. Yet she held to a thoroughly "Calvinistic" sense of divine judgment, supernatural agency, and deference to the spiritual "great commonwealth." The religious yield she anticipated from rejecting Augustine's theory of original depravity was not expanded "liberty" from biblical restraints but precisely the opposite. Showing sin to originate in human choice would "remove insurmountable difficulties from just and generous minds in accepting the Bible as Divine authority." In short, Beecher's "progress beyond Calvinism" anticipated new possibilities amid cultural transformation but ultimately looked to a spiritual vision of individual destiny that transcended the moral renovation of the commonwealth. Finally, the restorative potential of the gospel and, indeed, the efficacy of the pulpit itself, she informed her clerical allies, were contingent on the divinely inspired power of women.[77]

The social shocks of European revolution in 1848 gave Beecher and other mainline Protestants another unsettling venue on the proliferation of redemptive schemes. Following the demise of the Frankfurt Assembly, thousands of politically disillusioned, middle-class German liberals carried their hopes for social and political salvation to American shores. Educated, articulate, and steeped in German rationalism and romantic nationalism, the "Forty-eighters" found in American liberty new opportunity to combine antireligious sentiment with an unbending political faith in democracy, equality, and social justice. They established newspapers and political clubs throughout the country, especially in the West, where Chicago and Milwaukee became hubs of German political clout. Cultural groups, or Turnvereins, challenged organized religion with lectures, social gatherings, and Sunday schools based on humanitarianism.[78]

Protestant leaders, particularly German evangelicals, warned of the power that American liberty gave to this assertive and openly skeptical new group that embodied the new infidelity (Feuerbach was the acknowledged "patron saint" of many of these immigrants). Pennsylvania cleric John Ulrich complained that American social realities annihilated the distance between European intellectual theory and the popular American mind. He contended that a free press, paid agents, and publishing houses in New York, Philadelphia, Cincinnati, and St. Louis enabled "the religion of Strauss, Feuerbach, Hegel, Owen, [and] Carlyle . . . to [diffuse] its poison among all classes of society."[79] Illinois Lutheran divine Samuel Harkey told the 1859 Convention of the General Synod that "the Revolution of 1848 drove tens of thousands of rationalists to this country." This "multitude of infidels" have tried to "play the politician" and "become publishers of newspapers." They were the " 'lost sheep . . . of our own household [that] must be gathered into the fold."[80] The *Lutheran Observer* lamented that because religion carried no official political advantages in the United States, American liberty ironically reinforced German political rationalists in their unbelief.[81]

But gathered in the Forty-eighters would not be. Determined to expand their intellectual and political leadership beyond the German community, many of them capitalized on the political disintegration of the 1850s and entered mainstream politics. Carl Schurz's political success is well known. Chicago, where one of five citizens was German-born by 1860, became the heart of German political influence in the Midwest. Wilhelm Weitling and Joseph Weydemeyer cooperated in the early American labor movement and together edited the socialist *Die Republic der Arbeiter*.[82] Forty-eighters seized abolitionism as the consummate expression of their hatred of political tyranny and became one of the most radical antislavery contingents of the fledgling Republican party. Merging the American political lexicon with their own ethical rationalism, they voiced an unexcelled patriotic enthusiasm for American progress. An 1852 assemblage in Wheeling, Virginia, called on the United States to become the "new Rome." Steady expansion of the United States would affirm that "the Universal Empire of the Future belongs to them."[83]

Most ministers sanctioned patriotism in its proper place, but the German experience demonstrated that a politically centered ethical rationalism could draw fire from its anti-orthodox roots by claiming the mantle of American liberty as its own. The new social context of freedom, in other words, had become as troubling as heterodox ideas themselves. As one Methodist writer grumbled in his assessment of the intellectual contingent driving the revolutions of 1848, popular liberty inevitably made the ideals of such groups a "nucleus of attraction, a center of influence, which must either modify the elements around [them], or be modified by them in return."[84]

The intellectual and material components of the new unbelief compelled many clergymen to powerfully reassert spiritual values, since religion seemed to be specifically threatened. To be sure, clergymen announced skepticism's threat to the Republic as well. But the ease with which groups like the Forty-eighters assimilated unbelief and American political values convinced many divines that the new infidelity threatened the Protestant faith more than it did the nation. Almost any set of ideas couched in the language of liberty and democracy could claim sanctity, ministers believed, and opposition became ever more difficult. An "avowed and proselytizing infidelity" was abroad in the land, an Episcopal writer asserted. But ubiquitous claims of "divinity" now drove "error to its finest disguises, to the extremes of subtlety, and the nicest and closest imitations of the truth."[85] It is necessary, then, to examine this transatlantic ideological ferment, the ideas themselves that clergymen found so "new" and so troubling.

Redemption through Unbelief

Georg Hegel's dialectic of progress and amorphous spiritualism inspired the Continental speculation of the 1840s. Also driving the new idealism, materialism, and positivism was an anticlerical, political liberalism that declared church and state no longer competent to produce needed social and political change. German and French freethinkers chiseled new theories of human progress from a hardened materialist and rationalist stock that gave no visage to orthodox faith. Ideological diversity abounded, but orthodox guardians summed up substantive commonalities that they believed provided the foundations of a new unbelief: The new theorists shared a broad positivism hostile to spiritual truth. They reveled in a humanitarian faith that confined redemption to an earthly plane. They called for a mature skepticism that simply acknowledged the irrelevance of spiritual religion and pressed ahead with new progressive agendas. In return, ministers warned, these vanguards of popular progress promised a new world of benevolence, community, and charity, rising from the ashes of orthodoxy.

This heady brew of Continental thought had already inspired men like Thomas Carlyle and Emerson, but ministers were quick to cite this influence as symptomatic of a broader, more threatening infection. The general population was more likely to absorb new theoretical systems eclectically, even unknowingly, especially in light of the intellectual diversity fostered by American liberty. A Presbyterian editor put the new rationalism in its popular social context in 1851. Infidelity, he argued, spread not as an "avowed system" but as a *"fragmentary* being" whose errors "float loosely and at random through the public mind." Such heresies wielded "tremendous power though not apparent to the sight." It was a *"guerilla* form of warfare."[86] New York Lutheran divine Henry Schmidt prefaced a series of articles on European idealism with the warning that only a "semblance of piety" radiated from its constructive, positive facade: "In its former manifestations . . . it appears mainly [as] gross and trenchant scepticism, whose occupation is negation and destruction, with little or no care to give us aught in return. . . . In the place of this process we now meet with an attempt to construct a system of purely ethical spiritualism . . . the genuine offspring of the intellectual audacity and the practically self-sufficient spirit of the present age."[87] In uniting the "practical" and "theoretical" roots of the new unbelief, Schmidt expressed the transatlantic scope of Protestant worries.

The content and publication history of Feuerbach's *Essence of Christianity* put transatlantic substance behind clerical anxieties and show why ministers saw more than anticlericalism or parochial German resentment of Prussian hegemony in the new intellectual ferment. Feuerbach was a student of Hegel who, in Karl Barth's words, "scented the theological residue in the [master's] teaching—and stripped it off."[88] Like antebellum critics of German rationalists, Barth notes that Feuerbach offered no Voltairean indictment of religion as merely absurd. Rather, he viewed it as an intermediate step in human self-realization, which must inevitably transform theology into anthropology. His work influenced such contemporaries as Bruno Bauer, Richard Wagner, Karl Marx, and Friedrich Engels. At the conclusion of an 1848 lecture series in Heidelberg, however, Feuerbach made clear his hopes of triggering popular intellectual revolution rather than merely patronizing the speculations of academic elites.[89] This strategy symbolized for his American adversaries an activist, popular, and anti-Christian agenda common to divergent strands of the new infidelity. Feuerbach acknowledged no place for a socially responsible faith and charged that religious criticism now had to combine with positive, ideological construction. Unprecedented popular material and social progress would be the inevitable reward for man's trek beyond faith. Progress away from religion, he argued, was the essential road to personal freedom. Redemption from tyranny and social injustice depended on changing "the friends of God into friends of man, believers into thinkers, worshippers into workers, candidates for the other world into students of this world." Rather than "footmen of a celestial and terrestrial monarchy," Feuerbach demanded "free self-reliant citizens of earth."[90]

Feuerbach shared with Protestant critics of the new infidelity, then, a conviction that an intellectual watershed was at hand. Both agreed that nineteenth-century material, technological, and intellectual progress offered men novel opportunities for change. In the anticipations of Feuerbach and his compatriots, however, Protestants scrutinized an argument against faith that seemed at mid-century far more disarming and threatening than simple debunking of Scriptural truth. Feuerbach confidently ridiculed the "undecided, pusillanimous" faith of modern believers. He defined public criticism of his own work as little more than "simulated religious indignation." Though admitting his "negative, destructive" purposes in attacking Christian supernaturalism, he put greater emphasis on the "positive" need to relocate the "predicates of the divine" within their true human framework. This was a critical moment, "the culminating point of religion, i.e., the point at which the religious slides into the irreligious," he announced. His humanistic faith, he asserted, was decidedly populist, addressed not only to intellectuals but also to "universal man." His greatest hope matched the Protestant clergy's greatest fear—that "[my] fundamental ideas . . . will one day become the common property of mankind."[91]

Feuerbach's work reached a transatlantic, English-speaking audience directly through the efforts of once-orthodox British novelist and translator George Eliot (Marian Evans) and indirectly as the inspiration of German rationalists in America. Eliot's notoriety among Protestants stemmed from her English translation of David Strauss's *Life of Jesus*, which she brought to press in 1846. The work earned her the friendship of Carlyle, and Emerson paid her an extended visit in Liverpool during his English sojourn in 1848. A devotee of English radicalism and a writer for the *Westminster Review*, she shared Feuerbach's sympathy for an ethical, humanitarian morality. Congregationalist reviewer Charles Tiffany likened Evans's "anti-Christian" sentiments to those of Harriet Martineau and lamented that such "eminent ability" and "celebrity" had lent credibility to the essay. Indeed, the Feuerbach translation was the only major effort to which Eliot affixed her given name. That she preserved the work's unequivocal force was the only "silver lining" in its publication, Tiffany argued, since German rationalists in America too often "[entrenched] themselves from attack behind arguments and a subtle dialectic."[92]

Naturally, such arguments sent mainline defenders into a frenzy. Suddenly they faced challengers whose central argument against religion moved beyond debate over the validity of Christian doctrine and focused instead on the practicality and attainability of a better world outside the faith. From this view, religion had to be abandoned not because it had failed to sustain its own principles but because spiritual faith dehumanized people and interdicted true progress by needlessly siphoning human energy into the nonproductive pursuit of a nonexistent deity. The popular thrust, moral purpose, and sheer intellectual muscle behind the new rationalism drove the clergy's counterattack to new heights. Noted Reformed leader John Nevin told graduates of Franklin and Marshall College that by sanctifying purely "secular ends" and denying man's "supernatural and eternal" destiny, the new infidelity effectively "caricatured" gospel truth. The new age, Nevin argued, subtly sanctified its rational morality and "humanitarian philanthropy" as a purer faith beyond religion in order to "pass itself off as an angel of light." He warned that as believers ignored this confusion of sacred and secular purposes, their silence became "itself a species of infidelity," and their lives a *"living personal lie."* [93] The world was replacing religion with its own "human" schemes and associations, Maine Episcopal divine George Burgess told fellow ministers in 1850. With society pushing beyond mere "liberality of sentiment," though not yet into an "absolute unbelief," he cautioned, it had become harder than ever to detect infidelity. As spiritual foundations disintegrated, the only sure social assumption was that "every man stands for himself and we can presume nothing." [94]

Two pieces published in the Baptist *Christian Review* illustrate rising Protestant concern in the 1840s. In 1842, the journal's essay "Christian Doctrine the Sole Basis of Christian Morality" gently refuted claims that "nothing of the gospel is really indispensable except a life conformed to its moral code." The writer identified "moral elevation" and the "evangelical scheme" as inseparably tied to a single process of "repentance, confession, and self-abhorrence." To elevate human virtue— "mere change of opinion"—or an "outward reformation of life" above dependence on Christ and the "Supreme God" was effectively to "deny the faith once delivered to the saints." Practical morality apart from faith, he concluded, simply became a substitute for it. [95]

By 1849, the *Review*'s editors detected the spiritually inert, humanitarian edge of the new rationalism cutting a more threatening popular path. They delineated a new charge for the Baptists' most important theological journal. Toughening their 1842 language, they warned pastors that a new infidelity, "assuming the guise of benevolence and philanthropy," now constituted "one of the greatest obstacles" to the progress of Christianity. Ministers unable to explain their congregation's collective "hardness of heart," they cautioned, need only look to the "covert scepticism sown in their minds in connection with reforms of the day, that has undermined their faith." Looking backward, they called for reasserting the faith of the Baptist church fathers, emphasizing the denomination's historic evangelical stance, and affirming the spiritual priorities of faith.[96]

Noted Congregationalist divine Samuel Harris acknowledged the challenge of a new infidelity in a religious jeremiad delivered at Andover Seminary in 1855. Eight years earlier, Harris had argued that an uncontrolled democratic spirit might redefine the forces of progress outside the context of faith.[97] In the earlier piece, however, Harris directed his strongest fire at the liberal individualistic ethos and political apotheosis of "the people" as the most pressing culprit. In his Andover sermon, which broached wider terrain through publication in the orthodox journal *Bibliotheca Sacra*, Harris thundered that now "no enemy threatens the churches so deadly in its nature, or so formidable in its . . . resources, as infidelity." Whatever man's demonstrated natural desire and ability to improve his own lot, he railed, "all virtue and development, not springing from faith, are abnormal, and therefore essentially and radically wrong."[98]

Harris pointed out that infidelity had abandoned its old focus on "mere negation." It now exploited communicative resources for wide diffusion, and openly appealed to man's natural longing for peace, progress, and material well-being. Citing the increasingly popular social context of the new message, Harris warned that the taunts of the "workshops and factories, club-rooms and lecture-rooms" challenged Christianity to be a "religion of reform, and the rights of man and human progress, or it shall not be at all." He admitted the natural lure of the message. By announcing spiritual immortality as fiction, the opposition proclaimed itself the "special champion of . . . human development." By dismissing man's depravity, it elevated "human self-sufficiency and virtue." By denying the existence of future reward and punishment, it promised "to fit [humanity] for life and time."[99]

Harris refurbished ancient Augustinian defenses in claiming "faith in God the Redeemer" as the sole source of "human virtue, development, and salvation." Indeed, to sanctify any benevolent or humanitarian system of progress, he reasoned, was religious suicide, especially in light of the new challenges to faith. "Christianity must maintain its position as a system of redemption and faith, or it ceases to be essentially distinguished from infidelity itself."[100] Harris explained that the "entirely spiritual" nature of regeneration required for each individual "a spiritual act originating a new spiritual life." He could not reconcile his belief in regeneration through divine intervention with alternatives tied to impersonal social forces or confidence in the natural organic unity of mankind. Feuerbach insisted that the idea of faith was irreconcilable with true human benevolence and actually contradicted the brotherhood of mankind. Harris's solution was to put ministers on the razor's edge by demanding that infidelity be denied through the preaching of a "comprehensive" gospel that acknowledged the validity of temporal reform without degenerating into a purely "social" message. Christianity's "incidental capacities," he cautioned, did not mean that men should "preach Christ less." "In the face of infidelity . . . worldliness and indifference," he told his audience, the primary mission remained to "proclaim the gospel, grasp its central life . . . and preach it as the power of God unto salvation." Harris's fear of a new infidelity precluded a more accommodative course and drove him to defend faith's eternal verities over social progress.[101]

Within months of Harris's address, Presbyterian divine Theodore Dwight Woolsey assaulted the new shape of unbelief in a sermon to ministers of Connecticut's General Association on "the dangers of separating piety from philanthropy." Woolsey chanced a more speculative course, struggling to outline a future of humanitarian triumph over faith. Minister, Greek scholar, and for twenty-five years president of Yale College, Woolsey was no stranger to secular intellectual pursuits. Neither did he deny the validity of some of his opposition's insights. Indeed, he expressed "deep satisfaction" with the benevolent enterprises of the day, going so far as to thank secular reformers for rousing Christians to the realization that the "welfare of mankind" was an essential, although subordinate, component of Christian purpose. He admitted that the Protestant message earlier in the century had perhaps been justly criticized by outsiders for being too aloof from man's earthly concerns. There could not—indeed should not—be a retreat to feudal "monasticism" or merely "contemplative piety" of the post-Reformation era, he warned. Such self-imposed isolation would only further empower the enemies of the faith.[102] But Woolsey told ministers in 1855 that the certainty of God's ultimate triumph did not erase the risks or threats that lay immediately ahead. Ironically, he saw religion poised at the same critical juncture that so invigorated Feuerbach, though he pleaded an opposite outcome.

One of the fruits of human progress, Woolsey argued, was an unwarranted "sense of human power," a new conception of the "sources of man's improvement." Pleas for "human rights" and the "promotion of happiness" poured from the mouths of Christians and atheists alike, he contended, "while the glory of God, as a coincident but superior motive, has lost its power." [103] Woolsey avoided emphasizing distinctions among the new intellectual systems. Instead, he excoriated a common anthropocentric thrust behind new visions of human progress:

> Again, the great achievements of civilized man in this age have awakened *a lofty sense of human power*, and exalted man by the side of God. . . . The chorus of man's self-flattery is swelled by those, who, having nothing higher to worship, worship the divine in man—hero-worshippers, whose pantheistic eyes see no divine presence in the *burning bush*, that was unconsumed, but only in the *Moses* who headed the people. And the danger is, that *power*, however wielded—Titanic efforts in ever so bad a cause, shall claim idolatry.[104]

Woolsey hoped that piety, which he defined as a total personal devotion to God governing man's temporal and eternal striving, could still shape the humanitarian impulse. Still he projected for fellow ministers the evolution of a humanitarian spirit unchecked by faith. The advance of art, education, and material wealth, he began, begged only for human nature to "develop a *religion* out of itself" to complete the "humanitarian revolution." First, strictly spiritual ideas would be abandoned in favor of "humane feelings," while conversion would be valued only for "the good that it brings." Next, man's chief purpose would no longer be to serve God, but to "relieve distress, to repair injustice, to raise the degraded." Then the gospel would be valued as a purely civilizing force. Finally, man's hopes would rest not in salvation by Christ, but in "changes of government, improved prisons, emancipations of slaves, cultivation of intellect, cheap books, comfortable houses." A lust for accelerated progress would breed "self-righteousness and complacency." Finally, philanthropy would degenerate into a "naked humanitarianism," attacking Christianity "for repressing the flesh" while indulging "every propensity as leading to enjoyment." [105] For Woolsey, a newly contoured unbelief pressed the Church to confound faith's temporal and eternal priorities and thereby initiate a logical and inexorable process of spiritual disintegration.

In a regular sermon first preached in 1852 and published in 1858, New York City Presbyterian divine James Alexander reveals how ministers interwove complex intellectual and social changes in shaping their conceptions of a new infidelity. Alexander cited "modern unbelief" as the unwanted fruit of an information explosion and a swelling "gulf of Germanism" that aggravated the definitional chaos behind new ideas of progress. In the talk of "popular lecturers" about the "ideal, the spiritual, the divine," he warned, one finds the essence of infidelity's new strategy— to offer "counterfeits and caricatures of the very blessings . . . [of] true religion." The old "virus" of French unbelief depended too heavily on the interest of academics and elites and a "bloodless humanitarianism." Popular support proved superficial, Alexander argued, because it derived from political anger rather than from a "deliberate theory of religious unbelief." A half-century, however, had brought a complete transformation. "Antichristian systems" now "popularized themselves," embraced "freedom and social progress," and claimed to be the "benefactor of mankind." From pulpits and "liberal clubs" men talked of the "Spirit," the "God of History," the "union of Virtue and Beauty," while they effectively denied the revealed truth.[106]

Alexander reviewed American vulnerabilities. The nation housed not only the "books and arguments of false teachers" but also "the men themselves, the ready-made disciples, clamoring in our public assemblies, and inflaming a peaceful population." Antichristian clubs, societies, and institutes flourished through the "infusion of transatlantic people." Like Wayland, he attacked "unscriptural" principles grounding European socialism, while insinuating that sickness of another kind shadowed the American system and indirectly nurtured unbelief. If the "street-people of London" had generally given up faith, "are we not on the way?" Alexander asked. While our churches fill with "at least well-doing people," where are the "vastly greater numbers . . . who need the consolation of the gospel?" "I bring no charges," he conceded, but "I have the sickening faintness of one who beholds a great malady."[107] Alexander insisted that in the new democratic culture educated elites could not be the first line of defense against a new infidelity. He called for an unprecedented communal effort of believers "to preach the gospel and gather the Church." Hope lay not in "random assaults" on freethinking but in "childlike faith," the power of the "Holy Ghost," and simple recognition that "Divine Truth is its own defence."[108]

Whether clerical willingness to unravel a "darker side" of American progress played well among ordinary believers is difficult to establish, but one piece of evidence is at least suggestive. In 1843, the *Christian Secretary*, a prominent Baptist newspaper, emblazoned on its front page the full text of Nathaniel Hawthorne's "The Celestial Railroad."[109] Although scholars often contrast Hawthorne's critical visions with antebellum "Protestant optimism," his short story complements clerical harangues against a new infidelity. Hawthorne's modern travelers are undaunted by the trials that afflicted the pilgrims of John Bunyan's seventeenth-century tale. They surmount the "Slough of Despond" on a bridge of "French philosophy and German rationalism," sermons of "modern clergymen," and "books of morality." Though "Pope" and "Pagan" threatened Bunyan's voyagers in the Valley of the Shadow of Death, Hawthorne's rail passengers confront "a German by birth . . . called Giant Transcendentalist," a creature given to "strange phraseology" and shrouded by "fog and duskiness." His "capitalistic" Vanity Fair strikes his modern wayfarers as the "true and only heaven." They brand "piety" and "charity" as "useless anachronisms." [110]

Baptist readers apparently could not get enough of the tale. The story again filled the *Secretary*'s pages in 1848. [111] Repeated popular demands for republication had prompted the reprise, the editor explained. The *New Englander* shared Baptist enthusiasm for Hawthorne's lampoon, reprinting long passages and calling it the insightful centerpiece of the author's short-story collection *Mosses from an Old Manse*. [112] Rather than standing apart from orthodoxy, Hawthorne in this instance railed in tandem with mainstream clergymen about the humanistic pretensions behind a new infidelity.

Dismissing Protestant attacks on a "new infidelity" as mere bouts with windmills trivializes one of the most profound transformations in Protestant thinking to occur in the nineteenth century. In the religious jeremiads clergymen distinguished sacred and secular objectives because at mid-century they believed that the new social and intellectual power of transatlantic liberalism threatened to destroy those distinctions and relocate the divine within man. More than social order, political stability, or the millennium, they believed, religion itself was threatened. The new order had produced a muscular but illusory assault on religion, brimming with positivist enthusiasm for orthodoxy's impending doom. To be sure, they joined Augustine in asserting God's eventual triumph. Immediate realities, however, fed their suspicions that unprecedented intellectual and social change could make American liberty the nemesis of faith and the unpredictable arbiter of progress.

Protestant divines harped on a new infidelity not simply to spook believers or even to derail critics who questioned the divine inspiration of Scripture. What ministers feared most was that if the materialist ethos of the new economic and social order lulled the people into spiritual indifference, they would be rendered vulnerable to visions of human redemption keyed to popular material progress and unreined by the old doctrines of faith. In the midst of uncertainty, clergymen groped for understanding and confessed the blur of their own insights. "The unbelief of our day is forming, but not formed," James Alexander observed. Because the "process is incomplete," believers must search "tendencies rather than results." In the moment of uncertainty, Alexander prescribed vigilance: "As . . . the premonitions of the earthquake or volcano give inarticulate warnings before the earth is cleft and the lava boiling over, so we have a right to sit in judgment on the falsities beginning to prevail, even though we know but in part where unto they shall grow." [113]

Spiritual rather than civic discourse was the most important rhetorical vehicle by which ministers separated sacred and secular purposes and outlined the exclusive claims of the Protestant world. Indeed, the religious jeremiads were energized by the assumption that apart from the culture existed a uniquely empowered "oral community of the Word." This community thrived on premises at odds with a rising democratic culture. Its rhetorical anchor was the regular Sunday sermon, the most voluminous vehicle of Protestant communication. In its almost unilateral focus on the spiritual destiny of man, this vital center of day-to-day religious exchange powerfully reinforced jeremiadic countermands to the progressive, material alternatives of emergent liberal culture. Regular preaching also reveals the decidedly spiritual core of Protestant exceptionalism.

5

A Community of the Word

"Human *eloquence* and *learning* have often been employed in defending the *outworks* of Christianity," Lutheran divine Benjamin Kurtz wrote in 1850, "but *simplicity* and *truth* alone have preserved the *citadel*." Citing the Apostle Paul's example, Kurtz demanded pulpit preaching that put "frankness and simplicity" above "talents and rich imagery." Ministers strayed from the "unadorned but divine power" of evangelical preaching whenever they stopped short of "[telling] the people . . . that they are fallen, hell-deserving and perishing sinners" in need of Christ's "free and glorious salvation."[1]

The "citadel" of the simple "preached gospel," as Kurtz called it, was the Scripture, the regular sermon, and the spirit-fired, collective voice of believers. Vigorous clerical defense of this inner triad of faith at mid-century fit logically with religious jeremiads warning of the encroachment of liberal culture on the faith. Regular preaching served as a complementary offensive strategy that both responded to ministers' own jeremiadic alarms and tapped the popular access of the pulpit. In sum, the foundational level of spiritual discourse furiously reasserted the supremacy of both the "word" and the "Word." Protestant defenders commonly called upon the "preached gospel," not only to support evangelical outreach but also to anchor a spiritually separated community of believers.

The cultural commitments that sustained civic discourse strained against revitalized efforts to sharpen Protestant spiritual boundaries and assured a clerical search for internal compromise. Francis Wayland's self-flagellation and peer critique, for example, plumbed the multiple tensions that shaped a critical defense of the regular pulpit. This dimension of Protestant thought deserves closer attention. Recent analyses too often juxtapose the historian's scrutiny of accommodative preaching and the apparent critical silence of the ministers themselves. In fact, the unique capacity of the religious jeremiad to course the sermonic landscape unburdened by civic distractions yielded a rich interaction with cultural change and a thorough defense of regular preaching as provider of both spiritual outreach and the rhetorical boundaries of a "community of the Word." A jeremiadic foray into "preaching for the age" reached particular prominence in the early 1850s. The timing and thematic emphasis of these pieces enabled them to both reinforce and extend Protestant sermonic engagements with the culture. A historic defense of regular spiritual discourse assumed new relevance as worried ministers charted a constellation of cultural alternatives that had emerged by mid-century—acquisitive materialism, expansionism, cultural diversity, a communications revolution, and the rise of "new infidelity." Finally, these jeremiadic fortifications will be compared with the themes that *did* shape the most basic levels of mainstream Protestant communication.

Clerical sentries, then, seized upon a strategy that made both critical and evangelistical outreach to the larger culture serve a concomitant need for internal order and spiritual security. Yet the rhetorical insularity of this spiritually separated community of the Word provided its essential legitimacy among believers. A formidable language barrier distinguished its celestial citizens from ordinary mortals. Only the regenerate could decipher a spiritual discourse encoded by the Spirit and offering believers a unifying alternative to the fractious confrontations of liberal culture. North Carolina Presbyterian James Walker explained the barriers that preserved the "supremacy" of this distinctive community. Social "ties of gratitude and affection" must not bridge the great chasm that kept the believers' community "unspotted," he contended. As the "instrumental" means of the gospel, the Christian community must transcend ties with their "kindred in the flesh" and accept the burden of being a "peculiar people."[2] The purpose was to protect the sacred flow of unchallenged Scriptural truths from the atomistic forces of liberalism, lest the communicative heart of traditional faith crumble.

Clergymen viewed this inner world of communication as a sanctuary even from their own civic and speculative forays. It was a kind of spiritual haven where the rules of democratic culture and intellectual freedom did not apply. "Unquestioned truth" eclipsed "free inquiry." The language of sin, salvation, judgment, and "separation from the world" quelled that of nationalism, republicanism, and reform. The boundary of this exclusive community did not separate sanctified America from the world. Nor, it must be emphasized, did it suggest that believers should physically disengage from the culture. Indeed, the capacity to define a uniquely "superior" spiritual mode of discourse provided a critical avenue of evangelical engagement with both determined foes and honest seekers. Consequently, this communicative strategy worked on multiple levels: to expand the fold, to rebuke cultural complexity and diversity at odds with spiritual integrity and "simplicity," and to achieve communal identity that salved the strains of accommodation.[3]

In other words, delineation of a spiritually separated, communicative framework enabled ministers to claim an alternative agenda designed at once to rob liberal culture of potential recruits (make the evangelical commission restore the culture's amenability to orthodox faith) and to sustain critical distinctions between Christian and cultural striving. Reciting the culture's transgressions could then be matched with positive claims of universal truth and exclusive spiritual rewards. Thousands of regular sermons and intramural circulars, together with millions of pages of popular tracts, typically affirmed the subordinate status of temporal reforms and flayed "external morality." Material themes surrendered place to a withering fire of salvation messages, final judgment scenarios, and calls for believer unity unhinged from republican distinctions.

Listen to Congregationalist divine John Humphrey as he marked the gulf he perceived between the oral community of the Word and the larger culture. The unregenerate could never comprehend the "communion of saints," he charged. Only within this spiritually marked body were believers free to "delight in the same themes," to "discourse happily on the wonders of grace." The Christian could never sustain his pilgrimage alone, Humphrey contended. The earth remained "to saints as Babylon." In the ordinary pursuits of life the unregenerate could associate with believers as "amiable, cheerful, and intelligent men," but they could never "relish their society, or love them in their spiritual character."[4]

A regular sermon by African American luminary William Douglass reinforced Humphrey's boundaries and demonstrated important continuities between black and white preaching in the North. The pastor of St. Thomas African Methodist Episcopal Church in Philadelphia called up New Testament admonitions against "corrupt communication" and chastised believers for failing to consolidate their unity around spiritual discourse. He emphasized that even the absence of "corrupt" communication could not make up for an absence of "edifying" conversation shaping the "social intercourse" of believers. To allow "temporal subjects" to

replace "spiritual and eternal" themes exposed the faithful to the entice-
ments of the larger culture, inviting the "darkness of spiritual death."[5]

The spiritual discourse that supported this exclusive sphere of Christian community paradoxically emphasized the individual's solitary accountability before God and the temporal limitations of collective virtue.
Congregationalist minister Austin Phelps emphasized preaching as the
critical means of defining each individual's "probationary seclusion," his
"individual pilgrimage" to heaven or hell, and the impotence of organic
relations or cultural structures to facilitate his personal quest. But this
emphasis on an "isolated" destiny before God created a concomitant
need among believers for a regular flow of discourse promoting spiritual bonds that foreshadowed eternal community.[6] As a communicative
framework that assumed Christianity's superiority over culture, it limited
Protestant expectations for social reform and sanctioned religious exclusivity beyond the nationalistic or republican varieties. Ministers struggled
to preserve an exclusive "language of the regenerate." Against new cultural links between progress and the free exchange of ideas, the spiritual
discourse of the regular pulpit offered a refuge for the flow of spiritual constants. Calls for traditional faith bore the marks of historic pulpit fare, but the religious jeremiads make clear that immediate cultural
transformations provided critical sustenance.

The "Preaching for the Age"

In the face of an information explosion, Protestant critics mounted a
fierce defense of regular preaching as the anchor of spiritual community.
The political platform and lecture podium shifted the power of the spoken word away from the pulpit, but they also attested to its still-regnant
influence. As one clergyman noted, reading was merely "preparative" to
the "indispensable human voice" in sacred or secular causes.[7] Ministers
had a professional interest in such defenses, but worries about personal
place in the new order were shadowed by more fundamental probes of
religion's fate. Ministers' eroding stature as social spokesmen symbolized
a widening chasm between American society and the believer community itself. It also hardened clerical defenses of regular preaching and
believer interaction as securities against the chaos of liberal discourse.

Boston's *Puritan Recorder* and the *Western Recorder*, in Louisville, Kentucky, devoted space to announce prominently the breadth of this novel
challenge. The two newspapers lauded and summarized the "plain talk

about preaching" offered by Maine Congregationalist George Shepard. The writer (Louisville reprinted the original Boston piece) praised Shepard for explaining that the preacher and the Word now shared a "contested field" with "multitudes of gaping disciples." Speaking was now "a democracy," assailing the popular mind with an endless array of "counter voices." The attractive packaging of these multiplying "schemes and systems" pressed ministers toward a "sickly sentimentalism" unchastened by the "terrors of the Lord." Shepard insisted that human sinfulness remained the touchstone of evangelism and demanded that the unholy heralds of diversity return to the singular truths of the Bible. Here again is the irony that helped fire the Protestant quarrel. The "free inquiry" that ministers counted on to expose "error" and yield gospel unity was instead producing a faith-threatening diversity.[8]

The new secular communicators had completely restructured the responsibilities of speakers and hearers. Democratic discourse assumed the speaker's responsibility to amuse and titillate while it invited audiences to debate and disagree. Listeners enjoyed the creative task of consuming and refashioning as they pleased the raw materials hurled from the podium. Social diversity and the itinerant nature of the lecture and political circuits trivialized the relationship between speaker and audience. Their interaction rested on momentary realities, specialized concerns, or simply the sheer mesmerizing power of the speaker. Truth in this milieu became an evolutionary, rootless concept rather than a historic constant. Lecturers or politicians bent on moving "the people," ministers believed, had every motivation to identify virtue and truth with immediate public sentiment. To the extent that they succeeded in expropriating the preacher's authority and expanding popular choice, this new throng of diversity threatened the faith. Ministers hoped to snatch the pulpit from this cauldron of oratorical flux and shore up the sacred bridge between biblical truth and a spiritually needy flock. The task was not to be confused with "public speaking" or even with their own civic jeremiads. The flow of "truth" from Scripture to minister to congregation produced a supernatural bond among believers and gave the regular sermon ascendance in the hierarchy of Protestant communication. Democratic discourse threatened to destroy the sermon's unique purpose and with it the oral anchor that truly gave reality to the community of the Word.

Defending the preeminent place of the regular sermon kindled hot debate among ministers over what preaching style and substance best preserved the "simple truths" of the gospel. Baptist and Methodist devotion to extemporaneous, "Spirit-led" sermons, for example, clashed with Congregationalist and Presbyterian fondness for more carefully constructed displays of "pulpit eloquence." The written sermon, its defenders argued, preserved the natural symmetry of the gospel and minimized the risk of stumbling into repetitious, even heretical, babble. Detractors claimed dependence on the Spirit and often culled the Psalmist's exhortation "open thy mouth wide and I will fill it."[9] The conflict recalled the furor that had sent Anne Hutchinson packing from Massachusetts in an earlier day. Protestants for centuries had scanned the homiletic terrain, variously condemning antinomian ranting one minute and cold, lifeless rationalism the next. Nevertheless, spiritual discourse regularly elevated the gospel message and the human medium as a holy matrix beyond rational understanding. Amid the technological advance, reformist zeal, and rising political tensions of the 1850s, worried ministers held fast to the role of the regular sermon in sustaining a community of faith, as well as beckoning repentant seekers. Here, social and political turbulence could be exchanged for mutual affirmation of truths and spiritual unity on a plane of discourse insulated from cultural upheaval.

So twisted and confused had the rules of democratic communication become that ministers exhorted each other to separate their own speculative discourse from the peculiar sanctity and purpose of regular preaching. Pennsylvania Lutheran divine Charles Schaeffer defined the sermon as a *"transaction between the speaker and his hearers, superintended by the Holy Spirit."* The "stream of divine love," had to flow "copiously," he urged. The minister gripped his hearers with the "values and perils of the soul" and engaged them "to perform the work assigned to each." The sermon was not so much "discourse" as *"action,"* he contended.[10] Maine Congregationalist Edward Gilman insisted that *"the preaching of the gospel"* superseded "all other modes of Christian effort." "There must be a living preacher; he must speak with direct application . . . to his fellow men; and he must announce salvation through Christ, with a personal experience of its reality and its value."[11]

Neither Schaeffer nor Gilman prescribed social isolation, of course, and as was the case so often, clerical sensitivity to their own vulnerabilities provided the impetus to restore a balance that clearly subordinated material concerns. Congregationalist minister Austin Phelps lamented the cultural pressure on ministers to conflate civic and spiritual discourse as "an ordeal . . . which is one of the most singular that have ever tested the nerve of the Christian ministry." He warned ministers against a cultural humbling that fatally inverted priorities. The "mere correction of social wrongs" must not obtain a *"pervasive presence"* in the pulpit, he lectured.

The salvific mission lay "deeper than such themes." The "relation of Christian ethics to organic society" remained forever "collateral and not central." Instead of making regular mention of material concerns, the preacher "must generally forget them." Phelps carefully insulated spiritual discourse from subordinate digressions. "Essays, disquisitions, disputations, creeds there may be; but they are not preaching. . . . Preaching is Christian discourse, the roots of which run thriftily into a groundwork of distinctive doctrines." [12]

The referent phrase that acknowledged the supremacy of regular preaching was "gospel simplicity." Ministers might disagree as to what that simplicity entailed, but the term invariably indicted the intrusion of democratic complexity and intellectual prowess into the basic communication of the gospel. The "sincere milk of the Word," necessarily contradicted the "speculations and controversies . . . display and factions" of the age, Congregationalist Gordon Hall maintained. [13] "Out-of-the-way discourses," "learned disquisitions," and "ingenious speculations" crippled the "simple consolations" demanded by ordinary seekers. Hall blasted the materialism that contradicted this simplicity. "Gorgeous churches" and "genteel worshippers" stifled communication with the poor and signaled church complicity in sanctifying compromise "between God and Mammon." Hall struggled to marshal the expanding popular freedom to his cause. There must be more individuality, self-assertion, true liberty, he contended. Surely his definitions, however, would have confused the new American democrat. "Pride of reason" and a materialistic celebration of self must bow to unquestioning obedience to "the supreme undisputed sovereign—God, not the world—God, not God *and* the world." The regenerative power of faith, he concluded, preserved the exclusive web of communicants amenable to a world of spiritual absolutes. The world cannot comprehend a gospel learned only "through the teachings of the Holy Spirit." [14]

Few ministers believed that static simplicity on the cardinal tenets of faith meant replicating colonial Puritan preaching styles. Unable to turn back and unsure how to proceed, ministers attempted to strike a balance. They appealed to the democratic ear through flexibility in homiletic forms while asserting even more intensely the "changeless truths of the gospel." When Protestant leaders celebrated "religious liberty" and offered free grace to all, they sounded like true Jacksonian heralds. But within the spiritual community of faith, in the web of discourse that ministers believed mattered most, they demanded submission to Christ, unquestioning obedience to biblical truths, and deference to the spiritual "liberty" that was eternally most important. Blending adaptability with stern vigilance, the clergy struggled to bend without breaking in the democratic wind. As they exulted in the power of a preached gospel, they betrayed their confusion and anxiety over how to make regular sermons palatable to the American democrat without sacrificing historic faith at the altar of popular power. The struggle is mapped out across denominational lines in the three religious jeremiads that follow.

Addressing his peers on the "preaching for the age," Presbyterian divine William Goodrich laid out the new realities that had permanently reshaped the American audience. First, a pragmatic, commercial spirit had produced a popular "restless vigilance" and "nervous intentness." Gone was the congregation that could stomach the laborious, systematic track of old-style Puritan didactics. To grip the attention of men "never out of hearing of a railroad whistle," ministers risked distorting "foundational truths" in deference to the "sparkles and flashes" of immediate, "tangible result." Second, popular literature had established the market for lucid, tantalizing prose and exotic themes. The cultural pressure on ministers to mimic the popular press's "force, vivacity and gracefulness of style" carried equal temptation to "shrink from discussing the central truths of religion." Third, the "superficial resemblance" between the lecture and the sermon "provoked injurious comparison." If congregations goaded ministers to reproduce the "delights" of the lecture room, emphasis on conversion would be replaced by conciliation, Goodrich warned.[15]

Finally, he argued that the new infidelity's war on human oppression and injustice amounted to a "covert attack on the pulpit and preaching." This "designed disparagement," however, marked only one dimension of the assault. Infidelity's message of benevolence also broke down the "awful discrimination of character," beckoned ministers toward a "comfortable blending of all hearers into one body," and blurred the "broad line of separation" that distinguished the regenerate of Christ's kingdom from the world.[16] Goodrich explained the benevolent forces shaking the foundations of the preached Word:

> In many moral enterprises . . . the enemies of the Cross . . . are ready to join hands with the disciples of Christ, especially if the test points of religious character are dropped for the while. They have, in their view, a far better idea of brotherhood than that of the Church, one of much wider communion and more liberal feeling; and it is a trying task for one, at the present day, to turn to those whom he respects

for their morality, and with whom he sympathizes on great social
questions, and address them as godless men, and press on them the
discriminating truths of the gospel.[17]

For Goodrich, legitimate social concerns could not break down the
barriers between the believer's spiritual world and the society he unavoidably shared with the rest of humanity. He did not vilify social reformers,
but instead attacked the multiplying effects of "inferior" motives. Ministers unquestionably had to assuage human suffering, widen their field
of vision, and embrace legitimate social reforms, Goodrich decreed. But
elevating such motives above "future retribution" or "vivid impressions
of the eternal world" made "preaching thus *material*." It converted the
pulpit into another outlet for the commercial mentality, and the "natural
excitement of *progress*" that threatened to "[eat] out the heart of religion."[18] It is easy to sense here the anguish and frustration that informed
Goodrich's explication of a "trying task." To "respect" the moral fervor of
unbelievers admitted the inescapable reality of broader cultural bonds,
and, conversely, intensified a desire to maintain a critical separateness.

In 1854 Lutheran minister J. A. Brown issued similar warnings against
the "secularization of the ministry" in an address to the Synod of East
Pennsylvania. He concisely outlined the gulf between preaching the "unadulterated Word" and speculating on "the ways of God, in nature, providence, and grace." Let a minister's inquiries display "patient and profound investigation of the 'mystery of godliness,'" Brown declared, "but
let his pulpit resound with the simple doctrines of the cross, without any
mists of human speculation." Ministers had no commission to indulge
the "diseased taste" of the populace with lessons on "philosophy, politics,
[and] business."[19]

Even more intently than Goodrich, Brown explored the symbiotic
relationship between the core message and the vitality of the community of the Word. Pastor and flock, he maintained, were bonded by an
understanding far deeper than that "existing between a lecturer and
his audience."[20] Ministers and congregations faced material temptations
equally threatening to their spiritual kinship. Churches that inadequately
supported their pastors discouraged prospective candidates and drove
current divines to supplement their incomes with "worldly" pursuits. In
a broadside no doubt aimed at the practice of recompensing ministers
for "morality lectures," Brown blasted preaching "mainly for the love of
gain" as "trafficking in the blood of the Redeemer, and the treasures of
divine grace." "Sin," not morality, was the "awful fact" for Brown. On the

"truth of God, the unadulterated Word," hung the "health and destiny of the immortal spirit."[21]

New Jersey Baptist preacher John Carpenter shared common ground with Goodrich and Brown, but he homed in on the peculiar responsibilities of hearers. He called the regular sermon the vital "link in the chain of Christian truth" and exhorted his congregation to beware the indiscriminate consumption of information. The "priests of Satan" thrived on the "credulity of the simple and unsuspecting . . . , knowing that truth distorted [gave] error a plausible appearance."[22] Carpenter demolished the notion that intellectual freedom and inquiry were believer prerogatives within the context of Christian community and responsibility: "Take heed what you hear. Hear regularly. Hear with a sober undivided attention. Hear with a determination not to be led by momentary impulse. Hear with strict caution to guard against the artful attempts to impose error upon you for truth. . . . Take the scriptures as your standard. . . . We must be obedient hearers. The savior enjoined obedience upon those to whom he dispensed the word."[23] At a stroke, Carpenter crystallized the intellectual insularity he believed essential to preserving a community of the Word. Its defense required conscious repudiation of democratic culture and materialism as the dynamic of faith. On yet another level of communication, his determined invocation of "obedient hearers" mixes traditional instruction with an anxious explication of an essential symbiosis between pulpit and pew. The sermon, in other words, remained a viable catalyst to spiritual community as long as believers rejected a liberal world of "momentary impulses," "artful" error, and choice in order to remain unquestioning links in a chain of unquestioned truths.

Defending the community of the Word at times evoked hard internal criticism as well. The American Board of Commissioners for Foreign Missions took the offensive on two fronts in 1856. At a special meeting in Albany, New York, the board warned that its own evangelistic press had to remain auxiliary to preaching. The body also explained that oral communication of "the Word" and the salvation message necessarily defined the missionary effort. That the American Baptist Missionary Union enthusiastically affirmed and reprinted the board's resolutions in 1857 broadens the significance of the report.[24] The Prudential Committee of the American Board targeted the press and the school as most likely to "transcend their proper limits" and even demanded an end to direct missionary involvement in printing wherever possible. "*Preaching—literal* preaching," the committee mandated in its outline of missionary policy, is the "grand agency," the "chief instrumentality" for the salvation of men.[25]

The board singled out for special attack a commentary on foreign missions published in the *North British Review* in August 1856. Their barbs reveal motives far afield from social redemption or a material millennium. Consider the following argument by the *Review* writer, which the board quoted and then censured:

"Our object is to introduce Christianity with all the blessings which accompany it—true views of God, its ennobling motives, its pure morality, the elevation of life and manners, the civilization, the knowledge, even the material progress which are sure to follow in its train. . . . We may leave it to God himself to decide how the benefits of Christ will be extended to those whom it has pleased him to permit to live and die in ignorance of the Gospel."[26]

The committee pounced on such a mission rationale that squelched their conception of the "preached Word" and minimized the perils of the unsaved soul. "According to these views," they charged, "the *civilization* of pagan nations, rather than their rescue from *sin and endless death*, [is] the grand object of missions."[27]

Conscious of new social and material forces that weighed upon the pulpit and preaching, the American Board and ministers like Goodrich, Brown, and Carpenter struggled to check the power of the new competing oral culture. Clerical deference to the community of the Word forced them to subordinate even their own civic and speculative treatises in defense of the cause. Revels for American liberty and volleys against collective social sins quieted abruptly when ministers turned inward to the bread-and-butter message. Of course they resented the breakdown of their personal status within American society, and traces of bitterness are easily found in their harangues. Most, though, must have resigned themselves to their professional declension by the 1850s, however much they may have regretted it. Indeed, this breakdown itself was a key stimulus for critics celebrating the uniqueness and power of a spiritual community that could remain above cultural circumscriptions. That they could at the same time rail against slavery and temperance, gaming and Sabbath-breaking is not a contradiction in purpose. Social consciousness even facilitated religious dissent. Protestant leaders used these connections as a basis for attacking cultural arrogance, defining the peripheral status of material agendas, and maintaining the evangelistic effort. But easy assimilation of nationalism, social reform, and republicanism into the spiritual discourse of the community of the Word could only thwart their interests. Anxious ministers kept watch. One writer summed it up this way: "We rejoice in the incidental benefits of our religion but it will be an evil day when these become the prominent objects of its propagation."[28]

The laments of Baptist great Francis Wayland attest to how far the defense of regular preaching and spiritually separated community could go. Reflecting upon the ministry and his own career in the early 1860s, Wayland unleashed a blistering assault on accommodative preaching seeded with personal confessions. Calling for sermons that incited hearers to a spiritually separated life, Wayland chided the confusion of "weekly discourse on some social duty" with God's "communication to sinful men." The minister of God performed his divine calling only as "the medium of communication between the Spirit of God and his hearers," he charged. This most prominent of antebellum Baptist educators bristled at claims for the ministry as a "profession" instead of a spiritual calling. He confessed that a personal "ambition for scholarship and literary reputation" became the seedbed of his own "painful experience." "I think I erred," Wayland confessed, in exchanging "the work of saving souls" for the "work of education." Likewise, he divulged his gradual dependence on written sermons as an act of cultural deference that replaced dependence on the "Spirit of God" and constituted one of the "great errors" of his life.[29]

Wayland was not gunning for educators. The aging minister worried that for all its liberty, money, and material resources, transatlantic Christianity (he took additional note of British clerical anxieties) clung precariously to its historic "spiritual power." While cultural elites ordered innocuous messages from resplendent pulpits to "respectable citizens," the rejected poor and middle classes set their own material agendas beyond faith. He suspected that a lawyer and legislator who summed up religion's place among his professional peers also pronounced too accurately religion's place in the new order: "'They think religion a very useful thing for promoting the good order of society and reducing the number of policemen, and they are willing to contribute to its support; but that is all. As to its necessity for salvation of the soul,—or, in fact, as to its importance for anything else than the present life,—they have no belief at all." Here, for Wayland, was the predictable result of regular preaching that closed the critical gap between Christianity and culture. Yet as his sermonic legacy reveals, Wayland's *Letters on the Ministry of the Gospel* caps a long jeremiadic trajectory, one that outlines, in deeply personal terms, the cultural uncertainties that churned within the community of faith.[30]

Fire on the Front Lines

Clerical anxieties and remedies spelled out in religious jeremiads demanding simple preaching and preservation of an oral gospel admittedly beg the question: What kind of religious diet did ordinary preachers feed the folks week in and week out? The religious jeremiads expressed Protestant alarm at the church's weakening resistance to cultural compromise. Yet total despair was never pervasive, and periodic bursts of optimism remained a feature of the Protestant quarrel. Ministers' confidence in their own diagnostic powers inspired hope, but it was a hope dependent on the therapeutic puissance of their regular pulpit labors. The success of the day-to-day message in the trenches would determine the spiritual integrity of the community of the Word. That success ironically depended on the "democratic" will of believers to circumscribe their democratic power and remain steadfast in the traditional paths of spiritual discourse.

Following is an analysis of homiletic themes that shaped the preaching of five ordinary ministers from different denominations and regional settings. Together they represent an unpublished record of the themes and sketches that shaped at least one thousand sermons delivered between 1840 and 1859. None of these five men had exceptional or eccentric ministries. They include Jacob Dudley, Virginia Presbyterian; Henry Newton, Georgia Presbyterian; Charles Morton, New York Baptist; Samuel Kammerer, Ohio Lutheran; and Francis Asbury Hester, Indiana Methodist. The broad geographic spectrum represented here is intended to reveal common themes without minimizing regional differences. Donald G. Mathews and Anne Loveland have variously explained how Southern ministers made the accommodation of religion and slavery a basis for excoriating Northern materialism and defending their own region's cultural and spiritual superiority.[31] This tune played particularly well in justifications of the denominational splits of the 1840s and in addresses thematically centered on the growing sectional crisis. Yet the distinctions of contemporaries and historians can be coupled with equally revealing ties of purpose and concern that the confrontational pieces often obscured. As James Oakes has demonstrated, a liberal, acquisitive spirit generated materialistic conceptions of human progress in both sections. Moreover, Northerners like Wayland, Fish, and Bushnell did not need Southern prompts to illuminate cultural threats or Protestant vulnerabilities. Beyond jockeying for sectional position, ministers shared common concerns and a desire for Protestant spiritual ascendancy over the culture. These bonds produced a critical message amply expressed in both regions.

Jacob Dudley was raised by devout parents in the urban environs of Richmond, Virginia. Dudley never strayed from the South or the Southern Presbyterian piety that shaped his youth. Graduation from the University of Virginia led to three years at Union Theological Seminary and finally an 1840 ordination in the East Hanover Presbytery. Only the promise of better medical care in Philadelphia for his ailing wife compelled him to accept a one-year sojourn in the North. His ministry spanned forty-three years and was divided among rural churches in eastern Virginia. Between 1840 and 1860, Dudley completed a nine-year inaugural charge at Sussex Church followed by four years at Namozine Church in Amelia County. For the period 1855 to 1860, he served in Goochland County, northwest of Richmond.[32]

Dudley's thorough notes and preaching diary include sketches of ninety-eight sermons delivered 323 times from 1841 to 1860. These substantial remains give credence to the Virginia Synod eulogist who praised his willingness to eschew "popular applause" and hew to a Christocentric line emphasizing sin and salvation. Notable too was Dudley's willingness to regularly enlighten the unrepentant on the terrors of divine judgment. Consider the twenty-two sermons delivered at least five times that account for nearly half (156) of his recorded deliveries. Dudley spent little time enumerating the temporal rewards of moral living. Appeals for individual salvation are omnipresent. On seventy-seven occasions he bludgeoned his audience with the fiery stick of Jehovah's vengeance. For the unrepentant, "there will be no bounds to his wrath," Dudley warned in a homily first delivered in 1845. This "sudden and unexpected" destruction will be "intolerable and interminable—wave after wave and billow after billow will roll over you through all eternity." In another 1845 homily, Dudley told the unconverted to expect nothing less than the eternal "wrath and curse of God."[33]

Dudley's preaching complemented religious jeremiads calling for Christian separateness. "The Christian life is necessarily a warfare," he told the Namozine Church in 1848. Compromisers willing to break down this separation, he argued the same year, are more damaging to the community of believers than are its "declared enemies." In a homily with at least ten encores between 1846 and 1859, Dudley explained that the "word of the Lord" necessarily bound believers in a "self-denying," "exclusive" community. A spirit of cultural self-sufficiency and the "corruption of human nature" now combined to "choke the word" and thereby deny humanity its spiritual birthright. Another sermon reveals Dudley's frustration with a democratic culture of choices and compromise. Drawing on the gospel of Matthew ("he who is not with me is against me"), he rued a popular philanthropic spirit that seemed to establish a middle ground between traditional faith and unbelief. But Dudley was unequivocal: there could be no "neutrality in the cause of Christ." He wanted complete commitment to truths "beyond the reach of human reason" and practically beyond a world of unchecked liberty. Compromise and neutrality might be permissible, even "commendable" in ordinary human affairs, Dudley suggested. But the community of the Word required the hard-line language of exclusivity.[34] Born-again believers alone, Dudley charged, could withstand the responsibility and power of being a " 'peculiar people.' "

Dudley's sermon sketches and records suggest that he sustained his pulpit rigor over time. No doubt his certitudes of an unchanging faith offered respite to Virginia seekers bewildered by the cultural and political confusion that surrounded them. The Namozine Church recalled Jacob Dudley to their pulpit in 1867, and he remained there until his death in 1884.

Although Dudley left no record of preaching to slaves, outreach to the black population was a regular feature of most Southern Protestant ministries. Anne Loveland provides a useful examination of this ministry in her general study of Southern evangelicals and the social order. She also notes that sparse records make any examination of preaching to the black population especially difficult. Between 1830 and 1860, the gradual segregation of blacks into separate services, and eventually separate churches, marked a major change in Protestant strategy. Protestants cited overcrowded buildings (fewer ministers were available to fill plantation circuits) and the need to adapt preaching styles to black audiences as two reasons for the change. Ministers also assured slaveholders that the changes posed no threat to the South's peculiar institution. Significantly, Loveland concludes that evangelical preaching offered its strongest support to slavery by hewing a spiritual line that focused black hopes on eternal rewards. The devout slaveholder's concern for his slaves' spiritual welfare may often have been genuine, but his social stake in encouraging his slaves to fix their hopes on the hereafter was hardly obscure.[35]

Whatever the auxiliary interests of slaveholders, preaching that subordinated temporal to eternal aims was not necessarily a conscious clerical contribution to social control. Such messages dovetailed with sermons to white congregations North and South. The preaching diary of Georgia Presbyterian Henry Newton is suggestive. A lifelong laborer in Georgia home missions, Newton recorded thirty separate preaching engagements with slave audiences between 1852 and 1858. The Scriptural texts that anchored these sermons suggest that, beyond any stylistic variances he may have incorporated, Newton found black and white souls equally depraved—and equally capable of resisting the message of salvation.[36]

Strongly salvific themes, including his most frequently used text from Luke's gospel ("and yet there is room"), shaped Newton's preaching to both groups. Newton judged his African American charges frightfully "superstitious," but he complained as loudly about the materialism that galvanized white sinners. Meager turnouts of impenitent whites robbed him of the "liberty" to preach freely. Black seekers demonstrated the same "democratic" spirit. Newton recorded one afternoon service when unimpressed slaves voted him down with their feet. Their continual "passing in, out" finally halted the service. Still, he seems to have been equally pleased by successes in both camps. Slaveholders often discouraged "uncontrolled" emotion among slaves, but Newton marked emotionally wrought slaves "moved to tears" as important barometers of spiritual progress. Indeed, Newton tied his personal quest for "liberty" and "freedom" closely to the pulpit and the spiritual response of his listeners.[37] Consequently, his chronic scrutiny of black and white reactions to his preaching gave independent-minded slaves a measure of authority over the Presbyterian divine's sense of pulpit prowess. In sum, Newton preached with a spiritual consistency that offered little to blacks seeking temporal freedom or to masters wanting homilies on obedience. A message tragically silent on the injustice of slavery nevertheless reinforced a larger Protestant interest in protecting the supremacy of their spiritual agenda.

For forty years Baptist preacher Charles Morton lived with the uncertainty and mobility that characterized clerical life along the channels of westward settlement.[38] Born in Augusta, New York, in 1799, Morton grew up in the west central counties bordering the Erie Canal and spent his first years preaching there. His early career also clashed with the atomistic revival fires that swept through what Whitney Cross called New York's Burned-Over District. Nearly thirty congregations close to Morton's church in Manlius split or weathered serious infighting as a result of perfectionist zeal boiling at the fringes of mainstream revivalism. Eventually the area would produce the bulk of John Noyes's Oneida Community recruits and a large share of Millerites, who anticipated Christ's physical return to the Earth in 1843. Morton himself held protracted revival meetings with great success in 1833–34. Most important, amid economic boom and bust, intellectual turmoil, and personal travail (only three of his eight children survived to 1846), Morton fulfilled the ordinary responsibilities of a pastor to his congregation. He punctuated his travels with extended stays in several churches: Erie, Pennsylvania, in the late 1830s; Ashtabula, Ohio, in the next decade; and, after 1850, back to New York in Penn Yan and Corning.

Morton's preaching records survive for this third period in his career. They reveal an enormous output—more than 3,500 career sermons preached by 1853. His average 120-sermon annual output in the 1850s betrays no waning enthusiasm. As a comprehensive sampling of Morton's thematic emphasis in the regular pulpit, this period is particularly useful. It sandwiches his extended pastorates in Corning and Penn Yan between two stints on the road—one in 1853 when he was probably looking for a charge and another in 1858 when he blanketed the state with one-day engagements, no doubt in response to the revivalistic fervor of that year.

In 1853, Morton preached multiple sermons in Baptist churches in Hamilton (fourteen), Waterville (nineteen), and Penn Yan (nine) before returning to a thirty-month pastorate in Penn Yan.[39] For each pulpit message he recorded the date, his biblical text, and usually a paraphrased or quoted segment of Scripture that established his theme. His preaching strategy for this itinerant period is clear—subordinate "moral" themes to Christocentric texts emphasizing salvation, sin, and final judgment. Morton, for example, must have garnered good response to sermons drawn from John 3:3 ("Except a man be born again"), John 14:6 ("I am the Way"), and Titus 3:4–7 ("According to his mercy he saved us"). He repeated all three themes in Hamilton, Waterville, and Penn Yan. Of forty-five sermons preached from January to the beginning of his regular charge in Penn Yan, twenty-three focused specifically on salvation and impending judgment. Morton also hammered every congregation on the road with the theme "Let your light shine," a favorite Baptist exhortation to personal evangelism.[40]

During his 1858–59 sojourns Morton preached in more than eighty locations. After filling several New York City pulpits, he worked the Schenectady area and then traveled north to Malone near the Canadian border. He finally turned west to Buffalo and small towns south of Rochester. As he had six years earlier, Morton delivered an unbroken volley of salvation sermons, but this time he added a new twist. In harmony with the current Protestant jeremiadic emphasis on the spoken word, he assigned transcendent importance to texts that united preaching and salvation. From January 1858 to October 1859, Morton delivered 235 sermons. Ninety-eight of these drew from two New Testament texts that he had not used in 1853—Mark 16:15 ("Go ye into all the world and preach the gospel") and 1 Corinthians 1:21 ("It pleased God by the foolishness of preaching to save them"). Such narrow focus can only mean that Morton had struck homiletic gold—a thematic vein that tapped his personal concerns and resonated with audiences as well. He was almost as successful with Isaiah 45:22 ("Look unto me and be saved all the ends of the earth") and the parallel verses Titus 2:14 and Galatians 2:20 ("The Son of Man who gave himself for us") which accounted for 53 sermons. His determined output of Christocentric preaching reinforced conceptions of an oral community of the Word and a supranational, spiritual Protestant mission.[41]

As a regular pastor in Penn Yan (for thirty months) and Corning (for twenty-five months), Morton predictably supplemented the salvific theme with "pastoral" homilies on Christian nurture and obedience. Though he drew his themes from a wider range of texts during this sedentary period, some patterns are apparent. He referred nineteen times, for example, to Psalm 119.[42] The chapter emphasizes obedience to the law and connects personal holiness to a thorough knowledge of Scripture. His favorite single source from this chapter was verse 11: "Thy word have I hid in my heart." He also preached frequently from a variety of texts disparaging worldliness and materialism. It is likely that however varied Morton's textual base during these pastoral years, collective social themes rarely usurped his emphasis on personal salvation, holiness, and the eternal consequences of faith. On the few occasions when he *did* address social themes, he noted the digression specifically in his journal. While in Penn Yan he recorded a two-part sermon on temperance addressed to "young people." He acknowledged an address to the Temperance Society in Savona in 1856. In both Penn Yan and Corning he preached sermons specifically attacking Roman Catholicism. In general, however, such departures in the regular pulpit were rare.

The career of Lutheran divine Samuel Kammerer neatly paralleled that of Morton. Born in Lancaster, Pennsylvania, in 1799, he and his family moved to Ohio in 1801.[43] Kammerer was ordained in 1821 and spent his entire ministry preaching in and around Zanesville. He assumed his last charge in Adamsville in 1855 and was superannuated by the mid-1860s. The Evangelical Lutheran Church was powerful in southern Ohio and benefited from the tendency of German Lutheran immigrants to move directly to the nation's interior. German skeptics fleeing the political turmoil of revolutionary upheaval supplemented this flow after 1848.[44] Southern Ohio Lutherans like Kammerer faced particular opposition from the large contingent of German rationalists who settled in and around Cincinnati. Indeed, Baden revolutionary Friedrich Hecker established the first Turnverein in the United States in Cincinnati in 1848. The new immigrants tapped Cincinnati's publishing resources and peppered the countryside with decidedly antireligious German-language newspapers. For Lutheran divines like Kammerer, meeting this challenge made preaching in both German and English an even more urgent necessity by the 1850s.

Kammerer wrote his eighty-five sermon outlines in both German and English. None are dated, but it can be assumed that he, like most ministers who kept sketches, did so to build a repertoire of core sermons. Kammerer's homilies reveal themes that should not surprise us by now— the reality of human depravity, the need for personal salvation, and the necessity of subordinating individual will to divine purpose. Kammerer's forte, however, was crystallizing divine judgment. His homilies vaulted anxious listeners beyond millennial speculations to the threshold of death and eternity. Kammerer could recount "the blessed state of those who seek the Lord," but more than one-fourth of his sermons unraveled a gloomy forecast for the lost. The following exordiums are illustrative:

"An exhortation to be ready for death, judgment"
"The final state of the wicked"
"Reasons we must all appear before the judgment seat of Christ"
"Of death and judgment"
"How to prepare for death"
"The destruction of those who despise the word of God"
"The different ways to eternity"
"The judgment that shall come upon those who reject Christ and
      his Word"[45]

Such pulpit thrashings of the impenitent combined with equally vivid assurances of eternal, "perfect happiness" for believers. Sixteen of Kammerer's sermons instructed listeners on the "rest of God's people," the "salvation of those who come unto Christ," and the "glorious fruits and consequences of true evangelical faith." He touted the exclusivity of a community of the Word. In a sermon on "faith, hope, and charity," he underscored the last as a "branch of love" fully comprehended "only by the regenerate."[46]

Kammerer's spiritual discourse offered few sops to democratic pluralism or diversity. Exhortations for the penitent to seek "liberation from sin" blended with mandates for obedience, submission, and good works as evidence of personal salvation. He stressed the oral, Scriptural base of an otherworldly Christian community. Believers must "hear and obey" the "preaching of his word." The "new man" must live according to a "changed will," "sanctified desires," and "perseverance in good works." God called believers to "be separate" and "form a society of your own."[47] Like most evangelicals, Kammerer acknowledged the temporal benefits of faith. Social references, however, were peripheral and incidental to his incessant demands for individual repentance and spiritual separateness from the larger culture.

Like Virginia's Jacob Dudley, Indiana Methodist circuit rider Francis Asbury Hester began his thirty-year ministry in 1840. The newly licensed eighteen-year-old exhorter worried about "multitudes scoffing and ridiculing a mere boy attempting to proclaim the world of life." Assignments in and around New Harmony put him in head-to-head competition with itinerant lecturers from Robert Owen's experimental community. His dedicated, forceful preaching earned him a deaconship by 1845. Hester would eventually earn a doctor of divinity degree from Asbury University in 1872, but little formal schooling aided him during his early charges in southern Indiana between 1843 and 1860.[48]

Evident throughout the 128 sermon sketches that Hester wrote from 1846 to 1853 is his quest for "entire sanctification." He drew from Methodist founder John Wesley's holiness doctrine, which exhorted believers to pursue nothing less than complete subjection of human desires to the will of God. Most Baptists and Lutherans shrank from Methodist speculations about the pursuit of entire sanctification. At the level of regular preaching, however, Methodist pleas for holiness merged easily with general Protestant mandates for holy living and renunciation of sin. What holiness preaching like Hester's did reveal was another way in which Protestants isolated the community of the Word from the larger culture. Nearly one-third of Hester's sermons urged the faithful to pursue "internal righteousness," "be visibly distinct from the world," and eschew faith in the mere execution of religion's "external duties."[49] During the last five months of 1848 in Princeton, Indiana, he churned out sermons on spiritual separateness at a blistering pace. Eleven of nineteen pulpit messages attacked "moralists," ungodliness in the church, and spiritually-inert philanthropy.[50]

Otherworldliness under the yoke of Methodist Arminianism assumed peculiar significance. To be sure, Arminian "free will" theology opened the floodgates of grace to all, but free salvation also carried concomitant warning. Once converted, individuals still had "liberty" to stray from grace and plod again toward sin and eternal ruin. (Most Baptists taught the "perseverance of the saints" out of a conviction that Arminianism pointed toward salvation by works. Methodists vehemently denied the charge.) Consequently sin, not optimism about human potential, remained the salient theme issuing from the regular Methodist pulpit. Ministers like Hester hounded sinners toward the path of spiritual progress. In a pair of 1849 sermons, for example, he cautioned that "the sinfulness of our lives is evidence of the sinfulness of our hearts. . . . Grow in grace, [seek] entire sanctification. Unless we advance we will backslide."[51]

Hester's conception of spiritual progress, however, was contingent not on national or collective advance but on distinguishing spiritual improvement from material designs. One of every five sermons Hester sketched between 1846 and 1853 addressed believers on the eternal consequences of substituting "worldliness" and "outward morality" for "spiritual faith." In an 1851 homily, he asserted that "failing to grow in grace results in loss of spirituality and frequently apostasy. . . . How terrible the consequences of going away from Christ."[52]

Antebellum Methodists have long been noted for their communal worship gatherings (or "love feasts") and for an emphasis on the love of Christ as opposed to his wrath. Like Kammerer, however, Hester boldly proclaimed the eternal miseries of hell and final judgment in his regular preaching. In Edinburgh, Indiana, for example, he pummeled his congregation with ten successive sermons on the "wickedness" within Christendom, the nature of divine wrath, and the "certainty of endless future punishment for the impenitent." Human responsibility, not human potential, loomed largest in Hester's spiritual vision. "Man's wickedness will drive God to inflict punishment," he asserted.[53]

Hester was not impervious to national crises. He recorded a ringing indictment of national moral evils, intemperance, and licentiousness in a national fast day sermon in 1849. Separate from his regular sermon sketchbooks he kept an extended traditional civic jeremiad recounting the divine blessings and punishments that God providentially bestowed upon nations. This was not typical fare, however. His regular sermons incidentally acknowledged the temporal blessings of faith, but he offered no glowing visions of an earthly paradise as reason for men to repent. For Hester, "Zion" and the "kingdom" were the "Church," the worldwide body of believers. His sermons put the unregenerate on "the road to hell" and recounted for believers the eternal bliss of the "kingdom of heaven." His apocalyptic fare offered sinners the uncertainty of life and promised that Christ's return would be sudden, as a "thief in the night."[54] Hester was a true patriot, but his deep consciousness of a separated com munity of believers drove him toward cultural confrontation rather than conciliation in the regular pulpit.

Regular pulpit sermons of ordinary ministers like Dudley, Newton, Hester, Kammerer, and Morton dovetailed with Protestant jeremiads pleading for a simple, preached gospel. The quartet's production is equally significant for what it omits. Social reform emerges as a tangential concern at best. Their central themes and Scriptural references suggest little interest in conjuring millennial visions as a lure to the unconverted. Instead, they gave apocalyptic references an individualistic turn and fixed their hearers' gaze directly on the bliss or abyss of eternal judgment. Such a strategy fit the task of exalting the uniqueness of Protestantism and the special status of the community of the Word. Using the regular pulpit to elevate peripheral concerns could only deflect religious energies toward competing secular agendas. But this powerful yearning to preserve the old ways of faith represents neither mindless continuity with the past nor an insignificant backwater. The religious jeremiads demonstrate that Protestant ministers were not content to do battle with demons that haunted their ancestors. Their regular and jeremiadic preaching must be seen as a complex and complementary response to the perceived cultural crises of their own time.

One final example of how ordinary clergymen worked to insulate their spiritual discourse can be gleaned from "collective" sermons produced at annual Regular Baptist Association meetings. These circular letters were typically written by one minister on a topic collectively chosen by delegates. They were then approved by the assembly and published for local consumption. The hybrid homilies drew inspiration from both the religious jeremiad and the regular sermon. Frequent acknowledgment of secular pressures on the Protestant community intersected with recounting of the salvation message and often tedious Scriptural defenses of the basic doctrines that united believers.

This Baptist voice broadens an understanding of the mainstream Protestant message in three ways. First, Baptists joined Methodists in a broadly successful appeal to rural and working-class folks. Inclusive evangelism enabled the two camps to outnumber every other Protestant group by 1850. Second, local Baptist associations nationwide produced annual circulars. Finally, Baptist ambivalence toward such interdenominational bodies as the American Tract Society makes the letters a useful means of establishing continuity between the core message of these notoriously independent spirits and that of the more cooperative Protestant groups. Baptists cherished the independence of their individual churches and vehemently denied that they even constituted a "denomination." Such appendages seemed superfluous to the transcendent spiritual community of all believers. Rejection of infant baptism and other temporal "encumbrances" to the "soul liberty" of a pure "Bible faith" led Baptists to view themselves as specially appointed scions of Christian community. Their circular letters reveal this common understanding as essential to their associational integrity. Consequently, they provide an important link to collective Baptist sentiment.[55]

Circulars from Baptist associations in Indiana, Rhode Island, and South Carolina offer a geographically diverse sampling of this mainstream religious discourse. Regular Baptists outnumbered all other Protestant groups in Indiana (forty-eight associations) and South Carolina (eighteen associations) except the Methodists. Rhode Island's Baptist population (two associations) dwarfed the second-place Methodists. Under consideration here are eighteen circulars from the Edgefield Association in South Carolina, twenty from the Warren Association in Rhode Island, and forty-nine from the White Lick, Lost River, and Madison Associations in Indiana.[56]

Collectively, the circulars explained Christian purpose in language far afield from that of the developing democratic culture. Common were letters defending a single core doctrine such as the "new birth," the atonement, or the divinity of Christ. One overall theme emerged dominant between 1830 and 1860: Only a community of believers united in "one heart and soul" and committed to "one mind and one argument" could sustain the "bonds of grace." Sixteen Indiana circulars, for example, exhorted the faithful to seek unity in preaching and communal affirmation of the Word.[57] One 1837 circular demanded clear distinction between core and peripheral components of evangelism: "Our deliverance from the power of darkness and translation into the kingdom of Christ . . . does not depend upon speculative knowledge of the Bible, nor a conviction of the authenticity of the Scriptures . . . nor the inspiration of the Apostles . . . for all this may be believed without experimental knowledge of our translation."[58]

Eleven Rhode Island circulars made special appeals for unity based on common spiritual understanding. The 1844 writer explained that an age "singularly different" from apostolic times had not altered the responsibility of believers to remain a *"peculiar people."* The present could hardly be considered the threshold of millennial "glory," since "formal professions" were increasingly the only means of distinguishing the "children of light" from the "children of darkness." Separateness depended on sustained "*intimate and practical acquaintance with divine truth*," which secured the "*spiritual culture*" of believers from the "school of morals the world calls its own."[59] An 1856 South Carolina circular heralded Christian believers as "the highest and most responsible organization on earth." To fulfill its role as a "city set on a hill," the church must be prepared to reject error and discipline its own.[60]

According to many circulars, securing the inner web of Christian communication demanded practical action. An 1836 Indiana letter prescribed "great caution" in the reception of new members.[61] Another asked Baptists to select preachers with care to preserve "that doctrine our union says is the Bible doctrine."[62] One Hoosier writer ordered congregational resolve to orally "proclaim a departure from first principles."[63] Baptists' antipathy for episcopacy and "man-made" institutions prefigured their leadership among evangelicals in defending the community of the Word. They deemed extemporaneous preaching and the regular spiritual conversation of ordinary people as superior to organization and liturgical rigor. An 1851 Rhode Island circular recalled the pivotal role of simple "religious conversation" as an anchor of faith among the "primitive disciples." Christians must trod the "old path" away from new cultural standards that identified religious conversation with a "self-righteous spirit." The writer defined spontaneous and deeply spiritual discourse as the timeless, practical, and visible means of reinforcing the boundaries of true spiritual community.[64]

As a group, Baptists counted themselves the only Protestants completely dependent on personal communion with Scripture. One Hoosier writer referred to "liberty and the Bible" as an epithet peculiarly descriptive of Baptists' unique dependence on the "Word" alone.[65] South Carolina's Edgefield ministers told members that Baptist genius in preserving gospel simplicity bestowed upon them "solemn and weighty" responsibility and a "position peculiarly distinct" among evangelical Protestants. Consequently, they regarded themselves as master sleuths in flushing out enemies of sanctified discourse. Nearly half the Indiana circulars attacked "false teachers," propagators of "strange doctrine," "mockers" of the Word, and vendors of "vain philosophy." Equally guilty were selfish audiences who succumbed to "itching ears" and "heaped to themselves seducers and teachers." An 1841 South Carolina circular asked churches to expel members who persisted in such secular pleasures as gambling, theater, and like indulgences. If the Bible offered no specific injunctions, such activities nevertheless violated the principle of "'no corrupt communication'" among brethren. "Purity of speech" must mark believers as spiritually separated from the culture and affirm that every thought is "brought into captivity to the obedience of Christ."[66]

The letters often tagged such charges with invitations to "stand fast in the liberty wherewith Christ has made us free." The Warren Association's 1841 letter detailed the growing danger of liberty unbounded by faith. Such pleas certainly contradicted the moral freedom of a vigorous democratic order, but they also gave definition and purpose to the oral community of the Word. When these sacred boundaries appeared to be threatened, Baptist champions of "liberty and the Bible" declared the Scriptural bonds that united believers to be superior to the freedom that authored the new order.

Eighteen Indiana circulars cultivated Christian separateness by blasting worldliness and a concomitant compromise with Satan, the Antichrist, and innate human selfishness.[67] Writers repeatedly invoked these three adversaries as the chief purveyors of disunity and the destroyers of the Christian message. The church, if sapped of "vital piety" through worldly compromise, was little more than a "splendid sepulchre of souls, the gateway to hell."[68] Perhaps more than any single evangelical group, Baptists cultivated the personality of Satan as a vital, evil force. An 1856 circular demanded vigilance against the material, personal, and supernatural threats to the Christian community: "Guard against the world, the flesh, and the Devil as enemies to your God and to your souls."[69]

Not that Baptists, any more than other mainstream Protestants, wanted a cloistered community. The circulars called for unceasing evangelistic outreach from a core of affirmed, unquestioned truths, by regular preaching. The gospel needed to be spread to the ends of the earth, not because America was ushering in the millennium but because the future was uncertain. "We must believe and publish the doctrine of [man's] entire destitution of holiness . . . with the soul cheering, soul transforming doctrine of the atonement," an 1858 Indiana circular warned.[70] Regular, oral communication of the gospel, they believed, was essential to evangelism and vital religion even though not intrinsically salvific. For these guardians of the Word, the "natural man," remained a dangerous outsider, incapable of comprehending the spiritual discourse and purpose of the community of the Word.

"A Literature for the People"

Clergymen by the 1850s understood the waxing influence of the spoken word and struggled to maintain its power in the pulpit. The mainstream

Protestant message also found outlet in print, but speculative or weighty theological tomes, academic textbooks, or even popular religious newspapers are not the best gauges of this message. Editors and publishers depended on economic solvency as well as "truth" and recognized that controversy and a healthy smattering of secular news improved circulation. To find a coherent, sustained, and interdenominational effort to articulate mainstream Protestant thought we must look to the religious tract and its chief sponsor, the American Tract Society.

It would be easy but misleading to lump the American Tract Society with the myriad of reform societies that blossomed before the Civil War. The millions of pages that reeled from its presses, however, offer unique insight into Protestant spiritual discourse. The society was interdenominational and committed, in the words of its commissioners, to only those "great truths of salvation in which the mass of evangelical Christians agree."[71] It was national in scope. Finally, it focused its vision on the "lower ranks of society." In contrast to theological treatises "for the learned," the organization's annual report proudly proclaimed in 1839 that the society produced literature "for the people."[72] This trio of commitments compelled the group to distribute an intellectually and financially accessible message stripped of controversial content. It is clear that Protestant leaders had plenty of worries about the "liberated" press under American democracy. They exhorted their own house to subordinate the stratagems of a print culture to the oral traditions of the pulpit. Tracts, and even the Bible itself, necessarily remained "auxiliaries" to the preached word. The absence of a spirit-led Christian breathing fire into the words of grace effectively muted Christ's gospel, they believed. Still, the zeal of the society's leadership, its financial strength, and its expansive scope affirmed Protestant enthusiasm for the press as adjunct to evangelism.

Organized in 1825 and headquartered in New York City, the society consolidated smaller tract societies that had distributed materials locally for over a decade. East Coast Congregationalists composed the intellectual and financial soul of the early movement. Distribution over the first decade barely extended beyond New York State. Troubled by a failure to reach the spiritually "destitute masses," the society in 1841 established a "colportage" system—a network of regional agents to expand circulation. The group proclaimed that the eight denominational affiliations represented by its thirty-one commissioned agents and colporteurs in 1843 established its catholic spirit.[73] Society membership exceeded ten thousand at mid-century, and annual receipts topped $100,000.[74]

No body of printed sources provides better insight into the mainstream, noncontroversial Protestant message than the society's published materials. Evidence beyond faith in the size and chartered objectives of the society compels serious consideration of its product. The leadership drew freely from historic, interdenominational, and transatlantic sources for its 522 general series tracts that were in circulation by 1850. Authors included such luminaries as Lutheran Samuel S. Schmucker, Baptist Francis Wayland, and Presbyterian Albert Barnes. Church fathers dotting the tract landscape included John Bunyan, Richard Baxter, Jonathan Edwards, and Lemuel Haynes, the first African American Congregational minister in the United States. British evangelicals such as Thomas Chalmers and Hannah More contributed several pieces. Sixteen female authors had contributed tracts by 1850. The society often exchanged materials and coordinated overseas efforts with the Religious Tract Society in London. Both groups vigorously pursued an international audience and translated seminal works into more than a dozen languages.

The intellectual diversity of the society's contributing clergy is equally revealing. The speculative tomes of men like Wayland, Finney, Barnes, Bushnell, George Duffield, Nathan Lord, and Edward Beecher generated sharp clerical debate. Yet all of these ministers participated as contributing "directors" or "life members" of the society.[75] General cooperation and consensus on the essence of spiritual discourse, in other words, enabled mainstream Protestants to sustain a spiritual community that transcended but did not deny denominational strategies. Even the society's constitutional restrictions assured a mainstream message. No two members from the same denomination could serve concurrently on the powerful Publishing Committee. More important, the veto of a single committee member eliminated a tract from consideration.[76]

Tract themes and distribution statistics make the group's consensual arena transparent. The sounding of reform issues played second to a cadence of sin, salvation, and judgment messages. Table 1 illustrates this emphasis.[77] The society disseminated twenty-three general series tracts focusing directly on temperance by 1850. None approached distribution levels comparable to those of the sixteen most widely disseminated pieces. Indeed, these sixteen tracts all trumpeted spiritual themes—"The Lost Soul," "Prepare to Meet Thy God," "For Ever!"—and total distribution of these alone outnumbered the temperance essays almost three to one. The two leading temperance tracts—"The Fool's Pence" and "Who Slew All These"—had a combined press run of 724,000 by 1850. Production numbers for the most extensively printed tract, "Quench Not the Spirit" (a personal narrative cued to "the untried realities of eternity"), dwarfed that figure with a run of nearly a million copies. Even the title

Table 1. *American Tract Society Publication Totals to 1850 for Temperance Titles and Sixteen Most-Published Titles*

Tract Number	Title	Total Printed
Temperance Tracts Included in General Series of Tracts (522 titles)		
308	The Fool's Pence	388,000
247	Who Slew All These?	336,000
159	Rewards of Drunkeness	320,000
233	Dickinson's Appeal to Youth	304,000
221	Kittredge's Address on the Effects of Ardent Spirits	264,000
422	Reformation of Drunkards	212,000
398	Lost Mechanic Restored	192,000
240	Putnam and the Wolf	180,000
25	Effects of Ardent Spirits	172,000
313	Poor Man's House Repaired	146,000
300	Debates of Conscience on Ardent Spirits	108,000
239	Alarm to Distillers	100,000
249	Sewall on Intemperance	96,000
395	Eventful Twelve Hours	92,000
346	Jamie: or a Word from Ireland on Temperance	92,000
244	M'Ilvaine's Address to Young Men on Temperance	88,000
276	Bible Argument for Temperance	84,000
288	Four Reasons against the Use of Alcoholic Liquor	80,000
242	Hitchcock on Manufacture of Ardent Spirits	76,000
305	Barnes on Traffic in Ardent Spirits	70,000
475	The Ox Sermon	68,000
125	Traffic in Ardent Spirits	50,000
443	Tom Starboard, A Nautical Temperance Dialogue	44,000
	TOTAL	3,562,000
Sixteen Most-Published Tracts		
174	Quench Not the Spirit	908,000
50	The Swearer's Prayer	796,000
241	Hope of Future Repentance	704,000

Table 1. (*Continued*)

Tract Number	Title	Total Printed
273	The Lost Soul	612,000
4	Without Holiness No Man Shall See the Lord	604,000
26	Sin, No Trifle	528,000
8	On the Lord's Day	524,000
208	Worth of a Dollar	512,000
357	What Is It to Believe on Christ?	500,000
347	Prepare to Meet Thy God	492,000
292	Are You Ready?	488,000
191	Warning to Sabbath Breakers	484,000
320	I've No Thought of Dying Soon	480,000
68	Poor Joseph	472,000
368	Don't Put It Off!	452,000
260	For Ever!	452,000
	TOTAL	9,008,000

Source: American Tract Society, *Twenty-fifth Annual Report*, 1850; *General Series of Tracts*, 12 vols., 1825–50.

of the popular tract "Worth of a Dollar" was not a paean to frugality; it exhorted believers to devote individual time and resources to personal evangelism. Some of this imbalance is explained by membership overlap with the Temperance Society, which facilitated the Tract Society's more narrowly spiritual focus. The overwhelming dominance of spiritual themes over temperance or other "moral living" pieces, however, suggests the limits of that explanation. The society's own statistical explanation of its tract themes, published in the *American Tract Magazine* in 1831, reinforces the evidence presented here and reflects a pattern sustained throughout the antebellum era. Of 265 tract titles circulating by 1831, 60 percent focused on Christian doctrines and spiritual duties, and 25 percent were personal narratives that typically recounted conversion experiences or moments of spiritual enlightenment. Only 15 percent cautioned variously against non-Protestant faiths or "intemperance and other prevalent vices." The society's emphasis dovetails with antebellum pulpit themes. It is also consistent with increasing attacks on reformist zeal as a blind for the "new infidelity." From ministers desperate to preserve the uniqueness of Protestant faith, came clerical rumblings at the confusion of spiritual religion with secular reform motives, sounding broadly across communication channels.

Millennial scenarios are conspicuously absent in this tract catalog of core Protestant themes. They rarely appeared either as spur to salvation or as impetus to Christian service. A few pieces urged believers to "labor for the conversion of the world," to "preach the gospel to every creature," and to anticipate Christ's ascendancy over the "kingdoms of this world."[78] Scriptural disagreements notwithstanding, however, millennialists, millenarians, and the majority of ministers who drifted intellectually between the two extremes could easily embrace such general heralds. Indeed, David Nathan Lord, George Duffield, and Richard W. Dickinson, perhaps the three most outspoken mainstream millenarians in antebellum America, were all contributing members to the society. The point is that ideas about the millennium were simply too controversial, speculative, and diverse to be the centerpiece of spiritual discourse. Religious priorities and pragmatic considerations overruled apocalyptic speculation, as the society's strategy demonstrates.

The opposite was true with regard to final judgment themes. Titles such as "The Duration of Future Punishment," and "The Wrath to Come" abounded. In addition to the majority of tracts that mapped the road of repentance and salvation, twenty-eight titles alternately enticed readers with promises of eternal glory and searing accounts of the flames licking at the impenitent.[79] Publication statistics reveal the significance of this theme. Press runs for the twenty-eight tracts produced more than seven million copies by 1850, nearly a million more than the total for the society's top ten tracts. An innocuous melding of Christian and secular progress, as well as instruction on good behavior, lacked the drama, consequences, and finality of the high-stakes quest for eternal bliss or misery. The millennium, however interpreted, was only a nebulous halfway house to glory. In the tract "Sixteen Short Sermons," the group established the perimeters of Protestant consensus on the apocalyptic future. Centering on the "blessed hope" of believers, the writer stressed the sudden, unexpected nature of Christ's Second Coming. The great fact was that He would come "as a thief in the night" with "mighty angels in flaming fire" and "take vengeance on them that know not God." Only the born-again believer had the "blessed hope" of escaping "everlasting destruction" and finding rest in eternity.[80] Such a message motivated readers not with the prospect of an earthly paradise but with the hope of escaping hell.

To preserve the spiritual center of its message, the society pressed

a phalanx of old heroes to the fore. Though it is commonplace to expose antebellum clerics eagerly shedding traditional theological garb,
the American Tract Society committed itself in 1835 to packing American shelves with bound volumes of classic evangelical preaching. First,
a fifteen-volume "Evangelical Family Library" was compiled. Eventually
added were a forty-five-volume "Christian Library" and a forty-volume
"Youth's Christian Library," both of which included most of the original
fifteen books. The strategy was to reaffirm commitment to and continuity with the past. The Library collection gave new life to the works of
seventeenth- and eighteenth-century English dissenters, pioneers of the
evangelical homiletic tradition. Table 2 illustrates this historic emphasis.[81] The works of Richard Baxter, Joseph Alleine, John Bunyan, Philip
Doddridge, and John Flavel accounted for well over half of all family
library titles distributed by 1850 and 20 percent of the society's total
volume output. Baxter, the Puritan patriarch of Restoration England,
alone provided one-third of the library titles distributed. The society
even printed his works and Bunyan's *Pilgrim's Progress* in raised-letter
editions for the blind.

The volumes powerfully reinforced the society's push for spiritual religion. Baxter's *Call to the Unconverted* (1657) and Alleine's *Alarm to Unconverted Sinners* (1672) remained the sine qua non of evangelical homilies
for later Protestants. Among literary masterpieces, only Milton's *Paradise
Lost* approached Bunyan's *Pilgrim's Progress* in importance among Protestant leaders. The eighteenth-century equivalent of these heralds to faith
was Doddridge's *Rise and Progress of Religion in the Soul* (1745). Wilberforce confessed Doddridge's work as instrumental to his own conversion
and influential in the production of his *Practical View of the Prevailing
Religious System of Professed Christians* (1799). A tract society writer in
1850 updated the continuity by noting that Legh Richmond, an early
society secretary, attributed his own repentance to Wilberforce's influence. Richmond's subsequent penning of the "Dairyman's Daughter," the
tract society writer noted, yielded one of the most popular transatlantic
tracts (nearly a million distributed in England and the United States
by 1850).[82]

The society's volume and tract production dovetailed with a larger body
of regular spiritual discourse that resisted an easy melding of Christian and cultural purposes. To explain antebellum religion as an extension of reformist zeal can obscure the work of Protestant defenders who

Table 2. *American Tract Society Publication Totals to 1850 for Titles Included in "Evangelical Family Library" (five volumes contain more than one title)*

Title	Number Printed
Baxter's Call to the Unconverted	357,562
Bunyan's Pilgrim's Progress	188,797
Alleine's Alarm	165,427
Baxter's Saint's Rest	163,354
Doddridge's Rise and Progress	133,858
Pike's Persuasives to Early Piety	96,614
Flavel's Keeping the Heart	89,532
Flavel's Touchstone	80,716
Pike's Guide for Young Disciples	79,253
Nevins' Practical Thoughts	79,182
Baxter's Dying Thoughts	77,877
Baxter's Life	71,631
Edwards on the Affections	62,901
Memoir of David Brainerd	58,570
Memoir of Rev. Dr. Payson	56,680
Nevins' Thoughts on Popery	52,218
Memoir of Henry Martyn	51,870
Wilberforce's Practical View	50,782
Edwards' History of Redemption	45,842
Memoir of James Brainerd Taylor	46,787
Evidences of Christianity	32,901
TOTAL	2,042,354
Total for English Dissenters Doddridge, Alleine, Bunyan, Baxter, and Flavel	1,328,754
	(65%)

Source: American Tract Society, *Twenty-fifth Annual Report*, 1850.

labored on several fronts to sustain a more precise hierarchy. One minister summed up the task: There existed within the culture a separate "Christian community," and the "extension of its walls" required "bringing individual souls . . . to actual repentance." Claims on its power to correct social abuses and "meliorate the moral condition" of the "public conscience" remained legitimate but forever "occasional," "secondary," and "collateral" to its separate, primary mandate to "labor directly to promote the kingdom of Christ."[83]

Spiritual discourse also marked the perimeters of a community of the

Word in which believers reveled in truths and spiritual realities that they placed beyond the larger culture's comprehension. Consequently, simple, forceful messages of sin, salvation, and judgment became acts of cultural dissent in themselves. Themes of gospel simplicity, spiritual unity, and transcendent destiny had little in common with the cultural complexity and intellectual diversity that were the hallmarks of emergent liberal culture. An understanding of the clergy's hierarchy of civic and spiritual aims provides a better understanding of the extent, as well as the limits, of the antebellum Protestant quarrel with the Republic. In defending a destiny beyond the Commonwealth, Protestants also tapped a vein of exceptionalist zeal secured from the uncertainties that draped their republican and millennial visions.

Conclusion

When noted Unitarian divine Henry Bellows addressed the alumni of Harvard Divinity School in 1859, he quickly extinguished any anticipations of extended accolades. He chose "the suspense of faith" as his theme and urged battle against a cultural transformation that had gone far beyond his own liberal vision. Liberal and orthodox leaders alike, he charged, had proved unable to check the secular flow of liberty. The culture flaunted the "easy conscience of the people in the profound secularity of their lives." To declare genuine popular religious belief as anything but a "revered memory," he charged, was beyond what "a just discrimination would allow." The nation had created its own "substitutes for religion;" keeping the "forms of faith" while practically declaring "the irrelevancy of the things themselves."[1] His blunt religious jeremiad attracted high praise from the *New Englander*—not for its predictable indictment of orthodoxy but for its ironic consonance with forebodings that had long been issuing from orthodox pulpits. The Congregationalist reviewer also instructed Bellows in language that encompassed the essence of antebellum Protestantism's spiritual discourse: "The confusion and unbelief of the age," he protested, called for the "distinguishing principles of the gospel, as these have lived in believing hearts and minds from the Apostolic age until now." Dependence on "external institutions" instead of a more vital faith in the "distinguishing principles of the gospel" was no more than a "house built on the sand."[2]

The burden of this analysis has been to explain how and why the antebellum Protestant community sustained the capacity to resist uncritical cultural accommodation. By the 1830s, clerical critics worried that transatlantic materialism and emergent liberal culture had turned American liberty strangely against their forebears' hopes of Protestant triumph. They warned by mid-century that liberty had created a "new infidelity" far more threatening than Catholicism or Enlightenment assaults on biblical supernaturalism. This new liberal order offered its deepest bows to democracy and human freedom. It promised to raise a better world of benevolence, social justice, and humanitarian purpose from the ashes of the old faith. Liberty and American abundance, Protestant dissenters grumbled, had combined to elevate not the grandeur and authority of God but a grander potential within humanity itself. This radical change produced significant critical resistance across sectarian lines. Fears of weakness and cultural compromise within the community of faith provided a powerful internal impetus to this dissent. Finally, it drew added strength from a sense of separateness and superiority rooted more deeply in religious purpose and historic antecedents than in cultural confidence.

Protestant spiritual discourse, anchored by religious jeremiads and regular sermons, was the primary carrier of this quarrel with the Republic. It drew on historic conceptions of faith and mission and offered no easy endorsements of cultural arrogance. These messages placed faith's temporal benefits on a fulcrum that gave weighted advantage to a transcendent spirituality beyond the Commonwealth. They sustained in the process a significant measure of resistance to the confounding of Christianity and culture. Antebellum spiritual discourse did not betray the deep social pessimism and intellectual isolation that later characterized twentieth-century "fundamentalism." But this body of communication presented faith's capacity to improve society as a subordinate aim, offering benefits but not redemptive significance to material culture. It rebuked the pretensions of "Christendom" as a materialist threat to the eternal, spiritual claims of religion. Declaring Protestantism's exclusive, transcendent claims—not the material rewards of a coming millennium—was the strategy of choice for worried ministers. Liberty from the "yoke of sin" remained the radical, supernatural alternative to liberal culture's endorsement of the "peaceful progress of natural laws and a normal development of human nature."

In 1965, David E. Smith told scholars that exploring the interrelationship of American millennialism and nationalism offered possibilities for research that would "not be exhausted for some time."[3] More than a quarter of a century later, it is possible that we are approaching that limit. Historians of religion have given full due to American millennial thought and integrated this work carefully into the broader theme of how religion functioned as a vehicle of cultural values. Thanks to their efforts, we know that millennialism influenced Protestant thought and that ministers, in their civic discourse, often explained religion as boon to the Republic. Certain conclusions—that producing the millennium virtually defined antebellum Protestant purpose; that clergymen easily linked America and the kingdom of God; that belief in Christianity's cultural utility necessarily precluded meaningful dissent; that clerical complaints are best explained when linked to social or political purpose— must remain interpretive calls on the evidence if we are to sustain further inquiry and continue to expand our understanding of how Protestants responded to the rise of liberal America. Exploring a more critical dimension of Protestant thought is essential to illuminating the tensions and anxieties that shaped that response.

In the half-century after 1860, mainstream Protestantism plunged whole-heartedly into preserving one or the other half of the old evangelical equation. Social gospelers like Baptist theologian Walter Rauschenbusch cast Protestantism as the conscience of American culture. They labeled battles against individual sin anachronistic and declared a new war on the social chaos endemic to urbanization and industrialization. Rauschenbusch, the premier exponent of the new religious agenda, demolished old priorities that put eternity and judgment ahead of time and social improvement. Protestants obsessed with saving individual souls and building a spiritual kingdom, he explained, failed to comprehend Jesus the reformer. The Christian hope, he insisted, must be a "social hope" involving the "whole social life of man." It was not a matter of "getting individuals into heaven" but of "transforming the life on Earth into the harmony of heaven." Now the prospective paradise needed only brotherly love and cooperation to purge it of social and economic injustice and consummate the social transformation that Jesus had begun.[4]

Protestants hostile to evolutionary thought and the strident, muscular liberalism of the social gospelers retreated with varying intensity toward fundamentalism. Generally these divines refired the antebellum torch for the eternal dimension of faith, but without the penetrating and thoughtful critique of culture that shaped the antebellum religious jeremiads. To be sure, popular evangelists like D. L. Moody and his successor Billy Sunday furiously assaulted the rationalist thrust behind evolutionary naturalism.[5] But by the 1920s, a premillennial gloom limited fundamentalist will to sustain a credible, critical dialogue with the larger culture. The defense of extreme biblical literalism consumed the bulk of the movement's critical energies. The carefully constructed religious jeremiads of an earlier day would have struck these new evangelicals as an exercise in futility. Better to call men to conversion, spurn the larger culture, and await Christ's personal, cataclysmic vengeance on a degenerating world.

Fundamentalism and the social gospel, then, fragmented the antebellum Protestant struggle by isolating and alternately distorting its temporal and eternal components. Through either aloofness or assimilation, each Protestant contingent rejected the effort to sustain a socially and spiritually productive tension between Christianity and culture. Extremism engulfed the Protestant camp. One group tossed out sin and theology while the other forgot society. Reintegration of the antebellum Protestant strategy had to await the "neo-orthodox" revolt led by Reinhold and H. Richard Niebuhr. The two German evangelical theologians reinvigorated Augustinian notions of human sinfulness and declared the liberal-fundamentalist feud a plague on the church. They indicted fundamentalism as socially impotent and blasted Protestant liberalism for being spiritually bankrupt. Their aggressive intellectual force, as well as their intellectual proximity to modern scholars, has overshadowed the antebellum antecedents to their twentieth-century jeremiads. Nevertheless, certain similarities are compelling and invite analysis beyond the scope of this brief mention.

The Niebuhrs' writings have provided scholars with a rich store of social analysis and political and economic insights. A full understanding of their ethical and political positions, however, must also comprehend the theological and spiritual salvage mission that inspired the two men. As ministers, scholars, and prolific writers, they decried the cultural and spiritual impotence of modern Protestantism. Their early flirtations with social gospel optimism changed to resolute opposition by the 1930s. From their respective positions at New York's Union Theological Seminary and the Yale Divinity School, Reinhold and H. Richard Niebuhr worked to preserve spiritual religion from the materialism and secular idealism that denied its relevance. They sought to temper the political, social, and moral arrogance of humankind by linking each individual's ultimate destiny to divine faith. The gospel's central purpose was not to effect a material kingdom in history but to rescue man from the inescapable limitations of historical development and place his ultimate hopes in an omnipotent God through Christ. Only then, they believed, could individuals achieve indifference to material gain and attempt "proximate victories" over collective greed and selfishness within time.

Antebellum divines had feared the results of expanding liberty and materialism. In 1941 Reinhold Niebuhr concluded that a growing working class was "almost universally inimical to religion," and represented an antireligious sentiment "entirely new in history." Both liberal Protestantism and fundamentalism had responded to the challenge with a common "psychology of defeat." "Frantic" orthodoxy was little more than a smoke-screen for uncertainty and doubt. Liberalism tried to cloak its strategic theological retreats as "victorious engagements." It had allowed a potentially beneficial adaptive spirit to become a wholesale sellout to culture. As a tack for sustaining the relevance of religion in society, he warned, this approach "secularized religion itself" and made it little more than a "harmless adornment of the moral life."[6]

Niebuhr admitted that religion's spiritual dimension threatened to produce an unacceptable indifference to social chaos and human suffering. This vulnerability, however, represented a possible rather than a necessary result, he believed. The modern church's embarrassment about its eschatological tradition had produced a spiritually debilitating obsession with the "mundane interests of religious idealism." Only religion's otherworldly character could sustain its dynamic and socially productive conflict with sin, cultural pretension, and systematic evil, Niebuhr believed. By providing eternal hope beyond history and human power, Christianity was peculiarly adapted to rebuke the "primal sin" of human pride and to "condemn the world without enervating life."[7]

Niebuhr's thought most tellingly dovetails with antebellum clerical concerns in his apprehensions about the confluence of human freedom and human sinfulness. Sin and evil could never be erased from human history, Niebuhr believed, and the theological impotence of the modern church had wrongly allied itself with secular idealism in declaring sin an outmoded concept. Like his antebellum predecessors who railed that "infidel systems" were feeding on the lexicon of American liberty, Niebuhr pronounced liberal capitalism, communism, and fascism as impersonal, systemic variants of human pride. All defined redemption in terms of material well-being. Civilizations rose and fell, he argued, not because of human ignorance or technical or political flaws but because of collective sin—the willful denial of human finitude and the creation of secular "idolatrous religions." Man's penchant for self-worship inevitably corrupted his efforts and set limits to all human schemes. "The sin of man lies in the corruption of his will and not in his weakness," Niebuhr told the inaugural meeting of the World Council of Churches in 1948. Consequently, "the possibilities of evil grow with the development of the very freedom and power which were supposed to emancipate man."[8] The church must extricate itself from "vainglorious" political struggles and testify to the "final freedom" beyond history. Niebuhr's consciousness of universal sin against God forever separated his own vision from the Marxist critique of capitalism with which he often sympathized. In his worldview, technological freedom and power in the twentieth century confirmed not humanity's inevitable progress but its intractable infirmities. Niebuhr wanted a socially responsible religion, but he ultimately blamed the world's problems on spiritual, not material, failures.

The antebellum clergy's struggle to sustain both core and peripheral concerns found new life in H. Richard Niebuhr's work. While his brother dissected the collective sins of the culture, Niebuhr drilled the church on how cultural secularism had destroyed the theological foundation on which Christian community and a coherent religious vision depended. In his essay contributions to *The Church against the World* (1935), Niebuhr deplored the secularism that governed modern ideological conflict. Marxism accurately exposed capitalist avarice, he admitted, but its own economic determinism merely restated a transideological "economic faith." Communism's redemptive plan was merely a "variant of the capitalist religion." As the church complied with the terms of the debate it implicitly declared its own irrelevance by depriving itself of a unique communal vision. This flawed strategy of adaptation rendered the church a "captive" of modern anthropocentrism.[9]

Modern "idolatries" had perverted the core Christian message, Niebuhr thundered. Alienated from its historic theological roots, the church could no longer define its own purpose. Compromise and mimicry replaced independent conflict with the culture. Liberal Protestantism had mistaken its sympathy for universal social ideals of liberty, equality, and fraternity with true religion. Its proponents had forgotten that popular struggles against "self-righteousness and power politics" ultimately succumbed to their own success. The oppressed inevitably became the oppressors because human selfishness was not class-bound. In short, the ultimate Christian folly was to attempt religious revival by choosing among "revolting secular movements."[10]

Niebuhr's spiritual vision and social critique addressed modern ideological turmoil and the dislocations of industrial capitalism. Yet his sense of human sinfulness, his distrust of secular political culture, and his embrace of a transcendent solution beyond the social crisis recalled the themes of late antebellum dissenters. His conception of religious mission was not identical to theirs. Neither was it as far removed from their views as might be imagined. As earlier divines had struggled to balance faith's temporal capacities with eternal priorities amid expanding liberty, so Niebuhr confessed similar frustrations in his own time:

> How to be in the world and yet not of the world has always been the problem of the church. It is a revolutionary community in a pre-

revolutionary society. Its main task remains that of understanding, proclaiming and preparing for the divine revolution in human life. Nevertheless, there remains the necessity of participation in the affairs of an unconverted and unreborn world. Hence the church's strategy always has a dual character and the dualism is in constant danger of being resolved into the monism of otherworldliness or this worldliness. . . . How to maintain the dualism without sacrifice of the main revolutionary interest constitutes one of the important problems of a church moving toward its independence.[11]

Niebuhr's cause recalls that of antebellum divines who warned against a "new infidelity's" encroachment on the community of the Word. The social power of religion remained for Niebuhr an important but contingent cause.

The Niebuhrian vision has been praised for its political insights and cultural dissent. We must also give full attention to its antebellum antecedents. The Niebuhrs' spiritual remedies for cultural malaise did not turn on a strictly material response to their critical insights. Their assessments drew as much from historic Augustinian and evangelical roots—faith in the reality of sin, salvation, and judgment—as from a pragmatic assessment of modern historical realities. And like their antebellum predecessors, they worried about how to maintain religion's spiritual integrity and independence in an environment of unlimited freedom.

Finally, the fact that antebellum divines established a rhetorical framework for dissent within the context of orthodoxy is at least as worthy of note as the prescriptive analysis of neo-orthodoxy. The Niebuhrs wielded a heavier critical ax, particularly in their attack on church abuses. They benefited from witnessing transatlantic cultural pretensions—fascism, Stalinism, corporate capitalism—in their corrupted maturity. They honed their objections on a conviction that Protestants had responded to the challenge with a spiritual failure of nerve. But clerical worries that democratic freedom, materialistic idealism, and simple human selfishness could combine to make religion subservient to secular cultural aims were not new in the 1930s. Clergymen confronting the expansive freedom of emergent liberal culture in the late antebellum Republic had already surveyed the perimeters of the conflict.

Notes

Introduction

1. Several of these works are discussed below. Other examples include Maclear, "The Republic and the Millennium"; Berens, *Providence and Patriotism*; Walters, *American Reformers*, 24–28; Barkun, *Crucible of the Millennium*; Johnson, *Shopkeeper's Millennium*; and Maddex, "Proslavery Millennialism." The inspiration for many of these works was H. Richard Niebuhr, *Kingdom of God in America*. Two early works that discuss millennialism and Protestant social concerns are Bodo, *Protestant Clergy and Public Issues*, and Cole, *Social Ideas of the Northern Evangelists*. Older influential works on related themes include Tawney, *Religion and the Rise of Capitalism*; Weber, *The Protestant Ethic and the Spirit of Capitalism*; and Haroutonian, *Piety vs. Moralism*.

2. Hatch, *The Sacred Cause of Liberty*; Moorhead, *American Apocalypse*; Albanese, *Sons of the Fathers*. C. C. Goen argued that antebellum religious nationalism and buoyant millennial optimism helped spur disunion in 1860. Beleaguered by sectionally triggered denominational infighting and obsessed with America as the New Jerusalem, evangelical leaders rejected the conciliatory and rational path that could have helped avert war. Goen pronounced them guilty of a "moral failure of enormous proportions." See Goen, *Broken Churches, Broken Nation*.

3. Bellows, "Religious Liberty," 10–11; Phelps, "Theory of Preaching," 284, 295. The "Protestant quarrel" outlined in Phelps's essay in some ways anticipates the terms of dissent and cultural analysis usually associated with twentieth-century neo-orthodoxy. See, for example, H. Richard Niebuhr, *Christ and Culture*.

4. Most mainstream Protestants expected Christ's millennial reign to be the outgrowth of world evangelism and the conversion of individual souls. This "new world order" required the Holy Spirit's regenerative power but not the apocalyptic, "premillennial" return of Christ anticipated by some believers. Yet diversity of opinion expanded well beyond this chasm. Disagreement as to timing, accompanying historical contingencies, and the extent of earthly renovations made millennial speculations more a source of lively debate than a unifying, organizing rationale for evangelism or immediate cultural assessment. As Jon Butler aptly observes, "no single millennialist vision emerged in the early national period" (Butler, *Awash in a Sea of Faith*, 216). My analysis of regular preaching in Chapter 5 suggests that ministers were generally more interested in burdening listeners with the eternal consequences of unbelief than in tempting them with cultural optimism or millennial delights. In short, if most Protestants sighted a millennium

way station in God's certain triumph over evil, diversity, and uncertainty kept this "optimistic" long view from eliminating the immediate critical assessments and doubts about cultural change that complicated Protestant hopes. For a good contemporary summation of the debate see Nathan Lord, "The Millennium." Scholarly interest in millennialism as a vehicle of Protestant cultural endorsement has likewise been accompanied by significant diversity. A concise outline of recent millennial scholarship can be found in Dietrich Buss, "Meeting of Heaven and Earth." For a good discussion of the complexity within antebellum millennial expectations with less emphasis on the cultural dissent from which much of that complexity derived see Moorhead, "Between Progress and Apocalypse."

5. Charles G. Sellers offers the latest variant on this millennial theme in his sweeping analysis of antebellum capitalism: "Sanctifying entrepreneurial visions of a disciplined capitalist society, the mainline clergy channeled the Moderate Light's gradualist millennialism into a cultural imperialism that would create a Christian capitalist republic" (Sellers, *Market Revolution*, 211).

6. New social historians—Rhys Isaac, Gary Nash, and Sean Wilentz, for example—have denied the intellectual hegemony of early national elites. They argue that ordinary folks used liberty to conform religion and politics to their own republican and millennial expectations. See Isaac, *Transformation of Virginia*; Nash, *The Urban Crucible*; and Wilentz, *Chants Democratic*.

7. Parrington, *Main Currents in American Political Thought*, 1:148–63. Perry Miller, "From the Covenant to the Revival." Miller's essay was a historiographical jeremiad in its own right, a critical rejoinder to scholars who refused to consider religion as a motivational force in American political thought.

8. See Heimert, *Religion and the American Mind*; Bailyn, *Ideological Origins of the American Revolution*; Bellah, "Civil Religion in America"; and Tuveson, *Redeemer Nation*. On American political ideology, see, in addition to Bailyn, Wood, *Creation of the American Republic*. Heimert contended that the Revolutionary generation could trace its progressive republican vision to Jonathan Edwards's millennial ideas and to the "radical and emphatic definitions of liberty and equality" produced by the New Light faith of the Great Awakening. Bailyn also rejected Enlightenment rationalism as the primary source of Revolutionary thought, but he identified classical republican ideology as its intellectual core. Clergymen, he argued, were able exponents of classical ideals. Tuveson took a broader focus and explained how millennialism burst narrow theological confines and helped shape a national "sacred" republican mission to the world. Bellah defined nationalized faith as a "civil religion." He described a constellation of abstract principles—equality, justice, love, public spiritedness—that mollified American heterogeneity by sanctifying a collective intellectual identity.

9. Nathan Hatch found New England clerics sacralizing liberty and embracing a new republican eschatology by 1776. Cushing Strout called the amalgam "political religion." The genesis of this new faith is widely disputed. Its prevalence by 1825, however, has gained widespread scholarly acceptance. On the debate over the sources and limits of civil millennial thought see, for example, Strout, *The New Heavens and the New Earth*; Hatch, *The Sacred Cause of Liberty*, 170–75; Stout, *New England Soul*, 7; Endy, "Just War, Holy War, and Millennialism," 25; Bloch, "Social and Political Bases of Millennial Literature," and *Visionary Repub-*

lic; Berens, *Providence and Patriotism*, 164–70; and Davidson, *Logic of Millennial Thought*. For a particularly useful study of religion's broad impact on colonial culture see Patricia Bonomi, *Under the Cope of Heaven*.

10. Cherry, *God's New Israel*, 16–18. This definition draws on Emile Durkheim's argument that man's conceptual framework is actually, though not rhetorically, bounded by immediate social context. Consequently, religion's single resource for transcendent, "sacred" meaning is the collective moral mandates of society itself. Religion and its priests must affirm the cultural pretensions which sustain their own "reality." For an excellent collection of Durkheim's writings on religion, see Pickering, *Durkheim on Religion*.

11. Geertz, *Interpretation of Cultures*, 253–54.

12. Bercovitch, *American Jeremiad*, 176; Marty, *Protestantism in the United States*, 120–25; Turner, *Without God, Without Creed*, 83–84, 266–69. See also Stavely, *Puritan Legacies*; Clifford Clark, "Changing Nature of Protestantism," 832–46; Marsden, *Fundamentalism and American Culture*, 50; Marsden, *Evangelical Mind and the New School Presbyterian Experience*, 182–97.

13. For an important recent effort to blend modern social criticism with historic reticence, see Lasch, *True and Only Heaven*. Lasch's critique of Americans and the idea of progress adds to recent revisionism by restoring a sense of human limitation and material skepticism to such key figures as Jonathan Edwards.

14. See, for example, Perry Miller, *Life of the Mind in America*. 3–95; and H. Richard Niebuhr, *Kingdom of God in America*. Miller's respect for Puritan intellect did not obtain for nineteenth-century mainline Protestantism, which he tagged as hopelessly sentimental and critically impotent. In a useful examination of Miller's assessment, James Moorhead argues that leading antebellum Protestant "intellectuals" are unjustly described as "parochial, archaic or out of touch with life." They remained broadly influential in the popular Protestant community, and more culturally and theologically creative than Miller allows. See Moorhead, "Perry Miller's Jeremiad," 318. To Moorhead's thoughtful critique we may add that Protestant analysis and criticism of transformations in rationalist strategies (examined below) suggest both vital and critical religious and intellectual sensibilities at odds with what Miller called an antebellum "rigor mortis of the mind."

15. Bercovitch, for example, is on solid ground when he claims that Protestant political jeremiads (Fourth of July, Thanksgiving, national fast day, and other commemorative addresses) preached a message of "self-castigation and renewal" that never transcended the revolutionary limitations intrinsic to dissent "from within." Ministers predicted God's ultimate triumph and eschewed cultural rejection as "monastic" piety necessarily at odds with the evangelical mission. Consequently, republican loyalty, the missionary impulse, and confidence in an all-powerful deity ruled out Protestant "despair" and, as Bercovitch suggests, kept the political jeremiads from demanding radical political or material alternatives to middle-class hegemony. Accepting the absence of radical potential as a sufficient indication of Protestant optimism and accommodation, we may conclude with Bercovitch that these political sermons could serve the Standing Order as both chronic and ironic celebrations of an American status quo. But a narrow conception of dissent that explains religion's lack of revolutionary potential

over time also assumes a constant and comprehensive harmony between religion and culture that carries its own analytical limitations. The conclusion that the Protestant message inevitably apotheosized a progressive "American" dream indistinguishable from the Protestant mission relies too heavily on the explanatory self-sufficiency of Protestant civic discourse. The jeremiad assumes a static social and political purpose that resists analysis of its critical and profoundly religious turn when ministers addressed *believers* rather than "Americans." Bercovitch, *American Jeremiad*, xi–xvi, 176–210.

16. Bozeman, *To Live Ancient Lives*; Hatch, *Democratization of American Christianity*, 14; and Butler, *Awash in a Sea of Faith*. See also Lasch, *True and Only Heaven*, 247–56; Timothy L. Smith, "Afterword" in *Revivalism and Social Reform*, 257–58, and "Righteousness and Hope"; David D. Hall, "Of Common Ground"; and Bozeman, "The Puritans' Errand." For a review of recent Puritan studies, see Wood, "Struggle over the Puritans." On the Revolutionary period, see, for example, Endy, "Just War, Holy War, and Millennialism"; Valeri, "The New Divinity and the American Revolution"; and Weber, *Rhetoric and History in Revolutionary New England*. Weber examines the rhetorical legacy of Jonathan Edwards's New Divinity theology with an eye to the "multivalent aspect of Revolutionary rhetoric." He finds New Divinity discourse fully capable of harnessing otherworldly themes to a ritualized reworking of historical understanding in light of Revolutionary change.

17. Wiebe, *Opening of American Society*, 146. Charles Sellers's analysis of market capitalism's cultural dominance offers added insight into the scope and pace of change by the 1830s. He emphasizes that economic rebound after 1826 "set off the decisive phase of market revolution, cultural as well as economic." As a "cultural revolution," however, the expansive impact of the market incited Protestant resistance more substantial than Sellers acknowledges. See Sellers, *Market Revolution*, 237.

18. Appleby, *Capitalism and a New Social Order*, 50.

19. Wiebe, *Opening of American Society*. Wiebe's cultural conceptualization, especially his emphasis on a "revolution in choices," has been especially helpful in shaping my own views of clerical responses to cultural transformation. For a recent discussion of the debate over historical methodology in the study of religion, see Noll, "'And the Lion Shall Lie Down with the Lamb.'"

20. Hurst, *Law and the Condition of Freedom*, 6–7.

21. Bushnell, "Regeneration," 109.

22. Stout, *New England Soul*, 6, 148–65. Stout's interpretive tour de force invites a reconsideration of sermonic evidence beyond the confines of the colonial era as well.

23. Scott, *From Office to Profession*.

24. Handy, *A Christian America*.

Chapter 1

1. Francis Asbury Hester Diary, November 2 and 20, 1844, Francis Asbury Hester Papers.

2. Ibid., July 4 and 24, 1845.

3. Boles, *Religion in Antebellum Kentucky*; on the revival in New York, see Whitney R. Cross, *The Burned-Over District*. More recently, see Paul Johnson, *Shopkeeper's Millennium*.

4. Boles, *Great Revival*, xi.

5. Doggett, "Christ and Pilate," 322–26.

6. Bushnell, "American Politics," 192–94.

7. Augustine, *City of God*, 5.15–22; *Letters*, CXXXVIII, 9–15, in *Political Writings of Augustine*, 98, 106, 180. In many ways, Augustine's views of the state are not radically different from the nineteenth-century Protestant understanding. Augustine never urged complete Christian indifference to the state. Both traditions understood civil government as a divinely ordained check on human sinfulness that had temporal but not eternal significance. Both also insisted that Christianity could improve the condition of a commonwealth as a contingent result of pursuing its primary salvific mission. On Augustine's views of Christianity and the state see Herbert A. Deane, *Political and Social Ideas of St. Augustine*. On Augustine's legacy within the Protestant tradition, Deane notes, "Lutheran and Calvinist views of human nature and of political authority carry clear marks of their Augustinian origin" (234–35).

8. Skinner, *Foundations of Modern Political Thought*, 1:50, 91, 134–35, 182–85, 248–50; 2:50, 26.

9. "Confessions of Augustine," 483–88. See also Edward Beecher, *Conflict of Ages*, 279, and "The Life and Labours of St. Augustine," review essay in *Biblical Repertory and Princeton Review* 26 (July 1854). The critical potential of the Augustinian political tradition survived in spite of Thomas Aquinas's influential efforts to reconcile Christian and classical thought. On Aquinas, see Knowles, *Evolution of Medieval Thought* and Skinner, *Foundations of Modern Political Thought*, 1:50–51.

10. Skinner, *Foundations of Modern Political Thought*, 1:50.

11. Doggett, "Christ and Pilate," 322–25.

12. Scot, "Christ's Politician."

13. Baxter, "Holy Commonwealth," 77, 92.

14. Milton, "Paradise Regained," bk. 4, lines 313–21.

15. Bozeman, *To Live Ancient Lives*, 265–86.

16. Ibid.

17. J. C. D. Clark, *English Society, 1688–1832*.

18. Edwards, *Nature of True Virtue*, 21, 25–26, 78–79. For another perspective on this treatise, see Lasch, *True and Only Heaven*, 251–56.

19. Hatch, *Sacred Cause of Liberty*, 97–138. Note also the survival of explicit spiritual principles in early state documents. Pennsylvania's Declaration of Rights (1776), for example, outlawed any religious test for members of the state's House of Representatives, provided each member swore the following: "I do believe in one God, the creator and governor of the universe, the rewarder of good and the punisher of the wicked. And I do acknowledge the Scriptures of the Old and New Testament to be given by divine inspiration." Virginia's Declaration of Rights (1776) acknowledged that all citizens must practice "Christian forbearance, love, and charity toward each other." See Schwartz, *Roots of the Bill of Rights*, 262–75, 231–50.

20. Stiles, "The United States Exalted to Glory and Honor," 403, 454, 503.

21. Ibid., 505–6. On Stiles, see Morgan, *Gentle Puritan.*

22. "Relations of Law and a Reverential Spirit to Individual and National Prosperity," 392. On classical political thought in the Constitutional period, see Wood, *Creation of the American Republic.* For an assessment that stresses the complex intellectual traditions influencing early American political thought, see McDonald, *Novus Ordo Seclorum.* On contemporary Protestant reaction to the French Revolution, see Hatch, *Sacred Cause of Liberty,* and Bloch, *Visionary Republic.* For Jean-Jacques Rousseau's views on "civil religion" and pietistic religion as politically enervating, see Rousseau, *Of the Social Contract.*

23. Noah Webster, "Improving the Advantages and Perpetuating the Union," 30.

24. Noah Webster, "Nothing So Fatal to Truth and Tranquillity," 126.

25. Noah Webster to Thomas Dawes, December 20, 1808, in *Letters of Noah Webster,* 314.

26. Noah Webster, *Political, Literary, and Moral Subjects,* 336.

27. Ibid., 292.

28. Ibid., 271.

29. Ibid., 288.

30. Stewart J. Brown, *Thomas Chalmers and Godly Commonwealth in Scotland.*

31. Chalmers, "The Emptiness of Natural Virtue," 386, 390, 396.

32. Chalmers, "The Importance of Civil Government to Society," 338, 345–48.

33. Chalmers, "Sermon VIII: The Nature of the Kingdom of God," 306.

34. Wilberforce, *A Practical View of the Prevailing Religious System Contrasted with Real Christianity,* 375, 393.

35. Ibid., 394.

36. Howe, *Political Culture of the American Whigs,* 15. An insightful recent essay by Howe clearly demonstrates the influence of evangelicalism on antebellum political culture broadly conceived. Given that level of civic involvement (especially amid the laity's reformist zeal, as Howe emphasizes) in a liberal culture that daily probed new frontiers beyond the spiritual constraints of orthodoxy, it is hardly surprising that worried ministers across confessional-evangelical lines exploited the critical resources of spiritual discourse to interdict an accommodative free-fall. As we shall see, these defenders argued that erasing critical distinctions between spiritual and cultural agencies vitiated the transcendent spiritual loyalties that could also yield the collateral benefits that Howe explains. In essence, my study reinforces Howe's perceptive observation that recent scholarship has "vindicated the perception of the Progressive historians that American history has been characterized by profound conflict." See Howe, "Evangelical Movement and Political Culture." 1216–39.

37. Douglass, *Sermons,* 162–63.

38. In addition to Howe's thorough analysis of evangelical influence on Whig thought, see also Ashworth, *Agrarians and Aristocrats.*

39. "Desultory Remarks upon the Closing Year."

40. "Dangers of Our Country," 519.

41. *Episcopal Recorder,* March 17, 1849.

42. Schmucker, "Evangelical Lutheran Church," 402.

43. Catharine Beecher, "An Address to the Protestant Clergy of the United States," 21.

44. Ferm, *Crisis in American Lutheran Theology*, 129–30; Claude Welch correctly notes that rationalist challenges to orthodox theology spurred a mid-nineteenth century Protestant yearning for "restoration and recovery," among revivalists and conservatives alike. Welch's emphasis is on comparing and contrasting the theological positions of major transatlantic theologians, however, and not on developing the broader relationship and influence of this conservation effort on mainstream Protestant thought. Walter Conser addresses similar themes in his analysis of confessional Protestantism in an effort to contrast it with the cultural complacency of other mainline groups. See Welch, *Protestant Thought in the Nineteenth Century*; Conser, *Church and Confession*.

45. *Biblical Repertory and Princeton Review* 26 (July 1854).

46. Holmes, "Restoration Ideology among Early Episcopal Evangelicals," 157. On the nature of antebellum restoration movements, see also Shipps, *Mormonism*, 41–85.

47. William Warren Sweet, *Religion in the Development of American Culture* and *Revivalism in America*. See also Bodo, *The Protestant Clergy and Public Issues, 1812–1848*.

48. Griffin, "Religious Benevolence as Social Control," 423–44; Johnson, *Shopkeeper's Millennium*; Ryan, *Cradle of the Middle Class*, 103–4. See also Banner, "Religious Benevolence as Social Control." For a judicious assessment of evangelical motivation and the issue of social control within the context of nineteenth-century reform movements, see Walters, *American Reformers*, 21–37.

49. Hatch, *Democratization of American Christianity*, 14.

50. Butler, *Awash in a Sea of Faith*, 286–87. For Hatch's assessment of Johnson, see *Democratization of American Christianity*, 224–26.

51. "The Times, Morally Considered," 73.

52. "Eclipse of Faith," 108.

Chapter 2

1. Lincoln, "Perpetuation of our Political Institutions." Basler notes that by 1836, the lyceum was "one of the leading forums in the cultural activity of Springfield."

2. Ibid.

3. McLoughlin, *Cherokee Renascence*, xvi.

4. W. A. Scott, "Hope of Republics," 75; Lyman Beecher, *Plea for the West*.

5. Daniel Webster, "Adams and Jefferson."

6. "Eulogies on Adams and Jefferson," 260–68. Note similar attempts to distance Adams's and Jefferson's republican achievements from spiritual enlightenment in *Methodist Quarterly Review* 9 (August 1826): 317.

7. Bates, "Christian Patriotism," 290.

8. Lord, "On Special Efforts by the Church to Subvert the Unhallowed Institutions of the World," 447, 451. In the same year, a New York Lutheran pastor offered similar conclusions. See Thummel, "Nature of Christ's Kingdom and

Qualifications it Requires in the Believer," *Evangelical Lutheran Preacher*, 1–5.

9. Lord, "Special Efforts," 451.

10. On Wayland's early life, see Francis Wayland and H. L. Wayland, *Memoir*.

11. On Wayland as moralist, see Meyer, *Instructed Conscience*.

12. Wayland, *Memoir*, 2:140.

13. Wayland, "Moral Dignity of the Missionary Enterprise," 17. See also Chapter 3.

14. Wayland, "The Church of Christ," 322–23.

15. Wayland, "A Consistent Piety the Demand of the Age," 154–55.

16. Wayland, "The Apostolic Ministry," 19.

17. Wayland, *Memoir*, 2:136.

18. Ibid., 2:172.

19. See discussion in Chapter 5 of Wayland, *Letters on the Ministry of the Gospel*.

20. Noll, ed., *Charles Hodge*.

21. Hodge, "The Catholicity of the Gospel," 322, 324, 326–33.

22. Ibid., 324.

23. Davis W. Clark, "Allegiance Due to Christ," Davis W. Clark Papers.

24. "Circular Letter," Edgefield Baptist Association, *Minutes* (1834).

25. Young, "Sermon to the Society for the Propagation of the Gospel in Foreign Parts," 132.

26. Wayland, "Slavery to Public Opinion," 201–2.

27. Post, "Review of Democracy in America," 250, 289.

28. See Howe, *Political Culture of the American Whigs*, esp. Chapter 7. See also Ashworth, *Agrarians and Aristocrats*. Evangelical ideas certainly helped shape Whig rhetoric and gave Protestants an important avenue of social and political influence. But in the religious jeremiads, ministers harped incessantly on the danger of allowing cultural standards to define the purposes of faith. Consequently Protestant leaders often acknowledged social applications as backdrop to a more arduous defense of Protestant spiritual ascendancy.

29. "Some Characteristics of the Present Age," 436.

30. Harris, "The Dependence of Popular Progress upon Christianity," 436, 437, 443, 447.

31. Ibid., 444.

32. Ibid., 450.

33. Bushnell, "Regeneration," 113.

34. *Puritan Recorder*, cited in Cheney, *Life and Letters of Horace Bushnell*, 226.

35. Ibid., 225, 231, 338–39. For a recent analysis that emphasizes the intellectual power behind Bushnell's social views, see Howe, "The Social Science of Horace Bushnell."

36. Cheney, *Life and Letters of Horace Bushnell*, 339.

37. Bushnell, "Parting Words," 17–18. Bushnell made his core principle clear: "Assert, above all, and stand by the assertion of, a supernatural gospel; for there is, in fact, no other."

38. Bushnell, "American Politics," 200.

39. Ibid., 199–200.

40. Cheney, *Life and Letters of Horace Bushnell*, 192–93.

41. Ibid., 229.

42. Ibid.

43. Warren Baptist Association, *Minutes*, 1841.

44. "Religious Liberty in America," *Home Missionary*, 305–6, 310–11.

45. On James's popularity among American Protestants and his central place among English evangelicals, see Carwardine, *Transatlantic Revivalism*.

46. James, *James's Christian Professor*, 138, 140. In praising the book, an American Methodist reviewer looked beyond Wesleyan objections to James's Calvinist leanings and emphasized the author's transdenominational, transatlantic significance: "The name of John Angell James is, perhaps, almost as familiar in this country as it is in England. Few authors are read with more avidity; and probably few with more profit." The writer confessed that James's criticism of a rising "honorable," religion "exceedingly adverse" to spiritual vigor testified to the "remarkable similarity in the state of religion in England and America." See *Methodist Quarterly Review*, 7 (July 1847): 338–40.

47. James, *James's Christian Professor*, 141.

48. Tocqueville, *Democracy in America*, 2:104.

49. Phelps, "Theory of Preaching," 294–95; Wayland, *Letters on the Ministry of the Gospel*, 56. Also see William Lee Miller, *First Liberty*, 153–267.

50. Timothy L. Smith, *Revivalism and Social Reform*, 18–22. On the New School–Old School schism among Presbyterians, see Marsden, *Evangelical Mind and the New School Presbyterian Movement*.

51. Santee, "Signs of the Times," 290.

52. "Weakness of the Churches," 329–35. On Beecher, see Chapter 4.

53. "Individualism and Catholicism," 207–10.

54. Santee, "Signs of the Times," 290.

55. *Episcopal Recorder*, April 6 and September 21, 1850. One Presbyterian Covenanter even argued that since the Constitution, as the national "creed," made no reference to Christianity, it sanctioned a political order "comparable to any other infidel." See "The Christian Intelligencer—Civil Government," 208–9. Such demands for deference to exclusive religious claims betray republican suspicions that restrained Protestant blessings of the new liberal order.

56. Peter Bayne, *Bayne's Christian Life*, 291.

57. Finney, *Lectures to Professing Christians*. This work, together with *Lectures on Revivals*, circulated widely in Britain. The need for a biography of Finney has recently been filled. See Hardman, *Charles Grandison Finney*. On Finney's Jacksonian character, see McLoughlin, "Charles Grandison Finney," 97–107; and McLoughlin, *Revivals, Awakenings, and Reform*.

58. Finney, "Christian Perfection," in *Lectures to Professing Christians*, 341–46; Leonard I. Sweet, "View of Man Inherent in New Measures Revivalism," 221. Sweet's essay cogently reveals Finney's "pessimistic" views of human nature. For other views on Finney's perfectionism, see Timothy L. Smith, "Righteousness and Hope"; Hardman, *Charles Grandison Finney*, 324–49; and Weddle, *The Law as Gospel*.

59. Finney, "Rest of the Saints" and "False Professors," in *Lectures to Professing Christians*, 69, 438–40.

60. Finney, "Religion of Public Opinion" and "Rest of the Saints," in *Lectures to Professing Christians*, 116, 443–47.

61. James, *James's Christian Professor*, vi, 118. On James, Finney, and revivalism as a transatlantic movement, see Carwardine, *Transatlantic Revivalism*.

62. James, *An Earnest Ministry the Want of the Times*, 76, 192–94, 200–201.

63. On Fish's influence, see Timothy L. Smith, *Revivalism and Social Reform*, 49–50.

64. Fish, *Primitive Piety Revived*, 125, 150, 203.

65. Ibid., 124–28.

66. "Religion for the Republic," 171–72, 180.

67. On the Disciples of Christ as a democratic movement, see Hatch, "The Christian Movement and the Demand for a Theology of the People." See also Hatch, *Democratization of American Christianity*.

68. Hall, "Christian Simplicity," 444–48.

69. Archibald Alexander, "Faith's Victory over the World," in *Practical Sermons*, 408, 412–13, 416–17.

Chapter 3

1. "Our Country, as to the Future," 156.

2. Ibid.

3. Hietala, *Manifest Design*, 55–65; Wiebe, *Opening of American Society*; Bruchey, *Growth of the Modern American Economy*; De Voto, *Year of Decision*.

4. Pease and Pease, *Web of Progress*, 24–27; Sellers, *Market Revolution*.

5. Phyllis Deane, *First Industrial Revolution*, 232–37.

6. Hietala, *Manifest Design*. See also Merk, *Manifest Destiny and Mission*, and Van Alstyne, *Rising American Empire*.

7. Johannsen, *To the Halls of the Montezumas*, esp. Chapter 3.

8. *Baltimore American*, cited in *New York Evangelist*, December 7, 1839.

9. Sidney Mead, *Lively Experiment*. See also Tuveson, *Redeemer Nation*, 91–136.

10. Joseph P. Thompson, "Christian Missions Necessary to a True Civilization," 850; Willis Lord, "The Faithful Saying," 45, 49–53.

11. Bowman, "Traveler's Directory for Illinois," 420.

12. Nichols, "Chicago and the West," 512–13.

13. Ibid., 512. Compare the *New Englander*'s assessment of the Protestant role in the West with Augustine's similar approach to providential thought. See Augustine, *City of God*, V, 24; XV, 4, in Walsh et al., trans., 117–18, 327–28.

14. White, "Political Rectitude," 609–10, 630–31.

15. Wayland, "Moral Dignity of the Missionary Enterprise"; on the background of this sermon, see Francis Wayland and H. L. Wayland, *Memoir*, 1:164–68.

16. Wayland, "Moral Dignity of the Missionary Enterprise," 6, 12–18.

17. Wayland, "The Church of Christ," 324–25.

18. Lyman Beecher, *Plea for the West*.

19. "Conditions and Wants of the West," 250–53.

20. Ibid., 251, 257.

21. Hietala, *Manifest Design*, 186–87; Howe, *Political Culture of the American Whigs*, 93–95, 236; Johannsen, *To the Halls of the Montezumas*, 45–47; John Ashworth, *Agrarians and Aristocrats*, 73–84.

22. C. C. Goen, *Broken Churches, Broken Nation.*

23. "Christ in History," *New Englander,* 513–16.

24. Ellsworth, "American Churches and the Mexican War," 324.

25. *Christian Secretary,* April 11, 1845.

26. Norton, *Religious Newspapers,* 116–20.

27. *Western Christian Advocate,* cited in *Lutheran Observer,* July 2, 1847.

28. "Thoughts on the Infidelity of the Nineteenth Century," 195–96.

29. "Decrease in Northern Baptist Churches," *Tennessee Baptist,* January 18, 1849.

30. *Southern Presbyterian Review* 3 (January 1850): 377.

31. *Christian Index,* February 25, 1847.

32. Francis Asbury Hester Diary, October 30 and November 2, 1856, Francis Asbury Hester Papers.

33. "War with Mexico," 142.

34. *Episcopal Recorder,* February 8, 1851.

35. On Kossuth and the Revolutions of 1848, see Langer, *Political and Social Upheaval.*

36. "Kossuth in America"; Norton, *Religious Newspapers.*

37. Nevin's youthful struggle with what he later described as a spiritually enervating "crypto-rationalistic mode of thinking" helps explain the raw edge of his religious jeremiad discussed below. See Nevin, *My Own Life,* 120. On Nevin's background and especially his involvement in theological controversy, see Kuklick, *Churchmen and Philosophers.* See also Welch, *Protestant Thought in the Nineteenth Century,* and Conser, *Church and Confession.*

38. Nevin, "Man's True Destiny," 504, 512–13. For a view that suggests that clerical response to Kossuth demonstrates their absolute complicity with American religious nationalism see Daniel R. Miller, "American Christians and the Visit of Louis Kossuth," 5–17.

39. Nevin, "Man's True Destiny," 512–13.

40. Ibid., 510–11.

41. Ibid., 514–17.

42. Ibid., 519.

43. On antebellum clergymen and the issue of declining status, see Donald M. Scott, *From Office to Profession.*

44. Thornwell, "National Sins," 649–50.

45. "Overture for Christian Union."

46. "United Protestant Confession."

47. *Alta California,* cited in Van Alstyne, *Rising American Empire,* 131–32.

48. Mill, cited in Howard, *War and the Liberal Conscience,* 37. On Corn Law rhetoric, see McCord, *The Anti-Corn Law League,* 203.

49. Seward, cited in Van Alstyne, *Rising American Empire,* 146.

50. Daniel Wilson, "Introductory Essay," lxix–lxx.

51. See Bercovitch, *American Jeremiad*; and Martin Marty, *Protestantism in the United States,* 121–22. Bercovitch argues that American thinkers could generate little meaningful criticism of the American system because the nation itself had become the transcendent icon of worship. Melville, in Bercovitch's view, is Protestantism's closest link to meaningful dissent, though ultimately he too cannot reject the fundamental premises of the culture. Marty sees Melville as a Protes-

tant compelled outside Protestantism as evangelicalism "turned optimistic in its glorification of the trivial."

52. Melville, *Typee*, 150–53, 232–33.

53. Hetherington, *Melville's Reviewers*.

54. *Biblical Repository and Classical Review*, 3d ser., 5 (October 1849): 754.

55. Eleazar Lord, "Means of Promoting Christianity," 9.

56. Bunting, "Our Great Debt to all Mankind," 318–19.

57. Ibid., 317.

58. Coates, Beecham, and Ellis, *Christianity the Means of Civilization*.

59. Ellis, *Polynesian Researches*, 549–51.

60. *Methodist Quarterly Review*, 3d ser., 1 (January 1841): 43, 56, 58. For a similar missionary emphasis on spiritual over material means in the 1830s, see H. Southgate, "Spiritual Character of the Missionary Enterprise."

61. *Methodist Quarterly Review*, 3d ser., 1 (January 1841): 56–57.

62. Ellis, *Polynesian Researches*, 548–50.

63. J. L. Wilson, "The Certainty of the World's Conversion," 441.

64. Ibid., 430–31.

65. For a useful summary of the board's activity to 1850, see Anderson, *Memorial Volume of the First Fifty Years*.

66. Hopkins, "Sermon before the American Board of Commissioners for Foreign Missions," 440, 441–42, 446.

67. Ibid., 452–53, 454.

68. William Hutchison provides an important discussion of Board Secretary Rufus Anderson's efforts to separate spiritual and cultural purposes within the missionary movement. Anderson, however, was only one part of a much broader examination of missions that can be linked to the larger pattern of Protestant dissent examined in this study. Hutchison's work also provides useful perspective on the mission movement after 1860. See his *Errand to the World*, 62–90.

69. Missionary Society of the Methodist Episcopal Church, *Thirty-fifth Annual Report*, 109–10; Bradford Smith, *Yankees in Paradise*, 287.

70. "Report of Dr. Wayland," 220–22.

71. Ibid., 224–25.

72. "Prudential Committee Report," 25–31.

73. Ibid., 26–27, 32.

74. Sereno Clark, "Preaching the Gospel, the Instrument of the World's Conversion," 611, 623.

75. Ibid., 622–23.

76. Joseph P. Thompson, "Christian Missions Necessary to a True Civilization."

77. Ibid., 819, 834–35.

78. Ibid., 844, 825.

79. Ibid., 821.

80. Fisher, "Secular and Sacred Civilization," 721, 727.

81. Ibid., 727.

82. Bushnell to Dr. Bartol, Hartford, May 19, 1858, in Cheney, *Life and Letters of Horace Bushnell*, 414.

83. Bushnell, "Christ as Separate from the World," 449, 451–52.

84. Ibid., 454–56.

85. Hodges, "Christians Not of This World," 110.

86. Ibid., 115–20.

87. Samuel Steele Thompson, "The Righteous and the Wicked," unpublished MSS, Samuel Steele Thompson Papers.

Chapter 4

1. Nicholas Murray, "Defects in the Religious Character of This Age," 95.

2. *Christian Reflector*, February 26, 1840.

3. "Progress," *Christian Observatory*, 508–10.

4. Porter, "The New Infidelity." Porter became a leading authority on Continental thought. He combined clerical duties with a professorship at Yale in 1846 (and later became president of Yale in 1871). Together with Samuel Harris and Theodore Woolsey, he made the *New Englander* a major outlet for attacking the "new infidelity." Occasionally the journal acknowledged disagreement over defensive strategies, as in C. W. Clapp's "The Sphere of the Pulpit," in February 1857. For another perspective on the social and educational commitments of Woolsey and Porter, see Stevenson, *Scholarly Means to Evangelical Ends*.

5. *Thirty-fourth Annual Report of the American Bible Society*, 119–20; Moore, "English Infidelity," 4.

6. James, "Spiritual Religion the Surest Preservative from Infidelity," 179–80. See also Pearson, *Infidelity: Its Aspects, Causes, and Agencies*, 379.

7. Harris, "Infidelity: Its Erroneous Principles of Reasoning," 342–43.

8. Cashdollar, *Transformation of Theology, 1830–1890*. Cashdollar's study is especially useful for the post–Civil War era, when, he argues, positivism became the primary force behind Protestant theological creativity and change. Ministers appealing defensively to biblical authority were overwhelmed by greater numbers meeting positivism on its own terms and accepting it as a "facilitator of thought." Significantly, antebellum ministers assessing the new infidelity fulminated specifically about such potentialities.

9. On the Protestant response to Comte, see, for example, George Frederick Holmes's "The Positive Religion." Note also Cashdollar's useful discussion of Holmes, the English author of this piece. See Cashdollar, *Transformation of Theology*, 125–37, 267–72. His analysis emphasizes Holmes's interest in publicizing the merits of Comte's philosophy in two 1852 *Methodist Quarterly Review* essays, but this 1854 piece suggests that public notice was as important for the purpose of strategic demolition. Shedding the decorum of polite debate, Holmes called Comte's humanitarian faith "more repulsive and revolting than either the outrageous blasphemy of Voltaire, or the transcendental mythicism of Strauss. . . . Every one, who reflects for a moment, must see through the transparent gauze by which the delusion is barely veiled, and must estimate the tawdry puppet at its intrinsic worthlessness." See Holmes, "The Positive Religion," 358.

10. Marty, *The Infidel*, esp. 13–16, 198–201; Marty, *Protestantism in the United States*, 93, 118–25.

11. *Thirty-fourth Annual Report of the American Bible Society*, 106; "The Defects of American Civilization," 567; Moore, "English Infidelity," 27.

12. "Bayne's Christian Life," 550. John McClintock, *Review* editor from 1848

to 1856, developed an interest in the positivists that evolved into a spirited correspondence with August Comte. Like many ministers, McClintock was impressed with the intellectual power behind positivist philosophy and at the same time alarmed by its moral challenge to orthodoxy. Publicizing the new ideas became an essential strategy for attacking them. Yet the combat between McClintock and Comte also sustained a mutual respect, Comte at one point expressing gratitude to his "eminent adversaire," for giving outlet to his ideas. See Cashdollar, *Transformation of Theology*, 124–34.

13. *Lutheran Observer*, October 5, 1849.

14. Cole, *Social Ideas of the Northern Evangelists*, 168. Cole correctly speculates that spiritual preoccupations rather than social ideas may explain the seeming contradictions and insensitivities in evangelical economic thought. The suggestion explains why social analyses of Protestant motivation ultimately point to the need for fuller analysis of Protestant resistance to cultural accommodation.

15. Note, for example, Francis Wayland's charge to the Warren Baptist Association. See Warren Baptist Association, *Minutes*, 1847.

16. Troelstch, *Protestantism and Progress*; Tawney, *Religion and the Rise of Capitalism*; Weber, *The Protestant Ethic and the Spirit of Capitalism*.

17. Keith Stavely, *Puritan Legacies*, 206.

18. On Beecher as "eloquent profiteer," see David Mead, *Yankee Eloquence in the Middle West*, 134–41. See also Bode, *American Lyceum*.

19. Turner, *Without God, Without Creed*, 85, xiv. Turner argues that evangelicals themselves—by embracing moralism and carelessly abandoning the transcendent purposes of faith—were the primary authors of modern unbelief. In sanctifying rational agendas, they gave credibility to the very foes they sought to undo. Ministers felt the tensions but failed to understand them. Significantly, contemporaries played with the same irony that Turner unveils. Note Feuerbach's strategic stance: "I, on the contrary, let religion itself speak. . . . It is not I, but religion that worships man, although religion, or rather theology, denies this; it is not I, . . . but religion itself that says: God is man, man is God" (Feuerbach, "Preface to the Second Edition," xxxvi). Yet the explosion of religious jeremiads attacking a "new infidelity" reveals a far more critical and sophisticated Protestant understanding of cultural challenges than Turner allows. In addition, their spiritual discourse remained centered on ancient patterns of sin, salvation, and judgment despite speculative forays at the edges of theological debate. Finally, Turner's central question—"how the available *ideas* in the culture changed so as to make unbelief viable"—neatly summarizes the investigative agenda that fired antebellum Protestant resistance. Protestant defenders feared that emergent liberal culture sanctioned endless ideological choices and gave unprecedented viability to subtle but "fatal" sources of unbelief.

20. *Baptist Register*, November 18, 1847. On popular responses to the breakdown of the old economy in the late antebellum period, see Wiebe, *Opening of American Society*; Johnson, *Shopkeeper's Millennium*; and Wilentz, *Chants Democratic*.

21. Doerflinger, *Vigorous Spirit of Enterprise*. Significantly, Jonathan Edwards, whose writings remained powerfully influential among antebellum Protestants, registered serious concerns about the marketplace's encroachment on spiritual values. See Valeri, "The Economic Thought of Jonathan Edwards."

22. *Fourth Annual Report of the Newark City Tract Society*, 14.

23. Bushnell, "Prosperity Our Duty," 4–5.

24. Bushnell, "Parting Words," 22–23.

25. "Modern Theories of Social Progress," 10.

26. Abbott, *The Way to Do Good*, 187–88.

27. *Oberlin Evangelist*, September 1843, 160.

28. *Christian Observer*, February 7, 1845.

29. "European Views of American Democracy," 349–51.

30. James West Alexander, "Distrust of the Word," 111–12.

31. Sellers, *Market Revolution*, 228–31.

32. Significantly, Finney's personal lifestyle reinforced his war against materialism. See Hardman, *Charles Grandison Finney*, 339.

33. Finney, "Love of the World," 246–47.

34. Finney, "The Way of Salvation," 393. For a recent comparative perspective on antebellum views of salvation that includes Finney, see Glenn A. Hewitt, *Regeneration and Morality*.

35. Finney, "Christian Perfection," 363. Perry Miller acknowledges a distinction between Finney's views and liberal individualism. See his *Life of the Mind in America*, 34–35.

36. "The Spirit of the Age Viewed in Relation to the Duties and Trials of the Christian Ministry," 95.

37. "The Present Commercial Distress," 329–34.

38. Wilberforce, *Practical View of the Prevailing Religious System*, 358.

39. Bridgman, "High Standard of Piety Demanded by the Times," 373.

40. Dabney, "Principles of Christian Economy."

41. Ibid., 167.

42. Ibid., 166–67, 175, 180.

43. Wayland, "Moral Law of Accumulation"; Wayland, "Consistent Piety," 157.

44. Wayland, "Consistent Piety," 159.

45. Wayland, "Perils of Riches," 232–33.

46. Wayland, "Consistent Piety," 169; Wayland, "Perils of Riches," 233.

47. Wayland, "Consistent Piety," 173.

48. Wayland, "Perils of Riches," 241, 232.

49. Fish, *Primitive Piety Revived*, 31–32, 81–84, 183.

50. Ibid., 32.

51. Wayland, "Doctrine of Expediency," 302, 307.

52. Corey, "History of the Bible," unpublished MSS, n.d., Daniel G. Corey Papers.

53. Santee, "Signs of the Times," 293.

54. Bode, *American Lyceum*, 78; Wiebe, *Opening of American Society*, 166.

55. Tocqueville, *Democracy in America*, 1:328–29.

56. Norton, *Religious Newspapers of the Old Northwest*; Richards, *Gentlemen of Property and Standing*, 71–72. Richards emphasizes the significance of this print "revolution" for the abolitionist movement.

57. John Ulrich, "Signs of the Times," 350–53. The author is William Cowper.

58. Emerson, *Correspondence of Emerson and Carlyle*, 16–18.

59. Emerson to Carlyle, April 29, 1843, in ibid., 342–43.

60. "Pearson on Infidelity," 350–55, 376. For an analysis of the anti-Catholic dimension of Protestant thought, see Ray Billington, *The Protestant Crusade*.

61. Bode, *American Lyceum*, 12.

62. Ibid., 185–200, 225–28.

63. Ibid. See also Scott, "The Popular Lecture and the Creation of a Public."

64. Emerson, cited in David Mead, *Yankee Eloquence in the Midwest*, 17. On Emerson's interaction with his audiences, see Cayton, "Making of an American Prophet." On the exploitation of lyceums and the popular press by liberal and Unitarian ministers, see Douglas, *Feminization of American Culture*, 82–87, 227–56. Douglas emphasizes the cultural critique of the message of the northeastern liberal and Unitarian clergy as derivative of their own self-inflicted cultural marginalization. Substantive, hard-edged religious combat with the culture, according to Douglas, disintegrated in tandem with Calvinism and yielded a tenuous literary alliance of ministers and female writers whose innocuous, sentimentalized message ironically reinforced commercial capitalist culture.

65. "Infidelity in the United States," 204–8.

66. Owen and Campbell, *Debate on the Evidences of Christianity*, 14; *New York Evangelist*, cited in *Episcopal Recorder* December 22, 1832.

67. Moore, cited in *Thirty-fourth Annual Report of the American Bible Society*, 120–21.

68. "Bible Influence Indispensable to Society and the Institutions of Life," 5.

69. Porter, "The New Infidelity," 282, 294. Lutheran Samuel Schmucker gave succinct expression to the compatibility of "modern infidelity" with liberal culture. He chided it as a maddening exhibition of the "most irreconcilable diversity," starkly at odds with the "divine and unapproachable supremacy" of gospel simplicity and unity. Schmucker's sense of exclusive power and confidence, however, drew from historic spiritual assumptions. The culture's potential to support such diversity and choice clearly worried him. See Schmucker, *Modern Infidelity*, 16, 297.

70. "Circular Letter," Ontario Baptist Association, *Minutes*, (1851), 12–14, 16.

71. Angelina Grimké to Henry C. Wright, Groton, Mass., August 20, 1837, *Letters of Theodore Dwight Weld, Angelina Grimké Weld, and Sarah Grimké*, 1:420.

72. Angelina Grimké to Weld and John Greenleaf Whittier, Brookline, Mass., August 20, ibid., 1:428.

73. For a discussion of Beecher that emphasizes her cultural agenda as the product of an increasingly secular vision of female power based on personal "self-sacrifice," see Sklar, *Catharine Beecher*. For an excellent comparative biography of the Beecher family, see Caskey, *Chariot of Fire*.

74. Catharine Beecher, *Common Sense*, 334–35.

75. Catharine Beecher, *True Remedy*, 19, 233–36, 238, 242.

76. Catharine Beecher, *Common Sense*, 330–35. Sklar's useful analysis of Beecher's Calvinist departures nevertheless puts too great an emphasis on Beecher as alienated from Protestant spirituality and "allied . . . with the secular elements in American society" (Sklar, *Catharine Beecher*, 246–57). At least for the period before 1860, Beecher worried openly about the indiscriminate blending of Christianity and culture and emphasized the individual, transcendent process of redemption. Note her complaint in *True Remedy*: Too many, she argued, "keep

their consciences easy by performing various externals expected of them, such as attention to religious meetings, Sunday-schools, and certain benevolent associations. And they read the Bible, and keep up private devotions, and are strict in certain relative duties, as the method of saving *their own* souls. But these things being done, the main current of their thoughts and interests flow on, just as it would were there no such terrific dangers to their fellow-beings in that eternal scene, to which they are constantly passing away" (17–18).

77. Catharine Beecher, *Common Sense*, 330–35.

78. On the Forty-eighters' experience and influence in the late antebellum period, see A. E. Zucker, ed., *The Forty-eighters*.

79. Ulrich, "Signs of the Times," 350–53.

80. Harkey, "A Sermon Preached . . . at the Opening of the . . . General Synod," 18.

81. *Lutheran Observer*, September 28, 1849.

82. Zucker, *Forty-eighters*, 60–64, 161–62, 353–54.

83. Resolution cited in Eitel W. Dobert, "The Radicals," in ibid., 160–62.

84. "The Revolutions of 1848," 547.

85. *Episcopal Recorder*, February 9, 1850.

86. *Bibliotheca Sacra* 8 (January 1851): 228.

87. Henry Schmidt, "Infidelity: Its Metamorphoses, and its Present Aspects," 401.

88. Barth, "An Introductory Essay," xii.

89. Feuerbach, "Preface to the Second Edition," *Essence of Christianity*, xliii.

90. Feuerbach, *Das Wesen der Religion*, cited in Barth, "An Introductory Essay," xi.

91. Feuerbach, "Preface to the Second Edition," xxxvi–xxxix, xliii. On Feuerbach's relationship to nineteenth-century Protestant theological debate, see Welch, *Protestant Thought in the Nineteenth Century*, 170–89.

92. Tiffany, "Feuerbach's Essence of Christianity," 751.

93. Nevin, "Man's True Destiny," 511, 519.

94. Burgess, "A Charge Delivered to the Clergy of Maine."

95. "Christian Doctrine the Sole Basis of Christian Morality," 328–29, 323.

96. "Introduction," *Christian Review*, 4–5.

97. Compare below to Harris, "Dependence of Popular Progress on Christianity."

98. Harris, "Demands of Infidelity Satisfied by Christianity," 272, 285.

99. Ibid., 274, 285–86, 306.

100. Ibid., 285.

101. Ibid., 294–95, 313. See also Feuerbach, *Essence of Christianity*, 247–69.

102. Woolsey, "The Danger of Separating Piety from Philanthropy," 330–31.

103. Ibid., 334.

104. Ibid., 338.

105. Ibid., 339–41.

106. James West Alexander, "Our Modern Unbelief," 19–35. Alexander's religious jeremiad attracted attention in the South. The *Biblical Recorder*, a North Carolina Baptist newspaper, reprinted lengthy passages of the sermon and gave it front-page prominence. See *Biblical Recorder*, May 19, 1859.

107. James West Alexander, "Our Modern Unbelief," 24–25, 27–28.

108. Ibid., 38, 40–44.

109. *Christian Secretary*, October 6, 1843.

110. Hawthorne, "Celestial Railroad," 213, 224–26, 219. Bercovitch finds Hawthorne's critical vision atypical among Protestants, though he sees the author as thoroughly defined by the nationalistic dream. See Bercovitch, *American Jeremiad*, 205–9.

111. *Christian Secretary*, March 3, 1848.

112. *New Englander* 5 (January 1847): 56.

113. James West Alexander, "Our Modern Unbelief," 17.

Chapter 5

1. Kurtz, "How Should the Gospel Be Preached?" 525–26, 532.

2. Walker, "Private Christians in Their Relations to the Unbelieving World," 715–16.

3. Donald Weber explores this process of multiple rhetorical functions in an attempt to break down the distinctions between civic and spiritual discourse and thereby transcend what he sees as a too-rigid "either-or" dichotomy controlling scholarly debate over Revolutionary religious rhetoric. In the process, he refutes claims of New Divinity political aloofness by finding examples of ministers (Jonathan Edwards, Jr., for example) engrossed in the imperial struggle and imaginatively weaving political and temporal themes into a new historical/Revolutionary myth. The evidence, Weber argues, bears "irrefutable, eloquent witness to their secular engagement, their profoundly political voices." Like Weber's useful study, this analysis assumes a "cultural-linguistic dialogue," but with an emphasis on how ministers cultivated innovative rhetorical means (the religious jeremiad) to strategically analyze and stratify liberal culture's expanding mosaic of material and rhetorical options. In addition to discovering imaginative, integrative tendencies, we must explain how and why contemporaries offered explicit categorization of their own discourse in ways that still make the civic/spiritual dichotomy exploited by Hatch and others a relevant, though complex, avenue for analyzing clerical response to cultural ferment. See Weber, *Rhetoric and History in Revolutionary New England*, 5–13, 149.

4. Humphrey, "The Carnal Mind," 64–65.

5. Douglass, "The Sin of Grieving the Holy Spirit," in *Sermons*, 99–103. On black ministers in the antebellum North, see Fordham, *Major Themes in Northern Black Religious Thought*. Fordham points out that African American ministers generally reinforced Protestant mainstream spiritual discourse. Their civic themes pressed strongly for abolition, while white racism in all parts of the country gave them few reasons to talk of "excessive liberty." But the spiritual assumptions and doctrinal positions that guided regular pulpit preaching put African American divines squarely within mainstream Protestant thought. Rather than cultivating millennial hopes, for example, Douglass harped on the "uncertainty of time." Calls for collective morality only occasionally punctuated staple themes assuring divine vengeance upon individuals. In one sermon that traced the slave insti-

tution to a collective materialist spirit, Douglass matched scenarios of temporal punishment with even stronger warnings against the eternal fate of individuals who yielded to a national celebration of "avarice, pride and ambition." See Douglass, *Sermons*, 101–2.

6. Phelps, "Theory of Preaching," 295.

7. Sereno Clark, "Preaching the Gospel, the Instrument of the World's Conversion," 611.

8. "Plain Talk about Preaching," *Western Recorder*, October 8, 1851.

9. Psalm 81:10. See Clapp, "Sphere of the Pulpit," 136.

10. Schaeffer, "Homiletics," 304–6.

11. Gilman, "Permanence of the Pulpit," 436–37.

12. Phelps, "Theory of Preaching," 298–99, 301.

13. Hall, "Christian Simplicity," 447.

14. Ibid., 443–47.

15. Goodrich, "Preaching for the Age," 11–13.

16. Ibid., 12–13, 19.

17. Ibid., 18–19.

18. Ibid., 21–23.

19. Brown, "Duty, Spirit, and Reward of the Christian Ministry," 6–8.

20. Ibid., 10.

21. Ibid., 6, 14–15.

22. Carpenter, "Preaching and Hearing the Gospel," John M. Carpenter Papers.

23. Ibid.

24. *Baptist Missionary Magazine*, American Baptist Missionary Union 37: 17–25.

25. American Board of Commissioners for Foreign Missions, *Report* (1856), 61.

26. Ibid., 66.

27. Ibid.

28. "The Preaching of the Gospel, the Plan of the Almighty for the Conversion of the World," 25.

29. Wayland, *Letters on the Ministry of the Gospel*, 58, 71, 199–201.

30. Ibid., 131–32.

31. Loveland, *Southern Evangelicals*; Donald G. Mathews, *Religion in the Old South*.

32. On Dudley's background, see Presbyerian Synod of Virginia, *Minutes*, 1877, 261.

33. Sermons and sketches, Jacob Dudley Papers.

34. See sketches on Hebrews 12:4, Zechariah 8:13, Jeremiah 44:16, Matthew 12:30, Jacob Dudley Papers.

35. Loveland, *Southern Evangelicals*, 219–56. Loveland's work also notes the biblical, nonspeculative nature of antebellum Southern preaching. As this chapter suggests, mainstream popular preaching North and South followed similar patterns. On religion and the African American experience in the South, see also Genovese, *Roll Jordan, Roll*; Mathews, *Religion in the Old South*; and Hamilton, *The Black Preacher in America*. Hamilton argues that the black pulpit in the South also typically emphasized otherworldly themes. It is also plain, however, that black congregations resisted themes of "obedience" that equated duty to God with obe-

dience to the master. However genuine black faith in a transcendent destiny was, Hamilton emphasizes, some of that otherworldly emphasis resulted not from social passivity but from rigid surveillance of black ministers, particularly following the 1831 insurrection by black preacher Nat Turner. On Southern efforts to reconcile millennial thought with a social vision tied to slavery and Southern society see Maddex, "Proslavery Millennialism," 46–62.

36. "Preaching Record," Henry Newton Papers.

37. Ibid., August 1854.

38. On Morton's life, see biographical sketch, Charles Morton Papers.

39. Charles Morton, "Text Book No. 3," sermon texts 3521–66, box 1.

40. Ibid.

41. Ibid., nos. 4421–26.

42. Ibid., nos. 3567–4243.

43. On Kammerer, see brief biographical sketch, Samuel Kammerer Papers.

44. Augustus J. Prahl, "The Turner," in *The Forty-eighters*, 92.

45. Sermon sketches, Samuel Kammerer Papers,

46. Kammerer, "Faith, Hope, and Charity," sermon sketches, Samuel Kammerer Papers.

47. Kammerer, "A Promise for Those Persons Who Comply with the Conditions Specified in the Text," sermon sketches, Samuel Kammerer Papers.

48. Francis Asbury Hester Papers.

49. Hester, "Sermon Sketches," vols. 1, 2. Francis Asbury Hester Papers.

50. Ibid., 1:62–99.

51. Ibid., 1:122–24.

52. Ibid., 2:79–82.

53. Ibid., 160–214.

54. Ibid.

55. Gaustad, *Historical Atlas of Religion in America*, 168; *American Christian Record*, 640; Goen, *Broken Churches, Broken Nation*, 51–54; Burrows, *American Baptist Register*.

56. Indiana Regular Baptist Associations (White Lick, Lost River, and Madison), *Minutes*; Edgefield Baptist Association, *Minutes*; Warren Association, Rhode Island, *Minutes*.

57. "Circular Letter," White Lick Association, *Minutes* (1836); "Circular Letter," ibid. (1843); "Circular Letter," Lost River Association, *Minutes* (1839). On the interrelationship of "the Word," "the word," and the "bonds of grace," see "Circular Letters," Madison Association, *Minutes* (1840, 1841, 1842, 1847, 1848); White Lick Association, *Minutes* (1836, 1853, 1856, 1858); Lost River Association, *Minutes* (1831, 1832, 1838, 1839, 1844, 1855, 1856). In 1836, a White Lick circular included the following demand for separation from the culture: "The bonds of grace are nearer and stronger than those of nature; and in order to maintain uninterrupted communion with the Lord, and each other, practice all those duties enjoined by Christ, avoid all those who aim to prejudice the members against each other and are preaching strange doctrine; all such should be marked with disgrace. . . . Such are artful deceivers contending for opinions and notions. . . . Brethren, take the word of God for your man of council—there is no essential doctrine or duty but is clearly taught in God's precious word."

58. "Circular Letter," White Lick Association, *Minutes* (1837).

59. Warren Baptist Association, *Minutes*, 1844. For special emphasis on spiritual bonding and separation see *Minutes* (1843, 1844, 1846, 1849, 1850, 1851, 1854, 1855, 1856, 1857,1859).

60. Edgefield Baptist Association, *Minutes* (1856).

61. "Circular Letter," White Lick Association, *Minutes* (1836).

62. "Circular Letter," Lost River Association, *Minutes* (1839).

63. "Circular Letter," Lost River Association, *Minutes* (1844).

64. "Circular Letter," Warren Association, *Minutes* (1851).

65. "Circular Letter," White Lick Association, *Minutes* (1843).

66. Edgefield Association, *Minutes* (1841).

67. See "Circular Letters," Madison Association, *Minutes* (1836, 1838 1847, 1848); White Lick Association, *Minutes* (1836, 1840, 1855, 1858); Lost River Association, *Minutes* (1830, 1831, 1833, 1836, 1838, 1839, 1841, 1843, 1855, 1857).

68. "Circular Letter," White Lick Association, *Minutes* (1855).

69. "Circular Letter," Lost River Association, *Minutes* (1856).

70. "Circular Letter," White Lick Association, *Minutes* (1858).

71. American Tract Society, *Fourteenth Annual Report* (1839), 45.

72. Ibid., 43.

73. American Tract Society, *Eighteenth Annual Report* (1843), 27.

74. American Tract Society, *Twenty-fifth Annual Report* (1850), 161–225.

75. Ibid.

76. "Constitution of the American Tract Society," reprinted in American Tract Society, *Twenty-fifth Annual Report* (1850), 255.

77. For titles and publication figures, see American Tract Society, *Twenty-fifth Annual Report*, 230, 239–41. For a thematic description of individual tracts, see "Sketch of the Origin and Character of the Principal Series of Tracts." On the history of the American Tract Society, see Nord, "Evangelical Origins of Mass Media in America," and Thompson, "Printing and Publishing Activities of the American Tract Society." Figures and titles used in Table 1 are based on the 522 general series tracts contained in the society's twelve complete volumes of tracts. Incomplete figures for seven tract titles listed as part of a planned thirteenth volume are not included.

78. See, for example, "Training Children for the Conversion of the World," Tract No. 479 in *Tracts of the American Tract Society*, 7.

79. See publication figures and tract titles in American Tract Society, *Twenty-fifth Annual Report* (1850), 230, 239–41.

80. "Sixteen Short Sermons," Tract No. 72 in *Tracts of the American Tract Society*, 2:14–15.

81. Figures compiled from publication statistics in the American Tract Society, *Twenty-fifth Annual Report*, 228–29.

82. Ibid., 238.

83. Abbott, *The Way to Do Good*, 175–76.

Conclusion

1. Bellows, "Religious Liberty," 10–11; Bellows, "Suspense of Faith," 16.

2. "Dr. Bellows on 'The Suspense of Faith,'" 978.

3. David E. Smith, "Millenarian Scholarship in America," 537–38.

4. Walter Rauschenbusch, *Christianity and the Social Crisis*, 64–65. On the social gospel, see also Donald C. White, *The Social Gospel*; Gorrell, *The Age of Social Responsibility*; Handy, *The Social Gospel in America*; Szasz, *The Divided Mind of Protestant America*; and Hutchison, *The Modernist Impulse in American Protestantism*. For an important recent assessment that explains how social gospel leaders exploited the symbolic and material expressions of consumer culture, see Curtis, *A Consuming Faith*.

5. On fundamentalism's gradual rather than sudden shift away from social concern, see Marsden, *Fundamentalism and American Culture*.

6. Reinhold Niebuhr, *Does Civilization Need Christianity?*, 1–4. On the Niebuhrs and neo-orthodoxy, see Ottati, *Meaning and Method in H. Richard Niebuhr's Theology*; Fowler, *To See the Kingdom*; Grant, *God the Center of Value*; Kegley and Bretall, *Reinhold Niebuhr*; and Fox, *Reinhold Niebuhr*.

7. Reinhold Niebuhr, *Does Civilization Need Christianity?*, 231–36.

8. Reinhold Niebuhr, "The Christian Witness in the National and Social Order," reprinted in *Christian Realism and Political Problems*, 106. For Niebuhr's most extensive discussion of sacred and secular purpose see his *Nature and Destiny of Man*.

9. H. Richard Niebuhr, "Toward the Independence of the Church," 604–6.

10. Ibid., 613–15.

11. Ibid., 617–18.

Bibliography

Manuscript Collections

John M. Carpenter Papers. Record Group 1020. American Baptist Historical Society, Rochester, New York.

Davis W. Clark Papers. General Commission on Archives and History for the United Methodist Church. Madison, New Jersey.

Daniel G. Corey Papers. Record Group 1217. American Baptist Historical Society, Rochester, New York.

Jacob Dudley Papers. Manuscript Collection 702. Historical Foundation of the Presbyterian and Reformed Churches in the United States. Montreat, North Carolina.

Francis Asbury Hester Papers. Manuscript Collection 76. Depauw University Archives. Greencastle, Indiana.

Samuel Kammerer Papers. Lutheran Archives, Ohio Synod. Wittenburg University, Springfield, Ohio.

Charles Morton Papers. Record Group 1343. American Baptist Historical Society Archives, Rochester, New York.

Henry Newton Papers. Manuscript Collection 888. Historical Foundation of the Presbyterian and Reformed Churches in the United States. Montreat, North Carolina.

Samuel Steele Thompson Papers. File 665b. Wabash College Archives. Crawfordsville, Indiana.

Published Primary Sources: Reports

American Board of Commissioners for Foreign Missions. *Reports*. New York, 1854, 1856.

American Christian Record. New York, 1860.

American Tract Society. *Annual Reports*. New York, 1825, 1837, 1839, 1843, 1850.

Edgefield Baptist Association, South Carolina. *Minutes*. 1831–60. Southern Baptist Theological Seminary Archives. Louisville, Kentucky.

Fourth Annual Report of the Newark City Tract Society. Newark, New Jersey, 1856.

Indiana Regular Baptist Associations (Madison, White Lick, Lost River). *Minutes*. 1830–60. Franklin College Archives. Franklin, Indiana.

Missionary Society of the Methodist Episcopal Church. *Thirty-fifth Annual Report.* New York, 1854.

Ontario Baptist Association. *Minutes.* Penn Yan, New York, 1851.

Presbyterian Synod of Virginia. *Minutes.* 1877.

Thirty-fourth Annual Report of the American Bible Society. New York, 1850.

Warren Baptist Association, Rhode Island. *Minutes.* 1841–60. Southern Baptist Theological Seminary Archives. Louisville, Kentucky.

Published Primary Sources: Newspapers and Periodicals

American Biblical Repository (New York).

American Tract Magazine (New York).

Baptist Memorial and Monthly Record (New York).

Baptist Missionary Magazine (Boston).

Baptist Register (Utica, New York).

Biblical Repertory and Princeton Review (New York).

Biblical Repository and Classical Review (Andover, Massachusetts).

Bibliotheca Sacra (Robinson, New York).

Charleston Gospel Messenger (Charleston, South Carolina).

Christian Index (Penfield, Georgia).

Christian Observatory (Boston).

Christian Observer (Philadelphia).

Christian Reflector (Boston).

Christian Review (Boston).

Christian Secretary (Hartford, Connecticut).

Church Review (New Haven, Connecticut).

Covenanter (Philadelphia).

Democratic Review (New York).

Episcopal Recorder (Philadelphia).

Evangelical Review (Gettysburg, Pennsylvania).

Home Missionary (New York).

Literary and Theological Review (Boston).

Lutheran Observer (Baltimore).

Mercersburg Review (Lancaster, Pennsylvania).

Methodist Quarterly Review (New York).

Methodist Quarterly Review, South.

National Preacher (New York).

New Englander (New Haven, Connecticut).

New York Evangelist (New York).

Oberlin Evangelist (Oberlin, Ohio).

Quarterly Christian Spectator (New Haven, Connecticut).

Southern Presbyterian Review.

Spirit of the Pilgrims (Boston).

Tennessee Baptist.

Western Recorder (Louisville, Kentucky).

Published Primary Sources: Books, Sermons, Articles

Abbott, Jacob. *The Way to Do Good*. Boston, 1836.

Alexander, Archibald. "Faith's Victory over the World." In *Practical Sermons*, 407–23. Philadelphia, n.d.

Alexander, James West. "Distrust of the Word." In *The Living Pulpit*, edited by Elijah Wilson. Philadelphia, 1859.

———. "Our Modern Unbelief." In *Discourses on Common Topics of Christian Faith and Practice*, 13–47. New York, 1858.

Anderson, Rufus. *Memorial Volume of the First Fifty Years*. Boston, 1861.

Augustine. *City of God*. In *The Political Writings of Augustine*, edited by Henry Paolucci. Chicago: Regnery Gateway, 1962.

———. *City of God*. Abridged translation by Gerald Walsh, Demetrius B. Zema, Grace Monohan, and Daniel Honan. New York: Image Books, 1958.

———. *Letters*. In *The Political Writings of Augustine*, edited by Henry Paolucci. Chicago: Regnery Gateway, 1962.

Barnes, Albert. "Preparation to Meet God." In *Practical Sermons*. Philadelphia, 1841.

Bates, Joshua. "Christian Patriotism." In *Lectures on Christian Character*. Andover, Mass., 1846.

Baxter, Richard. "A Holy Commonwealth." 1659. In *Richard Baxter and Puritan Politics*, edited by Richard Schlatter, 68–124. New Brunswick, N.J.: Rutgers University Press, 1957.

Bayne, Peter. *Bayne's Christian Life*. Boston, 1855.

"Bayne's Christian Life." *Methodist Quarterly Review* 8 (October 1856): 548–68.

Beecher, Catharine. "Address to the Protestant Clergy of the United States." New York, 1846.

———. *Common Sense Applied to Religion*. New York, 1857.

———. *The True Remedy for the Wrongs of Woman*. Boston, 1851.

Beecher, Edward. *The Conflict of Ages*. Boston, 1854.

Beecher, Lyman. *Plea for the West*. Cincinnati, 1856.

Bellows, Henry. "Religious Liberty." Washington, 1852.

———. "The Suspense of Faith." New York, 1859.

"Bible Influence Indispensable to Society and the Institutions of Life." *Evangelical Review* 3 (July 1851): 1–33.

Bowman, Samuel. "Traveler's Directory for Illinois." *Methodist Quarterly Review*, 3d ser., 3 (July 1843): 402–20.

Bridgman, A. L. "A High Standard of Piety Demanded by the Times." *Evangelical Review* 7 (January 1856): 364–76.

Brown, J. A. "The Duty, Spirit, and Reward of the Christian Ministry: A Discourse Preached in the Lutheran Church in Lewisburg at the Opening of the Synod of East Pennsylvania." Philadelphia, 1854.

Bunting, Jabez. "Our Great Debt to All Mankind." In *Sermons by Jabez Bunting*. Vol. 1. New York, 1862.

Burgess, George. "A Charge Delivered to the Clergy of Maine." Reprinted in *Episcopal Recorder* (Philadelphia), August 17, 1850.

Burrows, J. Lansing, ed. *American Baptist Register*. Philadelphia, 1852.

Bushnell, Horace. "American Politics." Sermon printed in *National Preacher* 14 (December 1840): 189–204.

―――. "Christ as Separate from the World." In *Sermons for the New Life*, 434–56. 7th ed. New York, 1867.

―――. "Parting Words." Hartford, 1859.

―――. "Prosperity Our Duty." 1847.

―――. "Regeneration." In *Sermons for the New Life*, 106–26. 7th ed. New York, 1867.

―――. *Views on Christian Virtue*. Hartford, 1846.

Chalmers, Thomas. "The Emptiness of Natural Virtue." In *Sermons Preached in the Tron Church*. Glasgow, 1819.

―――. "The Importance of Civil Government to Society." In *Selected Works*, vol. 3. New York, n.d.

―――. "The Nature of the Kingdom of God." In *Selected Works*, vol. 4. New York, n.d.

"Christ in History." *New Englander* 6 (October 1848): 513–24.

"Christian Decision." *Episcopal Recorder* (Philadelphia), April 1850.

"Christian Doctrine the Sole Basis of Christian Morality." *Christian Review* 7 (September 1842): 321–41.

"The Christian Intelligencer–Civil Government." *Covenanter* 7 (February 1852): 208–12.

"Christian Simplicity." *New Englander* 12 (August 1854): 447–48.

Clapp, C. W. "The Sphere of the Pulpit." *New Englander* 15 (February 1857): 135–53.

Clark, Sereno. "The Evangelizing Church." *New Englander* 15 (May 1857): 221–41.

―――. "Preaching the Gospel, the Instrument of the World's Conversion." *New Englander* 12 (November 1854): 604–26.

Coates, Dandeson, John Beecham, and William Ellis. *Christianity the Means of Civilization*. London, 1837.

"Conditions and Wants of the West." *Christian Review* 1 (June 1836): 249–63.

"Confessions of Augustine." *Christian Review* 15 (October 1850): 483–504.

Dabney, Robert L. "Principles of Christian Economy." *Southern Presbyterian Review* 6 (October 1852): 157–86.

"Dangers of Our Country." *Quarterly Christian Spectator* 8 (December 1836): 505–19.

"Decrease in Northern Baptist Churches." *Tennessee Baptist*, January 18, 1849.

"The Defects of American Civilization." *Methodist Quarterly Review, South* 4 (October 1850): 559–69.

"Desultory Remarks upon the Closing Year." *Baptist Memorial and Monthly Record* 9 (1850): 392–93.

Doggett, David S. "Christ and Pilate." In *Methodist Pulpit South*, edited by William T. Smithson, 319–27. Washington, D.C., 1859.

Douglass, William. *Sermons*. 1854. Reprint. New York: Books for Libraries Press, 1971.

"Dr. Bellows on 'The Suspense of Faith.'" *New Englander* 17 (November 1859): 968–79.

"The Eclipse of Faith." *Church Review* 6 (April 1853): 101–18.

Edwards, Jonathan. *The Nature of True Virtue*. 1755. Reprint. Ann Arbor: University of Michigan Press, 1971.

Ellis, William. *Polynesian Researches in the South Sea Islands*. London, 1829.

Emerson, Ralph Waldo. *The Correspondence of Emerson and Carlyle*. Edited by Joseph Slater. New York: Columbia University Press, 1964.

"Eulogies on Adams and Jefferson." *Quarterly Christian Spectator* 2 (May 1827): 259–68.

"European Views of Democracy." *Democratic Review* 2 (July 1838): 337–56.

Evangelical Family Library. 15 vols. New York: American Tract Society.

Feuerbach, Ludwig. *The Essence of Christianity*. Translated by Marian Evans. 1841. Reprint. New York: Harper and Row, 1957.

———. "Preface to the Second Edition." In *The Essence of Christianity*, translated by Marian Evans. 1841. Reprint. New York: Harper and Row, 1957.

Finney, Charles. "Christian Perfection." In *Lectures to Professing Christians*, 339–82. New York, 1837.

———. "False Professors." In *Lectures to Professing Christians*, 21–35. New York, 1837.

———. *Lectures on Revivals*. Edited by William McLoughlin. Cambridge: Belknap Press, 1960.

———. "Love of the World." In *Sermons on Important Subjects*, 241–59. New York, 1835.

———. "The Way of Salvation." In *Lectures to Professing Christians*, 383–98. New York, 1837.

Fish, Henry Clay. *Primitive Piety Revived*. Boston, 1855.

Fisher, Samuel. "Secular and Christian Civilization." *Biblical Repository and Classical Review*, 3d ser., 6 (October 1850): 720–47.

General Series of Tracts. 12 vols. New York: American Tract Society, 1825–50.

Gilman, Edward. "The Permanence of the Pulpit." *New Englander* 13 (August 1855): 435–50.

Goodrich, William. "The Preaching for the Age." *New Englander* 12 (February 1854): 9–24.

Grimké, Angelina, and Sarah Grimké. *Letters of Theodore Dwight Weld, Angelina Grimké Weld, and Sarah Grimké*. Edited by Gilbert H. Barnes and Dwight L. Dumond. 2 vols. New York: American Historical Association, 1934. Reprint. Gloucester, Mass.: Peter Smith, 1965.

Hall, Gordon. "Christian Simplicity." *New Englander* 12 (August 1854): 440–49.

Harkey, Simeon. "A Sermon Preached . . . at the Opening of the . . . General Synod of the Evangelical Lutheran Church of the United States." Philadelphia, 1859.

Harness, William. *The Connexion of Christianity with Human Happiness*. London, 1823.

Harris, Samuel. "Demands of Infidelity Satisfied by Christianity." An address delivered in the Seminary Chapel at Andover, July 1855. Reprinted in *Bibliotheca Sacra* 13 (April 1856): 272–314.

———. "The Dependence of Popular Progress upon Christianity." *New Englander* 5 (July 1847): 433–51.

———. "Infidelity: Its Erroneous Principles of Reasoning." *New Englander* 12 (August 1854): 341–62.

Hawthorne, Nathaniel. "The Celestial Railroad." In *Mosses from an Old Manse*. 1846. Reprint. Boston: Houghton Mifflin, 1884.

Henry, C. S. "Importance of a Learned Order." *Literary and Theological Review* 3 (December 1836): 573–97.

Hodge, Charles W. "The Catholicity of the Gospel." In *The Living Pulpit*, edited by Elijah Wilson, 321–36. Philadelphia, 1859.

Hodges, C. W. "Christians Not of this World." In *Sermons*, 107–21. Burlington, Vt., 1850.

Holmes, George Frederick. "The Positive Religion: Or, Religion of Humanity." *Methodist Quarterly Review*, 4th ser., 6 (July 1854): 329–59.

Hopkins, Mark. *Evidences of Christianity*. 1863. Reprint. Boston, 1909.

———. "Sermon, before the American Board of Commissioners for Foreign Missions." In *Miscellaneous Essays and Discourses*, 430–57. Boston, 1847.

Humphrey, John. "The Carnal Mind." In *Sermons of John Humphrey*, edited by Heman Humphrey, 49–71. New York, 1856.

"Individualism and Catholicism." *Mercersburg Review* 6 (July 1854): 207–19.

"Infidelity in the United States." *Spirit of the Pilgrims* 6 (April 1833): 204–15.

"Introduction." *Christian Review* 14 (January 1849): 1–5.

James, John Angell. *The Anxious Inquirer*. New York: American Tract Society, n.d.

———. *An Earnest Ministry the Want of the Times*. New York, 1848.

———. *James's Christian Professor*. New York, 1838.

———. "Spiritual Religion the Surest Preservative from Infidelity." In *Lectures Delivered before the Young Men's Christian Association, 1848–49*. Vol. 4. London, 1876.

"Kossuth in America." *Mercersburg Review* 4 (January 1852): 81–82.

Kurtz, Benjamin. "How Should the Gospel Be Preached?" *Evangelical Review* 1 (April 1850): 524–34.

"Liberalism Not Charity." *Episcopal Recorder* (Philadelphia), September 21, 1850.

"The Life and Labours of St. Augustine." Review essay. *Biblical Repertory and Princeton Review* 26 (July 1854): 436–43.

Lincoln, Abraham. "The Perpetuation of Our Political Institutions." In *The Collected Works of Abraham Lincoln*, edited by Roy P. Basler, 108–15. 9 vols. New Brunswick, N.J.: Rutgers University Press, 1953.

Lord, Eleazar. "On Special Efforts by the Church to Subvert the Unhallowed Institutions of the World." *Literary and Theological Review* 1 (September 1834): 443–56.

Lord, Nathan. "Means of Promoting Christianity." *Literary and Theological Review* 2 (March 1835): 3–38.

———. "The Millennium: An Essay Read to the General Convention of New Hampshire." Hanover, N.H.: Dartmouth Press, 1854.

Lord, Willis. "The Faithful Saying." In *The Living Pulpit*, edited by Elijah Wilson, 44–62. Philadelphia, 1859.

Melville, Herman. *Typee*. 1846. Reprint. Edited by G. Thomas Tanselle. New York: Viking Press, 1982.

Milton, John. "Paradise Regained." 1671. Reprinted in *The Complete Poetical Works of John Milton*, edited by Harris Francis Fletcher, 391–436. Boston: Houghton Mifflin, 1941.

"Modern Theories of Social Progress." *Church Review* 5 (April 1852): 9–25.

Moore, Thomas V. "English Infidelity." *Methodist Quarterly Review, South* 6 (January 1852): 2–31.

Murray, Nicholas. "Defects in the Religious Character of This Age." *Literary and Theological Review* 5 (December 1838): 93–113.

Nevin, John. "Man's True Destiny." A Baccalaureate Address to the First Graduating Class of Franklin and Marshall College, August 31, 1853. Printed in *Mercersburg Review* 5 (October 1853): 492–521.

———. *My Own Life: The Early Years*. 1870. In Papers of the Eastern Chapter, Historical Society of the Evangelical and Reformed Church, No. 1. Lancaster, Pa., 1964.

Nichols, W. A. "Chicago and the West." *New Englander* 12 (November 1854): 510–24.

"Our Country, as to the Future." *Christian Observatory* 2 (April 1848): 155–58.

"Overture for Christian Union," (London, 1846).

Owen, Robert, and Alexander Campbell. *Debate on the Evidences of Christianity*. London, 1839.

Parrington, Vernon. *Main Currents in American Political Thought*. Vol. 1. New York: Harcourt, Brace, 1927.

Patton, W. W. "The True Theory of Missions to the Heathen." *Bibliotheca Sacra* 15 (July 1858): 543–69.

Pearson, Thomas. *Infidelity: Its Aspects, Causes, and Agencies*. New York, 1854.

"Pearson on Infidelity." *Biblical Repertory and Princeton Review* 26 (April 1854): 349–77.

Phelps, Austin. "The Theory of Preaching." *Bibliotheca Sacra* 14 (April 1857): 282–322.

Porter, Noah. "The New Infidelity." *New Englander* 11 (May 1853): 227–95.

Post, Truman. "Review of Democracy in America." *Biblical Repository and Classical Review*, 2d ser., 10 (October 1843): 247–90.

"The Preaching of the Gospel, the Plan of the Almighty for the Conversion of the World." Printed sermon. Lutheran Archives, Ohio Synod. Springfield, Ohio.

"The Present Commercial Distress." *Quarterly Christian Spectator* 9 (June 1837): 327–40.

"Progress." *Christian Observatory* 3 (November 1849): 508–15.

"Prudential Committee Report." In *Report of the American Board of Commissioners for Foreign Missions*. Boston, 1854.

Rauschenbusch, Walter. *Christianity and the Social Crisis*. New York: Macmillan, 1908.

"Relations of Law and a Reverential Spirit to Individual and National Prosperity." *Quarterly Christian Spectator* 9 (September 1837): 380–93.

"Religion for the Republic." *Church Review* 6 (July 1853): 169–83.

"Religious Liberty in America." *Home Missionary* 28 (January 1856): 305–11.

"Report of Dr. Wayland." *Baptist Missionary Magazine* 34 (July 1854): 218–26.

"The Revolutions of 1848." *Methodist Quarterly Review* 8 (October 1848): 535–52.

Rousseau, Jean-Jacques. *Of the Social Contract*. Bk. 4, VIII. Translated by Charles M. Sherover. New York: Harper and Row, 1984.

Santee, John W. "Signs of the Times." *Mercersburg Review* 7 (July 1855): 272–93.

Schaeffer, Charles. "Homiletics." *Evangelical Review* 5 (January 1854): 301–24.

Schmidt, Henry. "Infidelity: Its Metamorphoses, and Its Present Aspects." *Evangelical Review* 5 (January 1854): 399–413.

Schmucker, Samuel. *Modern Infidelity*. Philadelphia, 1848.

———. "Evangelical Lutheran Church." In *An Original History of the Religious Denominations*, edited by I. Daniel Rupp, 370–403. Philadelphia, 1844.

Scot, Thomas, "Christ's Politician." 1616.

Scott, W. A. "Hope of Republics." *National Preacher* 23 (January 1849): 61–76.

"Sketch of the Origin and Character of the Principal Series of Tracts of the American Tract Society." *American Tract Magazine* 6 (November 1831): 133–56.

"Some of the Characteristics of the Present Age." *American Biblical Repository* 3 (April 1840): 426–55.

Southgate, H. "The Spiritual Character of the Missionary Enterprise." *Literary and Theological Review* 3 (June 1836): 165–83.

"Sphere of the Pulpit." *New Englander* 11 (May 1853): 277–95.

"The Spirit of the Age Viewed in Relation to the Duties and Trials of the Christian Ministry." *Quarterly Christian Spectator* 9 (March 1837): 94–109.

Stiles, Ezra. "The United States Exalted to Glory and Honor." In *The Pulpit of the American Revolution*. 1860. Reprint. New York: Burt Franklin, 1970.

Thompson, Joseph P. "Christian Missions Necessary to a True Civilization." *Bibliotheca Sacra* 14 (October 1857): 818–54.

———. *Teachings of the New Testament on Slavery*. New York, 1856.

Thornwell, James Henley. "National Sins." *Southern Presbyterian Review* (January 1861).

"Thoughts on the Infidelity of the Nineteenth Century." *Methodist Quarterly Review, South* 4 (April 1850): 185–205.

Thummel, C. B. "The Nature of Christ's Kingdom and Qualifications It Requires in the Believer." *Evangelical Lutheran Preacher* 2 (May 1834): 1–5.

Tiffany, Charles. "Feuerbach's Essence of Christianity." *Bibliotheca Sacra* 14 (October 1857): 731–52.

"The Times, Morally Considered." *Charleston Gospel Messenger* 20 (June 1843): 65–75.

Tocqueville, Alexis de. *Democracy in America*. 2 vols. 1835. Edited by Phillips Bradley. Reprint. New York: Vintage Books, 1945.

Tracts of the American Tract Society. General Series. 13 vols. New York, n.d.

Ulrich, John. "Signs of the Times." *Evangelical Review* 7 (January 1856): 346–64.

"United Protestant Confession." London, 1846.

Walker, J. M. "Private Christians in Their Relations to the Unbelieving World." *Southern Presbyterian Review* 13 (January 1860): 712–27.

"War with Mexico." *New Englander* 5 (January 1847): 140–42.

Wayland, Francis. "The Apostolic Ministry." In *Sermons to the Churches*, 9–64. New York, 1858.

———. "The Church of Christ." In *Salvation by Christ*, 313–29. Boston, 1859.

———. "A Consistent Piety, the Demand of the Age." In *Sermons to the Churches*, 144–77. New York, 1858.

———. "The Doctrine of Expediency." *Bibliotheca Sacra* 1 (1843): 301–31.

———. *Letters on the Ministry of the Gospel*. Boston, 1863.

———. "Moral Dignity of the Missionary Enterprise." New York: American Tract Society, n.d.

———. "Moral Law of Accumulation." Providence, 1837.

———. "The Perils of Riches." In *Sermons for the Churches*, 206–42. New York, 1858.

———. "Slavery to Public Opinion." In *Sermons for the Churches*. New York, 1858.

"Weakness of the Churches: Its Causes and Effects." *Home Missionary* 28 (February 1856): 325–35.

Webster, Daniel. "Adams and Jefferson." In *Modern Eloquence*, edited by Thomas B. Reed, 15:2082–90. Philadelphia, 1901.

Webster, Noah. "Improving the Advantages and Perpetuating the Union." 1785. In *Noah Webster: On Being American*, edited by Homer D. Babbidge, Jr., 30–45. New York: Frederick Praeger, 1967.

———. *Letters of Noah Webster*. Edited by Harry Warfel. New York: Library Publishers, 1953.

———. "Nothing So Fatal to Truth and Tranquility." In *Noah Webster: On Being American*, edited by Homer D. Babbidge, Jr., 120–28. New York: Frederick Praeger, 1967.

———. *Political, Literary, and Moral Subjects*. 1843. Reprint. New York: Burt Franklin, 1968.

White, Charles. "Political Rectitude." *Biblical Repository and Classical Review*, 3d ser., 2 (October 1846): 602–33.

Wilberforce, William. *A Practical View of the Prevailing Religious System of Professed Christians, in the Higher and Middle Classes in This Country, Contrasted with Real Christianity*. 8th ed. Glasgow: William Collins, 1841.

Wilson, Daniel. "Introductory Essay." In *A Practical View of the Prevailing Religious System of Professed Christians, in the Higher and Middle Classes in This Country, Contrasted with Real Christianity*, by William Wilberforce, lxix–lxx. 8th ed. Glasgow: William Collins, 1841.

Wilson, J. L. "The Certainty of the World's Conversion." *Southern Presybterian Review* 2 (December 1848): 427–41.

Woolsey, Theodore Dwight. "The Danger of Separating Piety from Philanthropy." *New Englander* 13 (August 1855): 325–43.

Young, Thomas. "Sermon to the Society for the Propagation of the Gospel in Foreign Parts." *Charleston Gospel Messenger* 28 (August 1851).

Secondary Sources: Books and Articles

Albanese, Catherine. *Sons of the Fathers: The Civil Religion of the American Revolution*. Philadelphia, 1976.

Appleby, Joyce. *Capitalism and a New Social Order*. New York: New York University Press, 1984.

Ashworth, John. *Agrarians and Aristocrats*. Cambridge: Cambridge University Press, 1983.

Bailyn, Bernard. *The Ideological Origins of the American Revolution*. Cambridge: Harvard University Press, 1967.

Banner, Lois W. "Religious Benevolence as Social Control: A Critique of an Interpretation." *Journal of American History* 60 (June 1973): 23–41.

Barkun, Michael. *Crucible of the Millennium*. Syracuse, N.Y.: Syracuse University Press, 1986.

Barth, Karl. "An Introductory Essay." In *The Essence of Christianity*, by Ludwig Feuerbach, x–xxxii. Translated by Marian Evans. 1841. Reprint. New York: Harper and Brothers, 1957.

Bellah, Robert N. "Civil Religion in America." *Daedalus* (Winter 1967): 1–21.

Bercovitch, Sacvan. *The American Jeremiad*. Madison: University of Wisconsin Press, 1978.

Berens, John. *Providence and Patriotism in Early America, 1640–1815*. Charlottesville: University Press of Virginia, 1978.

Billington, Ray. *The Protestant Crusade*. New York: Macmillan, 1938.

Bloch, Ruth. "The Social and Political Bases of Millennial Literature in Late-Eighteenth-Century America." *American Quarterly* 40 (September 1988): 378–96.

———. *Visionary Republic*. Cambridge: Harvard University Press, 1985.

Bode, Carl. *The American Lyceum*. New York: Oxford University Press, 1956.

Bodo, John R. *The Protestant Clergy and Public Issues, 1812–1848*. Princeton: Princeton University Press, 1954.

Boles, John B. *The Great Revival*. Lexington: University Press of Kentucky, 1972.

———. *Religion in Antebellum Kentucky*. Lexington: University Press of Kentucky, 1976.

Bonomi, Patricia. *Under the Cope of Heaven*. New York: Oxford University Press, 1986.

Bozeman, Theodore. *Protestants in an Age of Science*. Chapel Hill: University of North Carolina Press, 1977.

———. "The Puritans' Errand into the Wilderness Reconsidered." *New England Quarterly* 59 (June 1986): 231–51.

———. *To Live Ancient Lives*. Chapel Hill: University of North Carolina Press, 1988.

Brown, Stewart J. *Thomas Chalmers and Godly Commonwealth in Scotland*. New York: Oxford University Press, 1982.

Bruchey, Stuart. *Growth of the Modern American Economy*. New York: Dodd, Mead, 1975.

Buss, Dietrich G. "Meeting of Heaven and Earth: A Survey and Analysis of the Literature on Millennialism in America, 1965–1985." *Fides et Historia* 20 (January 1988): 5–28.

Butler, Jon. *Awash in a Sea of Faith*. Cambridge: Harvard University Press, 1990.

Cashdollar, Ronald. *The Transformation of Theology, 1830–1890*. Princeton: Princeton University Press, 1989.

Caskey, Marie. *Chariot of Fire: Religion and the Beecher Family*. New Haven: Yale University Press, 1978.

Carwardine, Richard. *Transatlantic Revivalism*. Westport, Conn.: Greenwood Press, 1978.

Cayton, Mary. "The Making of an American Prophet: Emerson, His Audiences, and the Rise of the Culture Industry in Nineteenth-Century America." *American Historical Review* 92 (June 1987): 597–620.

Cheney, Mary Bushnell, ed. *The Life and Letters of Horace Bushnell*. New York, 1880.

Cherry, Conrad, ed. *God's New Israel*. Englewood Cliffs, N.J.: Prentice-Hall, 1971.

Clark, Clifford. "The Changing Nature of Protestantism in Mid-Nineteenth-Century America." *Journal of American History* 57 (March 1971): 832–46.

Clark, J. C. D. *English Society, 1688–1832*. Cambridge: Cambridge University Press, 1985.

Cole, Charles. *The Social Ideas of the Northern Evangelists, 1826–1860*. New York: Columbia University Press, 1954.

Conser, Walter. *Church and Confession*. Macon, Ga.: Mercer University Press, 1984.

Cross, Barbara. *Horace Bushnell: Minister to a Changing America*. Chicago: University of Chicago Press, 1958.

Cross, Whitney R. *The Burned-Over District*. Ithaca, N.Y.: Cornell University Press, 1950.

Curtis, Susan. *A Consuming Faith: The Social Gospel and Modern American Culture*. Baltimore: Johns Hopkins University Press, 1991.

Davidson, James West. *The Logic of Millennial Thought*. New Haven: Yale University Press, 1977.

Deane, Herbert A. *The Political and Social Ideas of St. Augustine*. New York: Columbia University Press, 1963.

Deane, Phyllis. *The First Industrial Revolution*. Cambridge: Cambridge University Press, 1965.

De Voto, Bernard. *The Year of Decision: 1846*. Cambridge: Riverside Press, 1942.

Doerflinger, Thomas. *A Vigorous Spirit of Enterprise*. Chapel Hill: University of North Carolina Press, 1986.

Douglas, Ann. *The Feminization of American Culture*. New York: Alfred A. Knopf, 1977.

Ellsworth, Clayton. "The American Churches and the Mexican War." *American Historical Review* 45 (January 1940): 301–26.

Endy, Melvin. "Just War, Holy War, and Millennialism in Revolutionary America." *William and Mary Quarterly*, 3d ser., 42 (January 1985): 3–25.

Ferm, Vergilius. *The Crisis in American Lutheran Theology*. New York: Century Press, 1927.

Feuerbach, Ludwig. *The Essence of Christianity*. Translated by Marian Evans. 1841. Reprint. New York: Harper and Brothers, 1957.

Fordham, Monroe. *Major Themes in Northern Black Religious Thought, 1800–1860*. Hicksville, N.Y.: Exposition Press, 1975.

Fowler, James W. *To See the Kingdom: The Theological Vision of H. Richard Niebuhr*. Nashville: Abingdon Press, 1974.

Fox, Richard Wightman. *Reinhold Niebuhr*. New York: Pantheon Books, 1985.

Gaustad, Edwin. *Historical Atlas of Religion in America*. New York: Harper and Row, 1962.

Geertz, Clifford. *The Interpretation of Cultures*. New York: Basic Books, 1973.

Genovese, Eugene. *Roll Jordan, Roll*. New York: Random House, 1974.

Goen, Clarence C. *Broken Churches, Broken Nation*. Macon, Ga.: Mercer University Press, 1985.

Gorrell, Donald K. *The Age of Social Responsibility*. Macon, Ga.: Mercer University Press, 1988.

Grant, C. David. *God the Center of Value*. Fort Worth: Texas Christian University Press, 1984.

Griffin, Clifford S. "Religious Benevolence as Social Control, 1815–1860." *Mississippi Valley Historical Review* 44 (December 1957): 423–44.

Hall, David D. "Of Common Ground: The Coherence of Puritan Studies." *William and Mary Quarterly*, 3d ser., 44 (April 1987): 193–229.

Hamilton, Charles. *The Black Preacher in America*. New York: William Morrow, 1972.

Handy, Robert. *A Christian America*. New York: Oxford University Press, 1971.

Hardman, Keith J. *Charles Grandison Finney*. Syracuse: Syracuse University Press, 1987.

―――. *The Social Gospel in America*. New York: Oxford University Press, 1966.

Haroutonian, James. *Piety vs. Moralism*. New York: Henry Holt, 1932.

Hatch, Nathan O. "The Christian Movement and the Demand for a Theology of the People." *Journal of American History* 67 (December 1980): 545–67.

―――. *The Democratization of American Christianity*. New Haven: Yale University Press, 1989.

―――. *The Sacred Cause of Liberty*. New Haven: Yale University Press, 1977.

Heimert, Alan. *Religion and the American Mind*. Cambridge: Harvard University Press, 1966.

Hetherington, Hugh. *Melville's Reviewers*. Chapel Hill: University of North Carolina Press, 1961.

Hewitt, Glenn A. *Regeneration and Morality: A Study of Charles Finney, Charles Hodge, John W. Nevin, and Horace Bushnell*. New York: Carlson Publishing, 1992.

Hietala, Thomas R. *Manifest Design*. Ithaca, N.Y.: Cornell University Press, 1985.

Holifield, E. Brooks. *The Gentlemen Theologians*. Durham, N.C.: Duke University Press, 1978.

Holmes, David L. "Restoration Ideology among Early Episcopal Evangelicals." In *The American Quest for the Primitive Church*, edited by Richard T. Hughes. Urbana, Ill.: University of Illinois Press, 1988.

Howard, Michael. *War and the Liberal Conscience*. New Brunswick, N.J.: Rutgers University Press, 1978.

Howe, Daniel Walker. "The Evangelical Movement and Political Culture in the North during the Second Party System." *Journal of American History* 77 (March 1991): 1216–39.

———. *The Political Culture of the American Whigs*. Chicago: University of Chicago Press, 1979.

———. "The Social Science of Horace Bushnell." *Journal of American History* 70 (September 1983): 305–22.

Hughes, Richard T., ed. *The American Quest for the Primitive Church*. Urbana, Ill.: University of Illinois Press, 1988.

Hurst, James Willard. *Law and the Condition of Freedom*. Madison: University of Wisconsin Press, 1956.

Hutchison, William R. *Errand to the World*. Chicago: University of Chicago Press, 1987.

———. *The Modernist Impulse in American Protestantism*. Cambridge: Harvard University Press, 1976.

Isaac, Rhys. *The Transformation of Virginia*. Chapel Hill: University of North Carolina Press, 1982.

Johannsen, Robert. *To the Halls of the Montezumas*. New York: Oxford University Press, 1985.

Johnson, Paul E. *A Shopkeeper's Millennium*. New York: Hill and Wang, 1978.

Kegley, Charles W., and Robert W. Bretall. *Reinhold Niebuhr: His Religious, Social, and Political Thought*. New York: Macmillan, 1956.

Knowles, David. *The Evolution of Medieval Thought*. New York: Vintage Books, 1962.

Kuklick, Bruce. *Churchmen and Philosophers: From Jonathan Edwards to John Dewey*. New Haven: Yale University Press, 1985.

Lamont, William. *Richard Baxter and the Millennium*. London: Croom Helm, 1979.

Langer, William. *Political and Social Upheaval, 1832–1852*. New York: Harper and Row, 1969.

Lasch, Christopher. *The True and Only Heaven: Progress and Its Critics*. New York: W. W. Norton, 1991.

Lerner, Gerda. *The Grimké Sisters from South Carolina*. Boston: Houghton Mifflin, 1967.

Loveland, Anne. *Southern Evangelicals and the Social Order*. Baton Rouge: Louisiana State University Press, 1980.

McCord, Norman. *The Anti–Corn Law League*. London: Allen and Unwin, 1958.

McDonald, Forrest. *Novus Ordo Seclorum*. Lawrence: University of Kansas Press, 1984.

Maclear, James F. "The Republic and the Millennium." In *The Religion of the Republic*, edited by Elwyn A. Smith, 183–216. Philadelphia: Fortress Press, 1971.

McLoughlin, William. "Charles Grandison Finney." In *Ante-Bellum Reform*, edited by David Brion Davis, 97–107. New York: Harper and Row, 1967.

———. *Cherokee Renascence in the New Republic*. Princeton: Princeton University Press, 1986.

———. *Revivals, Awakenings, and Reform*. Chicago: University of Chicago Press, 1978.

Maddex, Jack P. "Proslavery Millennialism: Social Eschatology in Antebellum Southern Calvinism." *American Quarterly* 31 (Spring 1979): 46–62.

Marsden, George. *The Evangelical Mind and the New School Presbyterian Movement.* New Haven: Yale University Press, 1970.

———. *Fundamentalism in American Culture.* New York: Oxford University Press, 1980.

Marty, Martin. *The Infidel.* Cleveland: World Publishing, 1961.

———. *Protestantism in the United States: Righteous Empire.* 1970. 2d ed. New York: Charles Scribner's Sons, 1986.

Mathews, Donald G. *Religion in the Old South.* Chicago: University of Chicago Press, 1977.

Mead, David. *Yankee Eloquence in the Middle West.* East Lansing: Michigan State College Press, 1951.

Mead, Sidney. *The Lively Experiment.* New York: Harper and Row, 1963.

Merk, Frederick. *Manifest Destiny and Mission in American History.* New York: Vintage Books, 1966.

Meyer, D. H. *The Instructed Conscience.* Philadelphia: University of Pennsylvania Press, 1972.

Miller, Daniel R. "American Christians and the Visit of Louis Kossuth." *Fides et Historia* 20 (June 1988): 5–17.

Miller, Perry. "From the Covenant to the Revival." In *The Shaping of American Religion*, edited by James Ward Smith and A. Leland Jamison, 322–68. Princeton: Princeton University Press, 1961.

———. *The Life of the Mind in America.* New York: Harcourt, Brace, and World, 1965.

Miller, William Lee. *The First Liberty.* New York: Alfred A. Knopf, 1985.

Moorhead, James H. *American Apocalypse.* New Haven: Yale University Press, 1978.

———. "Between Progress and Apocalypse: A Reassessment of Millennialism in American Religious Thought, 1800–1880." *Journal of American History* 71 (December 1984): 524–42.

———. "Perry Miller's Jeremiad against Nineteenth-Century Protestantism." *South Atlantic Quarterly* 86 (Summer 1987): 312–26.

Morgan, Edmund S. *The Gentle Puritan: A Life of Ezra Stiles.* Chapel Hill: University of North Carolina Press, 1962.

———. *Roger Williams: The Church and the State.* New York: Harcourt, Brace and World, 1967.

Munger, Theodore. *Horace Bushnell.* Boston, 1899.

Murray, James. *Francis Wayland.* Boston: Houghton, Mifflin, 1891.

Nash, Gary. *The Urban Crucible.* Cambridge: Harvard University Press, 1979.

Nichols, James Hastings. *Romanticism in American Theology: Nevin and Schaff at Mercersburg.* Chicago: University of Chicago Press, 1961.

Niebuhr, H. Richard. *Christ and Culture.* New York: Harper and Row, 1951.

———. "Toward the Independence of the Church." In H. Richard Niebuhr, Wilhelm Pauck, and Francis P. Miller, *The Church against the World.* Chicago: Willett, Clark, and Company, 1935. Reprinted in *Theology in America*, edited by Sydney Ahlstrom, 598–618. Indianapolis: Bobbs-Merrill, 1967.

――――. *The Kingdom of God in America*. New York, 1937.

Niebuhr, Reinhold. *Christian Realism and Political Problems*. New York: Charles Scribner's Sons, 1953.

――――. *Does Civilization Need Christianity?* New York: Macmillan, 1941.

――――. *The Nature and Destiny of Man*. New York: Charles Scribner's Sons, 1953.

Noll, Mark A. "'And the Lion Shall Lie Down with the Lamb': The Social Sciences and Religious History." *Fides et Historia* 20 (October 1988): 5–23.

――――, ed. *Charles Hodge: The Way of Life*. New York: Paulist Press, 1988.

――――, ed. *Religion and American Politics*. New York: Oxford University Press, 1990.

Nord, David Paul. "The Evangelical Origins of Mass Media in America, 1815–1835." *Journal Monographs* (May 1984): 1–30.

Norton, Wesley. *Religious Newspapers in the Old Northwest*. Athens: Ohio University Press, 1977.

Oakes, James. *Slavery and Freedom*. New York: Vintage Books, 1990.

Ottati, Douglas F. *Meaning and Method in H. Richard Niebuhr's Theology*. Washington, D.C.: University Press of America, 1982.

Pease, William H., and Jane H. Pease. *The Web of Progress*. New York: Oxford University Press, 1985.

Pickering, W. S. F., ed. *Durkheim on Religion*. London: Routledge and Kegan, 1975.

Rabinowitz, Richard. *The Spiritual Self in Everyday Life*. Boston: Northeastern University Press, 1989.

Richards, Leonard. *Gentlemen of Property and Standing*. New York: Oxford University Press, 1969.

Ryan, Mary. *Cradle of the Middle Class*. Cambridge: Cambridge University Press, 1981.

Schwartz, Bernard, ed. *Roots of the Bill of Rights*. Vol. 2. New York: Chelsea House, 1980.

Scott, Donald M. *From Office to Profession*. Philadelphia: University of Pennsylvania Press, 1978.

――――. "The Popular Lecture and the Creation of a Public in Mid-Nineteenth-Century America." *Journal of American History* 66 (March 1980): 791–809.

Sellers, Charles G. *The Market Revolution*. New York: Oxford University Press, 1991.

Shipps, Jan. *Mormonism: The Story of a New Religious Tradition*. Urbana: University of Illinois Press, 1985.

Skinner, Quentin. *The Foundations of Modern Political Thought*. 2 vols. London: Cambridge University Press, 1978.

Sklar, Catharine. *Catharine Beecher: A Study in Domesticity*. New Haven: Yale University Press, 1973.

Smith, Bradford. *Yankees in Paradise*. Philadelphia: J. P. Lippincott, 1956.

Smith, David E. "Millenarian Scholarship in America." *American Quarterly* 17 (Fall 1965): 535–49.

Smith, Timothy L. *Revivalism and Social Reform*. 1957. 2d ed. Baltimore: Johns Hopkins University Press, 1980.

――――. "Righteousness and Hope: Christian Holiness and the Millennial Vision in America, 1800–1900." *American Quarterly* 31 (Spring 1979): 21–45.

Snyder, K. Alan. *Defining Noah Webster: Mind and Morals in the Early Republic.* Lanham, Md.: University Press of America, 1990.

Stavely, Keith. *Puritan Legacies.* Ithaca, N.Y.: Cornell University Press, 1987.

Stevenson, Louise L. *Scholarly Means to Evangelical Ends: The New Haven Scholars and the Transformation of Learning in America.* Baltimore: Johns Hopkins University Press, 1986.

Stout, Harry. *The New England Soul.* New York: Oxford University Press, 1986.

Strout, Cushing. *The New Heavens and the New Earth: Political Religion in America.* New York: Harper and Row, 1974.

Sweet, Leonard I. "The View of Man Inherent in New Measures Revivalism." *Church History* 45 (1976): 206–21.

Sweet, William Warren. *Religion in the Development of American Culture, 1765–1840.* New York: Charles Scribner's Sons, 1952.

——— . *Revivalism in America: Its Origins, Growth, and Decline.* New York: Charles Scribner's Sons, 1944.

Szasz, Ferenc. *The Divided Mind of Protestant America, 1880–1930.* University, Ala.: University of Alabama Press, 1982.

Tawney, R. H. *Religion and the Rise of Capitalism.* New York: Harcourt Brace, 1926.

Thompson, Lawrence. "The Printing and Publishing Activities of the American Tract Society from 1825 to 1850." *Papers of the Bibliographical Society of America* 35 (2d quarter 1941): 81–114.

Troelstch, Ernst. *Protestantism and Progress.* 1912. Reprint. Philadelphia: Fortress Press, 1986.

Turner, James. *Without God, Without Creed.* Baltimore: Johns Hopkins University Press, 1985.

Tuveson, Ernest. *Redeemer Nation.* Chicago: University of Chicago Press, 1968.

Valeri, Mark. "The Economic Thought of Jonathan Edwards." *Church History* 60 (March 1991): 37–54.

——— . "The New Divinity and the American Revolution." *William and Mary Quarterly*, 3d ser., 46 (October 1989): 741–69.

Van Alstyne, Richard W. *The Rising American Empire.* New York: Oxford University Press, 1960. Reprint. Chicago: Quadrangle Books, 1965.

Walters, Ronald G. *American Reformers.* New York: Hill and Wang, 1978.

Wayland, Francis, and H. L. Wayland. *A Memoir of the Life and Labors of Francis Wayland.* 2 vols. New York, 1867.

Weber, Donald. *Rhetoric and History in Revolutionary New England.* New York: Oxford University Press, 1988.

Weber, Max. *The Protestant Ethic and the Spirit of Capitalism.* Translated by Talcott Parsons. New York: Scribner's, 1930.

Weddle, David L. *The Law As Gospel: Revival and Reform in the Theology of Charles G. Finney.* Metuchen, N.J.: Scarecrow Press, 1985.

Welch, Claude. *Protestant Thought in the Nineteenth Century.* Vol. 1. New Haven: Yale University Press, 1972.

White, Donald C. *The Social Gospel.* Philadelphia: Temple University Press, 1976.

Wiebe, Robert. *The Opening of American Society.* New York: Alfred A. Knopf, 1984.

Wilentz, Sean. *Chants Democratic*. New York: Oxford University Press, 1984.

Williams, Peter W. *Popular Religion in America*. Englewood Cliffs, N.J.: Prentice-Hall, 1980.

Wood, Gordon. *The Creation of the American Republic*. Chapel Hill: University of North Carolina Press, 1969.

———. "Struggle over the Puritans." *New York Review of Books* 36 (November 1989): 26–37.

Zucker, A. E., ed. *The Forty-eighters*. New York: Columbia University Press, 1950.

Index